ELLEN G. WHITE
Prophet of Destiny

ELLEN G. WHITE
Prophet of Destiny

BY

RENE NOORBERGEN

TEACH Services, Inc.
Brushton, New York

This book played a formative role in the development
of Christian thought and the publisher feels
that this book, with its candor and depth, still holds
significance for the church today.

Copyright © 2001 Judie D. Noorbergen
ISBN 1-57258-199-9
Library of Congress Catalog Card No. 2001090504

Facsimile Reproduction

This historical classic has been reproduced in its original form.
Frequent variations in the quality of the print are unavoidable
due to the condition of the original. Thus the print may look
lighter and appear to be missing detail, more in some places
than in others.

Published by

TEACH Services, Inc.
254 Donovan Road
Brushton, New York 12916

Introduction

SIMPLICITY HAS OFTEN been called the mark of true greatness; no single word could describe Ellen G. White as accurately as this one.

Born into a family where the deeper values of life took priority over social standing, surrounded by the grueling poverty of the early 1800's and severely handicapped, she found herself elevated from mediocrity to a position of guiding leadership in a great church, her actions aided and directed by a seemingly endless number of inspired revelations.

Surrounded by the throes of a great religious awakening, she emerged from obscurity in 1844, after her first vision, and soon found herself guiding a small band of devoted religious believers through disappointments, Civil War, Reconstruction and finally the climactic years surrounding the turn of the century. Convinced through her prophecies that the world was rapidly approaching its end, she led and counseled a large segment of the religious world of her time into a deeper spiritual and social awareness. But she did more than that. Her spiritual, medical and nutritional insight, gained through more than two thousand visions and prophetic dreams, provided her with a knowledge that was in many cases more than a hundred years ahead of her time. Medical researchers and nutritional experts still marvel at the forsightedness and accurate diagnoses of this woman, who, with only a third-grade education, managed to predict and guide health-related research to a point even beyond that which we have already reached today.

Yet, she remained humble.

Today, in a time when supernaturalism has again captured the minds of the masses through astrology and predictions forecasting calamitous events, the facts seem to indicate that even though many psychics claim to have "the answer," they solve no problems. They merely diagnose the symptoms, not the cause.

It is here that Ellen White shows her true greatness, for she goes deeper than any *psychic* ever has, and to confuse her inspired insight with the counsel of "spiritual seers" would be the greatest inaccuracy. Many more than ever are now turning to Ellen White, for during her lifetime and presently through her books, she not only counsels and guides, but she also points to the *cause* of all human misery —often illustrating it vividly by describing scenes shown to her while in vision.

Was she really a prophet? By comparing her life and work to that of the ancient prophets, and by using the tests of the ten criteria true prophets have to meet, many are convinced she was, even though she actually never boastfully laid claim to such distinction. Her introduction to a direct involvement with the prophetic power was marked by simple dignity, when, during a quiet moment of prayer, she felt taken up into heaven and brought into the presence of the heavenly host.

"As inquiries are frequently made as to my state in vision and after I come out," she once commented, "I would say that when the Lord sees fit to give me a vision, I am taken into the presence of Jesus and the Angels, and am entirely lost to earthly things. I can see no further than the angel directs me. My attention is often directed to scenes transpiring upon earth.

"At times I am carried far ahead into the future and shown what is to take place. Then again I am shown things as they have occurred in the past." [1]

During her lifetime, on numerous occasions, the question was asked whether she regarded herself as a prophet, and the answer was invariably the same.

"Why have I not claimed to be a prophet?" she would reply. "It is because in these days many who boldly claim that they are prophets are a reproach to the cause of Christ, and because my work includes much more than the word 'prophet' signifies." [2]

Exactly how much more she explained in the twenty-five million words she penned during her productive years; words now safeguarded in the vault of the Ellen G. White Estate offices in Washington, D.C.

Among the manuscripts held there are those of the thirty-seven books she wrote and published during her lifetime, and those of the thirty-two books published since her death, compiled from unpublished or out-of-print material. So tremendous is the appeal of her writings that some of her books —all hardbacks—have been sold in the millions, and have been translated into more than one hundred languages.

Taking her writings as an aid to a deeper understanding of the Bible, and to prophecy in general, it becomes quite apparent that the years ahead will be wrought in more controversy and hate than any other period in recorded history.

Yet—and this is undoubtedly her strength—she not only fore-casts the events, but she also points the way to escape from the final tragedy humanity is preparing for itself.

After having witnessed in vision the final events shaping the last climactic battle of the ages in true prophetic form, she described the outcome thus:

"The great controversy is ended. Sin and sinners are no more. The entire universe is clean. One pulse of harmony and gladness beats through the vast creation. From Him who created all, flow life and light and gladness through the realms of illimitable space. From the minutest atom to the greatest world, all things, animate and inanimate, in their unshadowed beauty and perfect joy, declare that God is love." [3]

And to acquaint man with the events that will move him to his unavoidable destiny, she relayed her visions.

Rene Noorbergen

Fairfax, Virginia
December, 1971

Contents

A Word of Appreciation

DEEPFELT APPRECIATION FOR his guidance and constructive criticism goes to Neal C. Wilson, a good friend, who, as a man with vision, greatly encouraged me in the writing of this book from the moment of its conception. His dedication to this project will always linger in my mind as a true example of sincere devotion.

Yet, encouragement and trust alone are never sufficient, and Arthur L. White, Secretary of the Board of Trustees of the Ellen G. White Estate, will always be remembered as the man who willingly placed all his knowledge and research on the subject of his grandmother at my disposal. Without him, the task would have been nigh impossible. His friendship, too, is greatly valued.

But there were others. Kenneth Wood's careful reading of the slowly developing manuscript, the advice of D. A. Delafield, and the untiring cooperation of other members of the Ellen G. White Estate also will not be forgotten.

xiii

More than ever do I wish to acknowledge the tremendous help my wife Judie has been in the writing of this book. The endless hours she spent on revisions, editing and research, not to mention her work on the final manuscript, saved many a valuable day. If real teamwork ever produced a readable book, then this one should certainly be considered!

R. N.

ELLEN G. WHITE
Prophet of Destiny

Chapter 1

Psychics Versus Prophets

IT WAS WITH a soul tormented by prolonged spiritual anguish that a frail seventy-eight-year-old woman passed through the uprooted streets of San Francisco. It was only days since the devastating earthquake had demolished the teeming metropolis, and in its wake was left nothing but ruins, death and a deep, deep hurt. . . .

Torn by compassion and understanding, she viewed the crumbling buildings, occasionally nodding her head in recognition as she compared actuality to the memory of what had been shown to her in vision. Gazing through the dusty windows of the rattling carriage, she fastened her misty eyes on the ravaged streets that had been visited by the wrath of God and sadly watched the demolition crews tear frantically at the remains of the once-so-proud buildings, hoping against all odds to uncover still more survivors of the quake.

Breathing the overpowering stench of death and destruction that engulfed the city like a shroud, she stared in shocked bewilderment at what the hand of God had wrought.

Slowly, carefully, the horses picked their way across the tons of rubble and broken glass strewn over the creviced streets, reaching for solid ground, forced on by the merciless whip of a grumbling coachman. Amidst the still falling debris and occasional wispy fingers of smoke that pointed skyward, he muttered under his breath and thought of his strange mission.

"Just drive around and show us San Francisco," the spokesman for the foursome in his carriage had asked him, and with a curious glance at the graying old woman who seemed to be the center of the party, he had agreed—though reluctantly.

Business was bad. Everything had virtually come to a standstill after the terrifying quake that had hit the city on April 18, 1906. It had been so destructive that some still called it the "judgment of God"; and the idea of taking sightseers, *tourists*, into his wrecked city and share with them his own private hurt was almost too much. Yet, they wanted to see the city and they'd already paid for it. So, with poorly controlled greed, he had nodded his agreement, flung open the door to his carriage and had harnessed the horses.

After all, for him it was just another job—and he needed it badly! But for her, the graying old lady, it marked the beginning of an agonizing appraisal of the judgment of God pronounced over a city that had become too evil to be ignored, most of all by the Almighty One.

Together with her son, W. C. White, the wife of her private secretary, C. C. Crisler, and her niece, May Welling, Ellen White roamed through the city, her eyes constantly wandering over the distressing panorama that met her scrutinizing look. The cries of the hundreds of dying and wounded had long since faded out into the vastness of eternity, yet the lingering echo of death was still very evident, and the fleeting expressions of guilt on the faces of the workmen and passersby made it seem as if they felt somehow responsible for the tragedy.

Choking from clouds of stony dust, the foursome witnessed the awesome results of the destruction of a doomed city. . . .

Ellen White saw—and trembled.

Regarded as a prophet by many and as a woman with a deep spiritual insight by others, she had seen the destruction of San Francisco pass before her mind's eye as early as 1902 when she warned:

"Not long hence these cities will suffer under the judgments of God. San Francisco and Oakland are becoming as Sodom and Gomorrah, and the Lord will visit them in wrath." [1] And on June 20, 1903, she continued her agonizing predictions:

"The judgments of God are in our land," she cried at that time, appalled at what had been revealed to her. "The Lord is soon to come. In fire and flood and earthquake He is warning the inhabitants of the earth of His soon approach."
And again she warned:

"I am bidden to declare the message that cities full of transgression and sinful in the extreme will be destroyed by earthquakes, by fire, by flood. All the world will be warned that there is a God who will display His authority as God. His unseen agencies will cause destruction, devastation and death.

"All the accumulated riches will be as nothingness." [2]

But as before, her pleadings concerning the fate of San Francisco were ignored.

A year passed during which time many of her inspired counsels were received and heeded, but San Francisco and Oakland remained under the waiting ax of the Eternal Judge. Not only Ellen White, but others also seemed to sense that the great city of the West was rapidly approaching a point of no return in the race to reach the absolute summit of immorality. A flood of revival meetings, religious crusades and scores of independent Bible workers begged the sinking city to repent, but time went on, and nothing changed.

Ellen White's anxiety increased. During the spring of 1906, while working on the final drafts of one of her books at her home in St. Helena, in Northern California, her distress grew immeasurably.

It was during her planned visit to Southern California that she received the final vision that spelled out the doom for the debauched city.

Traveling south to attend the dedicatory services of Paradise Valley Sanitarium near San Diego and Loma Linda Sanitarium in San Bernardino County, she had no foreboding that these days would be the decisive ones. This soon changed, however, when the last scenes of the devastating disaster were revealed to her in a vision on April 16, a mere two days before the quake.

"There passed before me a most wonderful [distressing, ed.] representation," she later wrote. "During a vision of the night, I stood on an eminence from which I could see houses shaken like a reed in the wind. Buildings, great and small, were falling to the ground. Pleasure resorts, theaters, hotels, and the homes of the wealthy were shaken and shattered. Many lives were blotted out of existence, and the air was filled with the shrieks of the injured and the terrified.

"The destroying angels of God were at work. One touch, and buildings so thoroughly constructed that men regarded them as secure against every danger quickly became heaps of rubbish. There was no assurance of safety in any place. I did not feel in any special peril, but the awfulness of the scenes that passed before me I cannot find words to describe. It seemed the forbearance of God was exhausted, and the judgment day had come.

"Terrible as was the presentation that passed before me, that which impressed itself most vividly upon my mind was the instruction given in connection with it.

"The angel that stood by my side declared that God's supreme rulership, and the sacredness of His law must be revealed to those who persistently refused to render obedience to the King of kings. Those who choose to remain disloyal, must be visited in mercy with judgments, in order, that, if possible, they may be aroused to a realization of the sinfulness of their course." [3]

The vision over—a new day pierced the nightly darkness . . . but to the San Franciscans, it was only the bright morning glare that preceded the storm.

Historians who have thoroughly studied the affairs of the city on the day prior to the terrifying catastrophe testify that there was nothing to indicate that the thriving metropolis was virtually on the brink of annihilation. There were no telltale signs pointing toward a shifting of the earth's crust. Business was as usual. Skid row was still going strong, deepening its alcoholic stupor with each passing hour, while the San Francisco brothels, known nationwide for their excessive aberrations, were experiencing an activity as never seen before. If the wrath of God was casting a shadow of its imminent judgment ahead, the city was blinded by its crime, corruption, vice and general lawlessness.

Then it happened.

At 5:12 A.M., while the unsuspecting city was still at rest, unbeknown to even the most active alarmist, the threatening San Andreas fault slipped over a segment of approximately 270 miles in length, shaking the very foundations of the cities along its destructive path. Gulf after gulf of raw uncontrolled power pulsated savagely through the crumbling streets, mixing its threatening thunder with the cries of the dying. Yet, to the night people, the morning itself seemed soft and innocent. Virgin spring had filled the dawn with a tremulous light, making the morning lovely enough for the birth of a world.

But when the sun hid behind the ravishing flames that night, all creation seemed to have died in the fire. Shocked, aghast, the unbelieving crowd stared at the smoldering ruins of their stricken city. Wringing their hands in quiet agony, they watched the smoke rise to the heavens from the still-active flames and silently waited for the expected news of the devastation of other major cities, for there was no doubt in their minds that the end of the world had come!

Much has been written concerning the true effects of the San Francisco earthquake of April 18, 1906. *Collier's* Magazine published one of the most accurate accounts thus far. According to the magazine, the "judgment of San Francisco" destroyed 490 city blocks and left between 225,000 and 256,000 homeless. Close to 800 people perished during the first few hours of the quake and the resulting fires. More than 1,500 were injured, many of them seriously. Property was destroyed at the rate of one million dollars every ten minutes, for, while the earthquake itself caused considerable damage, far greater devastation was wrought by the fires which at times burned with blast-furnace heat, ranging up to 2,000 degrees Fahrenheit.

For the first few hours after the quake, telegraph lines went wild.

"Rumors, tidings, catastrophe flew up and down the line. Chicago was in flames, a tidal wave had engulfed Seattle. New York had toppled into the sea. Confusion and chaos were besetting the world. San Francisco's fate—it seemed to them—was merely a tick of the clock of doomsday . . ."

When all the figures were in, the economic losses were disastrous. More than four hundred million dollars worth of damage was caused by the tragedy, and several insurance companies went bankrupt trying to pay off the resulting claims.

The morning of the quake, Ellen White, while en route to fill a speaking engagement at the Carr Street Church in Los Angeles, stopped. A newsboy's high-pitched voice suddenly brought back the memory of the visions she had received in clear and vivid detail about the destruction of San Francisco.

"San Francisco destroyed by earthquake," he screamed excitedly. "San Francisco destroyed by earthquake—the city's going up in flames. . . ." And buying a paper, with a heavy heart she began to read the results of the termination of God's patience.

A prophecy had literally been fulfilled.

The prophet wept. . . .

Philosophers will readily agree—as will most serious-minded historians—that when the time is ripe for a historical event of major proportion, the right man will rise to the occasion.

Many times during the centuries, this thought has prevailed; for strangely enough, whenever social upheaval or political strife necessitated unorthodox measures, extraordinarily gifted statesmen, conquerors or psychic seers have appeared on the scene, interjecting their often unsolicited advice into an already explosive situation. Few will wish to dispute the actions of historical statesmen, for, like the conquerors, they have become one with the history they helped forge, never to rise again. When we deal with psychic seers of old, however, it is a different matter, for they claimed to be able to see beyond their time and projected decisions that surround our lives today. They "peeked" into the events taking place in our century, and inasmuch as we live *with* and *in* the history they projected, they (the psychics) are still ours to deal with.

When the French astrologer Nostradamus attained his professional summit early in the sixteenth century and published his profound collection of prophecies in a book entitled *The True Centuries* (1555), he "reached" far beyond his days. Most of his prophecies covered time periods of hundreds of years, and many uncommitted searchers-for-truth regarded them as true revelations from the gods. This unreserved acceptance opened up the way for a grand revival of an old phenomenon: that of supernatural intervention in the daily affairs of man—and it skyrocketed Nostradamus to fame.

Born in the tumultuous age of Henry II and his wife Caterina de' Medici he attempted through his prophecies to relieve the pressures brought on by the political and social uncertainties that existed in those days and tried to substitute for them a highly developed degree of reliance on the unexplained phenomena of the supernatural. So far-reaching were many of his predictions that even today most of the world's best-known psychics have built their reputations on a carefully contrived rehash of his major prophecies.

There are a number of reasons that account for Nostradamus' popularity. In his day, astrology—the divination of the supposed influence of the stars on human affairs and terrestrial events by their position and aspects—was highly fashionable, and by claiming to have arrived at his predictions through a study of the stars, he gained instant fame. Then, too, faith in the power of witchcraft also played an important role in sixteenth-century life, and this also added its weight.

A study of his predictions place his P.A.Q. (Prophetic Accuracy Quotient) in the 80-percent-plus class, a psychic record difficult to match. Whether, however, he received his inspiration as a medium—consulting the so-called spirits of the dead—or as an astrologer is really immaterial, as both methods are unreservedly condemned in the Bible as heathen and idolatrous practices.

A clairvoyant he may have been, a prophet of Biblical dimension he most definitely was not. But this did not in the least dim his popularity, and the Europeans who swarmed to America's shores in the early days of this country's history brought with them the weird tales and awesome predictions of the French seer. Fortunately their effect on the early development of this country was barely noticeable, except in New England where witchcraft and religion clashed violently.

In the United States, the first half of the nineteenth century was a period of relative calm, both socially and economically. We were a pastoral people, living off rapidly spreading blotches of civilization, areas where the local community was thought to be the center of the world. But with the influx of immigrants, America changed, and so did its ways. With agrarian reform just around the corner, the convulsive development of industry and the feverish dreams of riches and fame funneled the youth of the land into the growing cities. Soon the results of the economic expansion began to show as the stresses and strains of the uncontrolled growth began to appear. Community life burst at the seams as the old ways made place for new sins.

While much of the population was in agreement with the new trend, the more conservative-minded took up a renewed study of the old, proved Biblical principles. Having as background not only the Bible, but also the folklore and traditional tales of the early psychic seers as well, they, in their desperation, decided to take a deeper interest in the "dark" prophetic books of the Bible, Daniel and Revelation. Within a short period of time, some began to draw detailed comparisons between the sociological and moral upheaval of America of the early 1800's to that existing in the days of Noah. Strangely enough, while most theologians accepted the retreat back to Noah's days without much concern, the Christian *laity* took it upon itself to find Biblical answers for the perplexing problems that faced them.

Unknown to one another, small groups of Christian lay-members formed and initiated deep, thorough studies of the Biblical prophecies, focusing their attention on Daniel, Revelation and the prophetic chapters of the Book of Matthew. For many years a religious re-awakening had been expected, based on the philosophy that man's self-serving ways will ultimately lead him to his own destruction, but now, however, for the first time, Biblical prophecies were drawn into this expectation giving a firmer basis to this conviction.

With fear and wonder these groups witnessed the gradual unfolding of the prophecies, but no matter how intensely they probed, the exact timing of the climactic events of the "last days" of human history stayed shrouded in mystery.

It remained for an ex-U.S. Army captain, William Miller (War of 1812), to make the discovery that was to become the backbone for the religious reformers. For fourteen long years—from 1816 to 1831—he diligently studied the Bible prophecies, comparing them to known historical events, and when he finally ventured into the open with the results of his investigation, he was ready to promote and preach that which he had discovered.

His study had been intense; the conclusion was frightening.

"As he concentrated month after month . . . in his reading and comparing of scriptures, he made a further discovery. He noted that while prophecies are generally couched in figurative language, they are fulfilled literally. He observed this not only by comparing scripture with scripture, but also by comparing scripture with history."

Finally he concluded.

"Finding all the signs of the times and the present conditions of the world to compare harmoniously with the prophetic descriptions of the last days, I was compelled to believe that this world had about reached the limits of the period allotted for its continuance. As I regarded the evidence, I could arrive at no other conclusion. I was thus brought, in 1818 . . . to the solemn conclusion that in about twenty-five years from that time, all affairs of our present state would be wound up." [4]

And while the uncommitted masses leaned heavily on the psychic predictions of Nostradamus (for the French), St. Odile (for the Germans) and those of St. Bearcan and Fionn Mac Cumhaill Ceninit (for the Irish), Captain Miller's warning led to a religious awakening that was unequaled in American history. Predicting the end of the world in 1844, Miller, aided by Charles Fitch, Joshua V. Himes, Josiah Litch, Joseph Bates and others, soon began to preach the Second Coming of Christ, an event he felt would coincide with other happenings foretold for the year 1844.

It was at this precise moment of historical uncertainty and anxious expectation that Ellen Harmon * entered the scene, and with her came a foreknowledge and insight into world and religious affairs unknown since Biblical times. The predictions of the old clairvoyants and psychic seers had not as yet run their course, but Biblical *time-prophecies* had, and the consequent feeling of approaching doom among the conservative religious believers was terrifying.

The world was indeed ripe for new spiritual counsel—not to *replace* the Bible but to strengthen it.

Ellen Harmon became the channel.

Was she indeed a prophet or merely a psychic?

The answer to this is partly hidden in the events surrounding the year 1844. With Biblical time-prophecies running out, the time was not only ripe for new spiritual counsel, but also for new spiritual movements. Confused and weary, people were ready to accept *anything* that would bring them in closer touch with the Unknown. A simple knock on the wall of a lowly wooden shack provided advantageous use of this susceptibility, creating a religion that embraced

* The maiden name of Ellen G. White.

the world before the end of that century. "Strange things began to happen on March 31, 1848, in the secluded village of Hydesville, New York, in the humble cottage of the teen-age Fox sisters. These became known as the 'Raps of Hydesville.' Methodists John and Margaret Fox and two of their younger daughters, Margaretta (fifteen) and Katie (twelve), were living at the time in this cottage while their own home was under construction. That particular night they were awakened by mysterious sounds—distinct rappings, or knockings—that could be heard all over the house.

"The children quickly imitated the raps by clapping their hands, Katie calling out, 'Mr. Splitfoot, do as I do.' For every clap there was an answering rap. She then held up her fingers—a different number each time—asking 'Splitfoot' to tell the number of fingers indicated. As correct answers were rapped out, Katie observed, 'It can see as well as hear.' . . . Mrs. Fox then asked the 'noise' to tell how many children she had (six living and one dead) and their ages. These were given, including the one who had died. So a 'code of communication' was developed. The unseen intelligence then indicated that it was the 'spirit' of a murdered peddler whose body had been buried in the cellar. It was seeking a human instrument through whom to acquaint the world with the facts of the man's mysterious disappearance—and to prove that his spirit still lived." [5]

"These crude communications were at first generally regarded by the public largely as fraud or a trick, and humbug and delusion, that would soon die out, and quickly be forgotten. At that time, Spiritualism (as it soon became known) was regarded by churchmen with aversion, and had no semblance of a religion, much less any form or organization as a church. Though given hostile reception at first—for mobs gathered, violence was threatened and the Fox family was castigated as sensational fakers seeking notoriety—tremendous changes soon took place. By 1854, in six short years, Spiritualism had extended to every part of the United States, and was active in Europe.

"The spread was indeed phenomenal. At the close of another decade, the claimed number of mediums practicing in the United States was thirty thousand. Judge J. W. Edmonds, of the New York Supreme Court, who became a Spiritualist in 1853, computed the number of American followers to be some three million. By the 1880's Spiritualism had reputedly spread over the entire surface of the earth. It excited the wonders of many jurists, scientists, philosophers, physicians, editors, poets, clergymen, statesmen and educators. . . . Even the eleventh edition of the *Encyclopædia Britannica* states that Spiritualism has 'spread like an epidemic.' " [6]

There is little doubt that the main attraction of this spirit-guided movement was the promise of becoming "one" with the mysterious and the weird, and it gave the believers a chance to become the "confidants" of invisible masters. Its spread was so explosive and so frightening that it led Katie Fox, one of the sisters who introduced the phenomenon to the people, finally to confess bitterly to a journalist of the *New York Herald* (October 9, 1888):

"I regard Spiritualism as one of the greatest curses the world has ever known."

To this, J. J. Morse, a renowned Spiritualist, added the following in his book, *Practical Occultism*, published in 1888:

"Shall we . . . come down to the plain simple truth, that the phenomenal aspects of Modern Spiritualism reproduce all the essential principles of the Magic, Witchcraft and Sorcery of the past? *The same powers are involved. . . . the same intelligences are operating.*"

But—it was born, and it was here to stay. And while Ellen G. White was writing her "Conflict of the Ages" series, tracing the struggle between the forces of good and evil, following a single unerring line of spiritual guidance, the demoniacal movements experienced periods of spasmodic growth, always changing, always fluctuating, forced on by the whims and often unrequested advice of disembodied entities, speaking through the mouths of unconscious mediums.

Whether it was due to the gullibility of the masses, their utter desperation or their experimental attitude, cult after cult based on "spirit messages" sprang into being, all of them promising life after death and all supplying "proof" of reincarnation based on a close personal contact with the spirit world.

With the psychic mediums guiding the spiritualist movements, it soon became an integral part of the religious confusion that reigned in the 1800's. Even President Abraham Lincoln, it has been reported, became so deeply involved with it that many of his major decisions, affecting not only the conduct of the Civil War, but also important matters of state as well, were made on the advice of disembodied voices speaking through spiritualist medium, Nettie Meynard.

Psychic mediums claimed to be guided by an invisible power, but so did Ellen G. White. Was there really a difference? Is there perhaps a possibility—no matter how vague or distant—that she may have been influenced by the same forces that controlled the mediums of her day—and those of today as well?

Because present-day psychics base their ability on the same power that controlled the psychics in Ellen White's day, *it is a question that must be faced, for much depends on it.*

One of the greatest living clairvoyants, Washington's Jeane Dixon, told me repeatedly while I was interviewing her for the book, *My Life and Prophecies*, that "the same spirit that worked through Isaiah and John the Baptist also works through me." On other occasions she defended Nostradamus' gift by saying that she was convinced he was a man of God. Mrs. Dixon often commented that "if it were not for the prophetic gift God has given me, I would not be able to do what I am doing today."

While researching background material for the book, we spent many hours together, examining her religious conviction and political strength. Even though in those particular sessions her answers indicated that she is firmly convinced she is the equal of the Biblical prophets, there can be no doubt that on *Biblical grounds* she cannot be regarded as a true prophet of God, inasmuch as she violates almost every prophetic test spelled out in the Bible.

On the other hand, another of today's well-known psychics, David Bubar, the subject of *You Are Psychic*, feels that it is not necessarily God or any *other* power that is responsible for the revelations and predictions, but that it is man's inert psychic ability which enables him to see beyond physical boundaries and beyond the self-imposed limitations of human imagination.

"We can 'touch' the future in very much the same way radar sends out its searching beams of energy," Bubar maintains. "When my outgoing energy beam meets with vibrations of events that have already happened or of those foreshadowing the future, it relays the information back to me and provides me with the ability to predict or to 'read' the past."

Unlike Jeane Dixon, Mr. Bubar does not claim to be the equal of any of the Biblical prophets, yet he does assert to have the ability to prophesy even though the theory behind his performance is entirely different.

But there are as many different explanations as there are psychics. Daniel Logan, the clairvoyant spiritualist medium, who gained nationwide fame through the publication of his

book, *The Reluctant Prophet,* believes that true spirit communication supplies the answer to revelations from the Unknown. The famous Virginia Beach psychic, Edgar Cayce,
firmly advocated that it was Jesus Himself who gave him
(Cayce) his ability to predict and diagnose.

Many, however, side with Daniel Logan in believing
that their information comes directly from the spirit world,
an abode in the Unseen dimension where untold millions
of so-called spirits of deceased are waiting for a chance to
communicate. Mediums whose performance is based on
this usually move into a state of complete unconsciousness,
while voices purporting to be those of unknown entities or
departed spirits speak through their mouths, displaying an
uncanny knowledge of current affairs and making prophecies
intending to prove that they possess ultimate and indis-
putable wisdom.

There are a few other possibilities, and one more is
certainly worth mentioning. Since the Second World War,
the Eastern European countries, Russia in particular, have
been engaged in a crash program to discover the basic
principles of psychic phenomena. One of their pet theories
is that a psychic is someone whose brain, very much like a
computer, sorts and computes myriads of known facts, and
that based upon its subsequent evaluation, the brain flashes
out information that appears to be a foolproof prediction.

Perhaps psychic mediums are a combination of the first
and third of these possibilities or perhaps a combination of
all three, inasmuch as Jeane Dixon fuses her faith in her
God-given ability with an even stronger faith in astrology,
palmistry, spirit communication and a certain degree of reincarnation.

Yet as different as they may be, the psychics do agree on
one point, and that is their abhorrence of being tested by
someone regarded as an expert in their field of parapsychology.

"How can a parapsychologist who is not a psychic devise a way to test a psychic?" they ask. "The very fact that he is devoid of psychic ability proves his complete ignorance of psychic affairs." Perhaps they have raised a valid point. However, all of them, without exception, will gladly open their Bibles to show how similar their extrasensory gift is to that of the Biblical prophets. They proudly refer to it in trying to justify their ability, and this is the worst thing any psychic can do. It opens up the way for the use of Biblical references to *test* their ability, and if they regard the Bible as authoritative enough to be utilized as an absolute standard, then it should also be qualified enough to judge—and if need be, condemn.

And it is precisely on this point that true prophets and psychic mediums can be separated.

James Bjornstad, author of the paperback, *Twentieth Century Prophecy*, a small yet powerful book dealing with the prophetic phenomena as displayed by Edgar Cayce and Jeane Dixon, has made a number of interesting comparisons between the abilities of these two great psychics and the Biblical requirements for a true prophet. His conclusion, *based strictly on Biblical references*, is for them truly devastating.

Comparing all those who profess to have the extrasensory psychic gift (astrologers, mediums, clairvoyants, clairaudients, palmists, crystal gazers, telepathists, etc.) and submitting their abilities to the same basic set of Biblical standards, one arrives at the mind-shattering conclusion that all psychic mediums—and this includes such greats as Edgar Cayce, Jeane Dixon, Daniel Logan, Gerard Croiset, Peter Hurkos, Arthur Ford, etc.—*without exception* not only violate many basic Biblical principles, but also more often than not act in stark *contradiction* to the Biblical norms for a true prophet.

The occult covers a vast field of activities, and expecting

to find one single Bible text applicable to all psychic phenomena would be asking too much. Yet there are ten very fundamental tests that beg for attention.

At a time when 10,000 professional astrologers control the daily activities of 40 million people in the United States through 1,200 daily astrology columns and 2,350 horoscope computers; when roughly 140,000 fortune-tellers, mediums, clairvoyants and psychic seers have created a 42-million-dollar-a-year business; and when three major universities offer credit courses in witchcraft, magic, astrology and sorcery, a foolproof method to separate the psychics from the prophets has become essential!

The tests for a true prophet, all found in the Old and New Testaments of the Bible, pointedly indicate that those prognosticators not measuring up to these stringent qualifications cannot lay claim to the rare distinction of being true prophets of God.

They can be summarized as follows:

1. A true prophet does not lie. His predictions will be fulfilled (Jer. 28:9).
2. A true prophet prophesies in the name of the Lord, not in his own name (II Pet. 1:21).
3. A true prophet does not give his own private interpretation of prophecy (II Pet. 1:20).
4. A true prophet points out the sins and transgressions of the people against God (Isa. 58:1).
5. A true prophet is to warn the people of God's coming judgment (Isa. 24:20, 21; Rev. 14:6, 7).

These first five tests alone are already sufficient to damage the reputation of most of the so-called prophets, but crowned with the second group of five, they are truly devastating.

6. A true prophet edifies the church, counsels and advises it in religious matters (I Cor. 14:3, 4).

7. A *true prophet's words will be in absolute harmony with the words of the prophets that have preceded him* (Isa. 8:20).
8. *He recognizes the incarnation of Jesus Christ* (I John 4:1-3).
9. *He can be recognized by the results of his work* (Matt. 7:16-20).

Finally he must be able to meet the requirements listed in Deuteronomy 18:19, A *true prophet acts in accordance with the will and approval of God.*

". . . *thou shalt not learn to do after the abominations of those nations. There shall not be found among you any one . . . that useth divination [fortune-teller], or an observer of times [astrologer], or an enchanter [magician], or a witch, or a consulter with familiar spirits [medium possessed with a spirit or a 'guide'], or a wizard [clairvoyant or psychic], or a necromancer [medium who consults the dead].*

"*For all that do these things are an abomination unto the Lord.*"

Based on these texts, it becomes obvious that not everyone who prophesies is a prophet of God—for a *true prophet* is not a psychic who performs with the aid of a mental or "spiritual" crutch, but is someone who has no degree of freedom either in tuning in or controlling the prophetic impulses or prophetic recall. These impulses are superimposed over the prophet's conscious mind by a supernatural personal being, having absolute knowledge of both past and future, making no allowance for error or human miscalculation.

To be even more precise, the actions of a true prophet are not in contradiction to basic Biblical doctrines, but rather support and strengthen precepts already outlined.

Chapter 2

A Humble Life

"WHO REALLY *was* Ellen G. White?"

Many times since I initiated the search for the "Ellen White story," curious friends have asked this question with increasing frequency, and the answer is never one that can be given in a short, precise statement, for even though at birth and death the same emotions touched her as touch everyone, it is exactly here that all comparison ends. True, birth and death mark the outer limits of life for all, but it is the events in between that determine greatness or mediocrity.

As the daughter of Robert and Eunice Harmon, she entered life on the wintry night of November 26, 1827, by the yellowish flame of a candle, warmed by the soft glow of embers in an open fireplace. Eighty-seven years later, when her life ended in the writing room of her St. Helena home those who had known her intimately believed that it had reached complete fulfillment.

Her life had indeed been a full one. Nevertheless, those not acquainted with her work could not fully comprehend the overpowering sadness that spread across the land and around the world from the little Northern California town when she died. Death had invaded the privacy of her home on the rays of the afternoon sun one balmy summer afternoon and had taken her life as quietly as it had begun—thus completing a cycle of earthly existence.

Death marked the end of life for a great woman.

It marked the end of a prophet.

Eighty-seven years are not much when measured against the aeons of time, but in those few years, she experienced enough to fill the memories of an entire generation.

At the time she was born in Gorham, Maine, John Quincy Adams "reigned" as the country's sixth President, but when she died, Woodrow Wilson, the twenty-eighth President of the United States, lived in the White House. Her death took place just two years prior to the birth of another illustrious American, John F. Kennedy.

During her lifetime, twenty-two United States Presidents were inaugurated, and the country underwent a transition from relaxed tranquillity to feverish activity. While she lived, the casual and often uncomplicated life of the early settlers was transformed into an existence where money, crime and industrial strife shaped industries and forged financial empires—and hundreds of thousands of young Americans died on the fields of battle, first at home, then abroad.

Contradictions ruled the masses when she was alive, and while others claiming to possess the gift of prophecy took advantage of the gullibility of the people, enticing their followers to seek contact with the spirit world, Ellen lived a life of strict dependence on God. Only in recent years is it beginning to reveal its true significance.

In quest for details I consulted Arthur White, her grandson and one of the administrators of her literary Estate in

Washington, D.C., hoping to uncover some intimate personal glimpses of the woman who has often been called "one of the truly great women of the turn of the century."

Arthur smiled when I asked about his memories of her.

"I remember her as a quiet, kindhearted grandmother who was always full of love," he mused, allowing his mind to drift back over the years to the early part of the century. "But I don't remember too many details, as I was only seven when she died . . . and that was all of fifty-seven years ago." The "few" details he does recall, however, can fill a book, for his memory, augmented by the immense documentation in the Estate's vault, goes much deeper than his initial reaction indicated.

Biographies of her as printed in the *Dictionary of American Biography, American Biographical History* and the more recently published *Notable American Women* do not exceed the basic outlines, but the voluminous information and the many articles written about her by her contemporaries, as well as her own biographical sketches, portray her as a woman driven by only one desire—to elevate humanity.

Uneventful until her ninth year, Ellen's life took a drastic turn when, on the way home from school one afternoon in Portland, Maine, alarmed by the angry shouts of a classmate, she reeled around. For a moment she stood there, transfixed, while the girl raised her hand and viciously hurled a stone at her head. The impact was so great that Ellen was thrown to the ground. Upon returning to consciousness, she found herself in a merchant's store where she had been carried by worried bystanders. Refusing to be driven home, she pulled herself up and clung to the arm of her twin sister. Bleeding profusely from a head wound, she staggered home, supported by her sister and a schoolmate, once again falling unconscious before reaching her house.

For a full three weeks, she wavered between life and

death, and when she finally regained enough strength to get
around, she was burdened with a disfigured face and the
aftereffects of a serious head injury.

"It influenced her health to such a large extent," Arthur
White commented, "that it forced her to forgo further
schooling. In fact, she never quite got beyond the third
grade. Of course she tried again at a later time, but it soon
became obvious to both her teachers and her parents that
the strain and the tension of school life were more than she
could bear. So she had to stop once more. Yet this may
have been a real blessing for her, because there is every
indication that this illness made her more dependent on
spiritual values, and it was this subsequent concentration on
spirituality that guided her straight into the direction of
God."

In later years, Ellen often looked back on her ninth year
with an odd mixture of emotions, for it terminated one
phase of her life and at the same time introduced her to
what was to come. Following her misfortune, she became an
avid Bible student, fascinated by the religious revival taking
place around her. Being intensely religious, she did not miss
a chance to associate with others who shared her interest,
inasmuch as her regular friends shunned her after the acci-
dent.

Ellen White's story is basically a religious one, and when
in her fourteenth year she spoke of having two dreams that
seemed to have a deeper significance than ordinary dreams,
her close friends understood.

Referring to one of those dreams, Ellen wrote:

"I seemed to be sitting in abject despair, with my face in
my hands, reflecting like this: If Jesus were upon earth, I
would go to Him, throw myself at His feet and tell Him
all my sufferings. He would not turn away from me; He
would have mercy upon me, and I would love and serve
Him always.

"Just then the door opened, and a person of beautiful form and countenance entered. He looked upon me pitifully, and said: 'Do you wish to see Jesus? He is here, and you can see Him if you desire it. Take everything you possess, and follow me.'

"I heard this with unspeakable joy, and gladly gathered up all my little possessions, every treasured trinket, and followed my guide. He led me to a steep and apparently frail stairway. As I began to ascend the steps, he cautioned me to keep my eyes fixed upward, lest I should grow dizzy and fall. Many others who were climbing the steep ascent fell before gaining the top.

"Finally we reached the last step, and stood before a door. Here my guide directed me to leave all the things that I had brought with me. I cheerfully laid them down. He then opened the door, and bade me enter. In a moment I stood before Jesus. There was no mistaking that beautiful countenance; that expression of benevolence and majesty could belong to no other. As His gaze rested upon me, I knew at once that He was acquainted with every circumstance of my life and all my inner thoughts and feelings.

"I tried to shield myself from His gaze, feeling unable to endure His searching eyes; but He drew near with a smile, and laying His hand upon my head, said, 'Fear not.' The sound of His sweet voice thrilled my heart with a happiness it had never before experienced. I was too joyful to utter a word, but, overcome with emotion, sank prostrate at His feet. While I was lying helpless there, scenes of beauty and glory passed before me, and I seemed to have reached the safety and peace of heaven. At length my strength returned, and I arose. The loving eyes of Jesus were still upon me, and His smile filled my soul with gladness. His presence awoke in me a holy reverence and an inexpressible love.

"My guide now opened the door, and we both passed out. He bade me to take up again all the things I had left without. This done, he handed me a green cord coiled up closely. This he directed me to place next to my heart, and when I wished to see Jesus, take it from my bosom, and stretch it to the utmost. He cautioned me not to let it remain coiled for any length of time, lest it should become knotted and difficult to straighten.

"I placed the cord near my heart, and joyfully descended the narrow stairs, praising the Lord, and telling all whom I met where they could find Jesus." [1]

To Ellen, lonely and disfigured, it was a hope-giving dream. She began to see the way out of her misery, and eager for help, she called to her mother.

"What can I do?" she begged, her face transformed into one, single, desperate plea for help. "Mother, can't you show me how to go on from here?"

Eunice Harmon clearly struggled to find an answer that would be fair and would help her daughter; yet at the same time she didn't know how to advise her.

"I just don't know how, Ellen," she whispered softly, placing her hand gently on her daughter's shoulder. "Perhaps you should go and see Elder Stockman. . . . He's a man we can trust."

Encouraged, Ellen left the house and hurried to the man who had made a name for himself in Portland by preaching about the soon Second Coming of Christ.

Quietly Stockman listened to her and compared her story with what he had previously heard concerning this unusual young woman. When Ellen finally ended her appeal for spiritual help by recalling for him her recent dream, he thoughtfully stared at her, suddenly feeling his emotions forcing tears to well up in his eyes.

For a moment he just sat there, unable to find words. Then he stood up and walked over to her.

"Ellen, you are only a child," he said, taking off his glasses and wiping away a tear with the back of his hand. "But yours is a most singular experience for one of your tender age. Jesus must be preparing you for some special work." [2]

"Your agony of mind, your perplexities, your doubt and despair indicate to me that the Spirit of the Lord is striving with you. . . . Go free, Ellen," he advised after counseling with her at length. "Return to your home trusting in Jesus, for He will not withhold His love from any true seeker." [3]

It was a different girl who walked home that day. Thrilled with Stockman's advice, she determined to search for other ways to grow and share her newfound faith. For more than a year and a half she struggled along, studying, talking religion and attending religious meetings conducted by William Miller and his associates who preached that Christ would return in October, 1844.

With the interest of the entire Harmon family now focused on the newly formulated Millerite doctrines, serious difficulties developed between them and the Methodist Church of which they were members, resulting ultimately in their expulsion in late 1843. Not long thereafter the national controversy about the Millerite beliefs reached a decisive stage, and when on October 22, 1844, the expected celestial event tarried, Ellen was heartbroken—that is until December of that same year when she experienced her first vision. Seventeen years of age, with seriously impaired health, weighing a bare eighty pounds and suffering from a weak heart and a diseased lung, she was a far cry from what one might expect of a prophet. What troubled her most, however, was the uncertainty as to how the vision would be accepted by her fellow believers, and in her earliest preserved letter, written after December, 1844, she told of her doubts.

"After I had the vision, and God gave me light," she wrote, "He bade me to deliver it to the band, but I shrank from it. I was young, and I thought they would not receive it from me. I disobeyed the Lord, and instead of remaining at home, where the meeting was to be that night, I got in the sleigh in the morning and rode three or four miles." [4] Torn between faith and fear, the seventeen-year-old fled to the home of a friend where she spent the remainder of the day, torturing herself with doubt.

Whereas psychics proudly claim to have the Spirit of Prophecy, Ellen was wary of it, for she regarded her inspiration as a privilege, a sacred trust, and instead of boasting of her supernatural experience, she tried to hide it.

She did not know that an interesting incident had occurred only weeks prior to her vision. Near to the time of the expected Second Advent, and in the midst of the tumultuous last months, Hazen Foss, a young Millerite, hesitantly related to some of his close friends that he had received a vision explaining the experience of the Advent believers. Following the October disappointment, his friends, recalling what he had told them, pressed him to render his vision to them again. He bluntly refused. Then "very strange feelings came to him, and a voice said, 'You have grieved away the Spirit of the Lord.'" [5]

Of this Ellen Harmon knew nothing until a few weeks later when she received an invitation to speak at the Poland, Maine, church and share with the anxious congregation her prophetic experiences. For more than two hours she held her audience captive, reporting the details of her vision while Hazen Foss, who had declined an invitation to attend the meeting, stood outside the closed door and listened. She did not know about this, or realize that her presentation had had a devastating effect on him, until the next morning.

She had scarcely finished her breakfast when there was a knock on the door and someone asked to speak to her. Ellen walked into the hallway.

"I am Hazen Foss," he introduced himself rather hesitantly, as though half expecting her to recognize his name or recoil in absolute horror. "I want to speak with you.

"The Lord gave me a message to bear to His people, and

I refused after being told the consequences. I was proud; I was unreconciled to the disappointment. I murmured against God, and wished myself dead. Then I felt a strange feeling come over me, and a voice said, 'You have grieved away the Spirit of the Lord.'

"Ellen, I shall be henceforth as one dead to spiritual things. I heard you talk last night. *I believe the visions are taken from me, and given to you.* Do not refuse to obey God, for it will be at the peril of your soul. I am a lost man. You are chosen of God; be faithful in doing your work, and the crown I might have had, you will receive." [6]

For a long time that morning Ellen and Hazen conversed and compared experiences. So great and lasting was the impression the visit made on her young mind, that years later in 1890, she was still able to recollect almost the entire conversation.

Recalling his words, she wrote, "Horrified at his stubbornness and rebellion, he 'told the Lord that he would relate the vision,' but when he attempted to do so before a company of believers, he could not call it to mind. In vain were his attempts to call up the scenes as they had been shown to him; and then in deep despair he exclaimed, 'It is gone from me; I can say nothing, and the Spirit of the Lord has left me.'

"Eyewitnesses described it as 'the most terrible meeting they were ever in.'" [7]

Commented her grandson Arthur White after having studied all the documents relating to that meeting:

"On comparing dates, they discovered that it was not until after he had been told that the visions were taken from him that Ellen Harmon was given her first revelation. Although Hazen Foss lived till 1893, he never again manifested interest in matters religious." [8]

The biographical information available on Ellen White

places her marriage to a young schoolteacher-turned-Miller-ite-preacher, James White, on August 30, 1846. The files of the Estate contain enough documentation to indicate that the mutual attraction was just as much of a spiritual nature as it was physical. Said James White in his biographical work, *Life Sketches of James and Ellen White*, "When we first met, we had no idea of marriage at any future time. But God had a work for both of us to do, and He saw that we could greatly assist each other in that work. As she should come before the public, she needed a lawful protector; and God having chosen her as a channel of light and truth to the people in a special sense, she could be of great help to me. But it was not until the matter of marriage was taken to the Lord by both, and we obtained an experience that placed the matter beyond the reach of doubt, that we took this important step."

He did not say exactly what the "experience" was, but their first meeting had indeed provided the two of them with a lasting memory.

For Ellen it all began in February, 1845, in Orrington, Maine. William Jordan, a close friend, invited her to accompany him and his sister on a sleigh ride to Orrington, where, as he told her, he had to deliver a horse and a sleigh belonging to James White, a preacher. Delighted at the chance to join them, Ellen traveled the 135 miles from Portland to Orrington, the sleigh being pulled over the snow-covered fields by the steady gait of a dark brown stallion.

Great consternation awaited her in Orrington. Tremendous friction had arisen between the hard-working conservative townspeople and a small band of religious fanatics who, with their shouting and noisy demonstrations, had angered the normally peaceful citizenry to the point where they were threatening them with arrest or even violence.

When asked to help and talk to the excited group of

troublemakers, Ellen at first refused, then changed her mind and met with them in an attempt to persuade them to relinquish their useless fanaticism.

For a while it appeared successful, but after having made a quick visit to nearby Garland, Exeter and Atkinson, Ellen returned to find that much of the same situation had developed again. Once more she tried to mediate in her role as peacemaker, but the anger of the crowd had greatly increased during her absence, and when after the evening meeting she received a vision telling her to leave early the following morning, she did so. Rising at dawn the next day, James White and some close friends rowed the visitors over a distance of twenty miles down the Penobscot River to Belfast where they were to take the steamer to Portland. Were Ellen and James aware of the mutual attraction that was beginning to spring up between them during that first meeting? Both their memoirs are silent on that point, but it seems a reasonable assumpton that he must have been seen in her company many times during those days in the small town, for as soon as he returned to Orrington, an unruly crowd of irate citizens awaited him at the river's edge and beat him mercilessly. It appears that Ellen's futile attempts to pacify the fanatical group had given the people the false impression that she had agreed with them, and James White had become the unwilling victim of their wrath!

A year and a half passed during which time James and Ellen were involved in numerous religious activities, most of them separately, some jointly, for soon after Orrington, James became Ellen's frequent companion as she traveled from town to town, preaching and recounting her visions to the often crowded churches. "On such occasions, they were always accompanied by one of her sisters. In reply to a charge based upon an evil insinuation regarding their association, she once commented proudly, 'I rejoice in God that not a spot or blemish can be fastened upon my name or character. Those who are vile themselves will be the ones who will try to think evil of me.'"[9] And on August 30, 1846, Ellen and James were married.

Seldom has anyone tried to build a marriage on less than the Whites possessed, for it simply would not have been possible. For a year they lived with Ellen's parents in Gorham. Aghast at their poverty, close friends, the Howlands of Topsham, offered a few upstairs rooms in their rather spacious home as living quarters for James, Ellen, and their newborn son Henry—and they gladly accepted. With borrowed furniture, at times sharing the Howlands' food, but often going without; working and living on faith, their marriage was destined to doom—or so outsiders said. But to them there was a world to conquer, people to warn and spiritual confusion to overcome. With Ellen's mind attached to the words "Make known to others what I have revealed to you," as spoken to her in vision, they pressed on. The commission had come to her soon after her first vision in 1844, and when she tried to write again, she realized that a new strength had invaded her hands. She was soon busily copying her visions in letter after letter, mailing her revealed knowledge to friends and fellow believers. In time, even James joined in some of the copying. To him, spare time was almost nonexistent, for determined to provide means for the support of his little family and their evangelistic efforts, he began hauling stone on the railroad, later switching to chopping cordwood in the nearby forests. . . . In this way he worked from dawn till dark for fifty cents a day.

"While at Topsham, Maine," Ellen writes in her memoirs, "we received a letter from Brother E. L. H. Chamberlain, of Middletown, Conn., urging us to attend a conference in that State in April, 1848. We decided to go if we could obtain means. My husband settled with his employer, and found that there was ten dollars due him. With five of this

I purchased articles of clothing that we very much needed, and then patched my husband's overcoat, even piecing the patches, making it difficult to tell the original cloth in the sleeves. We had five dollars left to take us to Dorcester (South Boston), Mass. Our trunk contained nearly everything we possessed on earth." [10]

From Massachusetts they journeyed to Connecticut to the conference and then on to New York for another. "We had no means with which to travel," Ellen wrote of this episode. "My husband's health was poor, but the way opened for him to work in the hayfield, and he decided to accept the work.

"It seemed then that we must live by faith. When we arose in the morning, we bowed beside our bed, and asked God to give us strength to labor through the day. . . ." [11] Quoting in her memoirs from a letter written by her husband on July 2, 1848, to the Howlands, she enlarged on this experience.

" 'It is rainy today, so that I do not mow, or I should not write,' he confided to the Howlands. 'I mow five days for unbelievers, and Sunday for believers, and rest on the seventh day, therefore I have but very little time to write. . . . God gives me strength to labor hard all day. . . . Brother Holt, Brother John Belden, and I have taken one hundred acres of grass to mow, at eighty-seven and one half cents per acre, and board ourselves. Praise the Lord! I hope to get a few dollars here to use in the cause of God.' " [12]

With this hard-earned money, James and Ellen pressed on from conference to conference, six in all. The next summer, still destitute, they began the preparation of the publication of their first periodical, *The Present Truth*. With that simple and unassuming beginning—an eight-page semimonthly publication—the first step was set on the road to the creation of a worldwide publishing venture, all based on guidelines given to Ellen in a series of visions starting in 1848.

"I have a message for you," she said to her husband early in November of that year. "You must begin to print a little paper and send it out to the people. Let it be small at first; but as the people read, they will send you means with which to print, and it will be a success from the first. From this small beginning it was shown to me to be like streams of light that went clear round the world." [13]

Not until the summer of the following year was the venture officially launched when the first issue consisting of one thousand copies came off the press to be paid for when the money became available. With a borrowed horse and buggy, James traveled to Middletown, Connecticut, to pick up the first load of magazines from the printer, paying for it with the money that came in from interested readers.

Looking at the present (1972) chain of forty-six publishing houses, the outgrowth of a simple beginning, critics sometimes have remarked, "They were successful for they knew what they were after." However, even though Ellen's visions gave her and her husband the mental and spiritual support for their publishing efforts, it was their sincere dedication to their work that forced them on, publishing in Connecticut, Maine and then New York, too. It was in Rochester that they secured a handpress as a means to save money.

In a letter dated April 16, 1852, to their dear old friends the Howlands, Ellen confided about the problems they had encountered since moving to Rochester, New York.

"We are just getting settled in Rochester," she wrote. "We have rented an old house for one hundred and seventy-five dollars a year. We have the press in the house. Were it not for this, we should have to pay fifty dollars a year for office room. You would smile could you look in upon us and see our furniture. We have bought two old bedsteads for twenty-five cents each. My husband brought me home six old chairs, no two of them alike, for which he paid one dollar, and soon he presented me with four more old chairs without any seating, for which he paid sixty-two cents. The frames are strong, and I have been seating them with drilling.

"Butter is so high that we do not purchase it, neither can we afford potatoes. We use sauce in the place of butter, and turnips for potatoes. Our first meals were taken on a fire-board placed upon two empty flour barrels. We are willing to endure privations if the work of God can be advanced. We believe the Lord's hand was in our coming to this place." [14]

It was in Rochester that Uriah Smith, described by many of his contemporaries as "a handsome young man with charming manner" entered the "official" household of the Whites, and with him came a fresh outlook on the development of the growing publishing work.

Starting as a pressman in the office of *The Review and Herald*, he soon attracted the attention of James White. Educated at the Phillips Exeter Academy, his mind was keen and sharp, but no matter how much he attempted to lighten the work load of James White, he could not raise the appalling standard of living that had attached itself to the Whites.

The years spent in Rochester were most arduous for them. Money was scarce, their scanty provisions barely kept them alive, and disease often threatened them with extinction.

"We toiled on in Rochester through much perplexity and discouragement," Ellen writes. "The cholera visited the city, and while it raged, all night long the carriages bearing the dead were heard rumbling through the streets to Mount Hope Cemetery. This disease did not cut down merely the low, but took victims from every class of society. The most skillful physicians were laid low, and borne to Mount Hope.

"As we passed through the streets in Rochester, at almost every corner we would meet wagons with plain pine coffins in which to put the dead." [15]

But—the tide turned, and when in 1855 the Whites moved to Battle Creek, Michigan, to continue the publishing work in a building provided for by friends, it was the first time in their marriage that they were able to occupy a home all by themselves.

Here, too, Uriah Smith began to exhibit his true value, for that very same year, the now twenty-three-year-old pressman's name began to appear as editor on the masthead of *The Review and Herald.* It was not a desirable job, for so primitive was the equipment he was forced to work with that he once confided after trimming the edges of tracts with a pocketknife:

"We blistered our hands in the operation, and often the tracts in form were not half so true and square as the doctrines they taught." So hard did he work on the growing magazine that even though its reputation grew steadily and its financial position improved year after year, he felt forced to take a year's leave in 1869 to overcome his physical exhaustion. His early introduction to the Advent movement, however, began to show, for in later years his function as secretary of the General Conference of Seventh-day Adventists and all-round church pioneer earned for him a reputation as a dedicated church leader.

But this was all still in the future when he joined the Whites in their move to Battle Creek. While both James and Uriah directed the publishing efforts in the *Review* office, Ellen continued to lay the spiritual foundation.

With visions supplying her with divine guidelines about the course of her work in connection with the growth and development of the Advent Movement, she soon concentrated all her efforts on her conviction that Christ's Second Coming was still very imminent. Her major vision given her in Lovett's Grove, Ohio, in 1858 strengthened her belief inasmuch as it revealed to her the intricacies of the cosmic battle between good and evil. It also signified the begin-

ning of her greatest literary work, *The Great Controversy*;
however, her deep glow of inner satisfaction was sadly
jolted when a fourth son, her infant boy, Herbert, died on
December 14, 1860, approximately three months after birth.
"When that tender branch was broken, how our hearts
did bleed none may know but those who have followed their
little ones of promise to the grave," she cried by pen. "But
oh, when our noble Henry died, at the age of sixteen, [1863]
—when our sweet singer was borne to the grave, and we no
more heard his early song—ours was a lonely home." [16]
Saddened by the grip of death, the Whites renewed their
work. Writing out her visions, publishing books and magazines, counseling with the leaders of the newly formed
Seventh-day Adventist Church (the outgrowth of the early
Millerite Movement) and guiding the growth and development of the Church, now became the central issues around
which her life revolved.
It was during that same year that the loosely knit state
organizations of the growing Advent Movement sent dele-
gates to a meeting in Battle Creek, to form what is now
known as the General Conference of Seventh-day Adventists, using for it the name selected at a meeting in 1860 for
the newly organized body of believers. Backed by her many
visions, both James and Ellen White became deeply involved
in the new organization, so much so that the presidency of
it was offered to James—but he refused.
Once the new Church was organized, developments followed each other in quick succession. Only weeks later, on
June 6, Ellen, in vision, received a comprehensive view of
the relation of spirituality to physical health, and of the
many benefits of nature's own remedies. Impressed by what
she relayed to them, the leaders of the newly formed church
decided on a church-wide health-educational program. The
backbone of it formed six pamphlets of sixty-four pages

each, entitled, *Health, or How to Live,* compiled by the husband-and-wife team.

It was a gentle beginning for what was to become a dynamic work, for on Christmas Day, 1865, Ellen received additional inspiration, guiding her to the establishment of a health institute that should not only take care of the sick, but should teach basic principles of preventive medicine. With Dr. George Lay and Dr. Phoebe Lamson as medical staff, the Western Health Reform Institute opened less than one year later, on September 5, 1866, and became the forerunner of a vast chain of Seventh-day Adventist medical institution encircling the globe. It is interesting to note that a twelve-year-old boy, John Harvey Kellogg, who had helped set the type for the *How to Live* pamphlets had by that time become so engrossed in and fascinated by the principles of preventive medicine that a few years later the Whites decided to sponsor him through medical school. Finishing his studies in 1876, he returned to Battle Creek and took charge of the medical institution, soon to be known as The Battle Creek Sanitarium.

Medical institutions of this type were highly unusual in the country, inasmuch as hydrotherapy formed much of the basis on which the newly opened sanitarium operated. But soon its popularity became so great that a mere two months after he treated his first sanitarium patient, Dr. Lay reported its success to be "far beyond our most sanguine expectations." And no wonder, for *The Health Reformer* of November, 1866, states that "patients had been received from Canada, Vermont, Rhode Island, New York, Ohio, Indiana, Michigan, Illinois, Wisconsin and Iowa."

With Ellen's inspired principles of health having been vindicated by the Health Institute, she now became even more in demand as a lecturer on the principles of healthful living, yet it was as a temperance speaker that she drew some of the largest crowds ever recorded in the 1860's and 1870's.

Typical of these was the meeting held at Groveland, Massachusetts, where, without the aid of an electronic public-adress system, she spoke to a gathering of more than twenty thousand people, all of whom arrived at the campground by carriage, boat and train, hoping to hear this remarkable woman speak. Capturing their attention at the afternoon meetings, Ellen forcefully presented her case for Christian temperance.

"Every seat, and all the standing room throughout the entire enclosure was full; some, following the example of Zacchaeus, climbed trees to get a sight of the speaker," one witness described the session. "Standing at the upper part of the campground, the eye swept over a living sea of humanity." [17] So numerous were her public appearances in those years that the Michigan volume of the *American Biographical History* concluded, "As a speaker, Mrs. White is one of the most successful of the few ladies who have become noteworthy as lecturers, in this country, during the last twenty years. Constant use has so strengthened her vocal organs as to give her voice rare depth and power. Her clearness and strength of articulation are so great that, when speaking in the open air, she has frequently been distinctly heard at the distance of a mile. Her language, though simple, is always forcible and elegant. When inspired with her subject, she is often marvelously eloquent, holding the largest audiences spell-bound for hours without a sign of impatience or weariness."

"The subject matter of her discourses," the same biographer stated, "is always of a practical character, bearing chiefly on fireside duties, the religious education of children, temperance, and kindred topics."

By this time (mid-1870's) her reputation as an inspired speaker on religion, health and temperance had extended throughout the country, and the hundreds of speaking engagements she filled, together with the arduous travels, her writing, and at the side of her husband, guiding the publishing efforts of the Seventh-day Adventist Church, undermined her physical endurance greatly. It became apparent when an influenza epidemic struck the country, including Battle Creek, Michigan, their hometown, in late 1874. Shortly after she contracted the disease, pneumonia threatened, and the doctors feared that she had already been touched by the hand of death; however, James suggested one more approach to healing—one he was certain would not fail.

"I shall never forget the solemnity of the occasion," her son William C. White remembered, recalling that dreadful day of January 3, 1875, when in utter desperation James White and two co-workers, Uriah Smith and J. H. Wagoner, knelt down in the living room of the White home, to beg God to spare her life.

"Then mother undertook to pray, and in a hoarse, labored voice, she uttered two or three sentences of petition.

"Suddenly her voice broke clear and musical, and we heard the ringing shout, 'Glory to God!' We all looked up, and saw that she was in vision. Her hands were folded across her breast. Her eyes were directed intently upward, and her lips were closed. There was no breathing although the heart continued its action.

"As she looked intently upward, an expression of anxiety came into her face. She threw aside her blankets, and, stepping forward, walked back and forth in the room. Wringing her hands, she moaned, 'Dark! Dark! All dark! So dark!' Then after a few moments' silence, she exclaimed with emphasis, and a brightening of her countenance, 'A light! A little light! More light! Much light!'

"This we understood afterward, when she told us that the world was presented to her as enshrouded in the mists and fog of error, of superstition, of false tradition, and of worldliness.

"Then as she looked intently and with distress upon this scene, she saw little lights glimmering through the darkness. These lights increased in power. They burned brighter, and they were lifted higher and higher. Each one lighted other lights, which also burned brightly, until the whole world was lighted.

"Following her exclamatory remarks regarding the lights, she sat down in her chair. After a few minutes, she drew three long, deep breaths, and then resumed her natural breathing. Her eyes rested upon the company that had been assembled for prayer. Father, knowing that after a vision everything looked strange to her, knelt by her side, and spoke in her ear, saying, 'Ellen, you have been in vision.'

"'Yes,' she said, her voice sounding far away as though she were speaking to someone in another room.

"'Were you shown many things?' father asked.

"'Yes,' she replied.

"'Would you like to tell us about them now?' he asked.

"'Not now,' was her response." [18]

"Returning from his publishing house office later that same afternoon, James, with concern, rushed to Ellen's room and asked,

"'Ellen, there is to be an important meeting in the church this evening. Do you wish to attend?'

"'Certainly,' she answered. So she dressed for the meeting, and with father, walked down through the snow to the church." [19]

Only hours had passed since the prayer session had ended, but whereas at that time she had virtually been on the brink of death, she was now completely healed. Her influenza and hoarseness were gone, and no longer did she show signs of weakness and exhaustion.

A heavy silence greeted Ellen White as she walked up to

the platform and began to talk about the vision. Beaming brightly, she announced that she had been shown new methods and possibilities to be explored for the advancement of the gospel. When she mentioned that she had observed printing presses running in many foreign lands, printing periodicals, tracts, books and other religious material, James White interrupted his wife.

" 'Ellen, can you tell us the names of those countries?' he queried, eagerly, probing into parts of the vision that seemed to be related to their publishing work.

She looked at him, hesitated for a moment and then answered:

" 'N-o, I do not know the names. The picture of the places and of the printing presses is very clear, and if I should ever see them, I would recognize them. But I did not hear the names of the places. Oh yes, I remember one, the angel said, "Australia." ' "

"At the time when this vision was given," William White explained, recollecting the events surrounding the 1875 revelation, "we [Seventh-day Adventist Church] had one publishing house, and were contemplating the establishment of a second one in California. . . . It was several years before we had presses of our own in Switzerland and Norway, and ten years before we had work of any kind in Australia, the country that was especially mentioned in the relation of the vision." [20]

James White's interest in this vision was sincere, for he occupied a very select place in his wife's work, since he was not only her husband, but her co-worker as well. While Ellen concentrated on giving religious guidance to the Church, James converged all his attention on church administration and the establishment of church-affiliated educational institutions and publishing companies. As a direct result of his endeavors, the *Review and Herald Publishing Association* and the *Pacific Press Publishing Association* were formed, together with Battle Creek College, the forerunner of Andrews University in Berrien Springs, Michigan. The Battle Creek Sanitarium grew and flourished under his successful leadership.

Though enthralled by his wife's vision concerning the future of the publishing work, he did not live long enough to see it realized. Did he have a foreboding of his approaching death? No one will ever know, yet Ellen's writings seemingly pointed to that direction.

"We had an appointment to attend a tent meeting at Charlotte," she recalls, "[and] on the way, my husband seemed cheerful, yet a feeling of solemnity rested upon him. . . . Little did I think, as we traveled on, that this was the last journey we should ever make together. The weather changed suddenly from oppressive heat to chilling cold. My husband took cold, but thought his health so good that he would receive no permanent injury. On our return home, my husband complained of slight indisposition, yet he engaged in his work as usual. Every morning we visited the grove near our home, and united in prayer.

"On the following Monday he had a severe chill, and the next day I too was attacked. Together we were taken to the Sanitarium for treatment. On Friday my symptoms became more favorable. The doctor then informed me that my husband was inclined to sleep, and that danger was apprehended. I was immediately taken to his room, and as soon as I looked upon his countenance I knew that he was dying." [21] Ellen stayed by his side all that day and the next until 5:00 P.M. Saturday afternoon, August 6, 1881, when he died.

The sudden tragedy fell upon her with a crushing weight. A relapse resulted, and when on August 13 his funeral service was held, she had to be carried to the church to attend. Departing two weeks later for the West, she hoped to lose herself once again in her work, although without her husband. On the way to California, she stopped in Boulder, Colorado, to rest among the pines.

"From our cottage I could look out upon a forest of young pines, so fresh and fragrant that the air was perfumed with their spicy odor," she confided to her diary. "In former years, my husband and myself made this grove our sanctuary. . . . Again I have been among the mountains, but alone. None to share my thoughts and feelings as I looked once more upon those grand and awful scenes! Alone, alone! God's dealings seem mysterious, His purposes unfathomable; yet I know that they must be just, and wise, and merciful." [22]

Arriving in California and making her home with friends, after the trying weeks following James's death, it almost appeared as if she had begun to regard his death as a challenge to add his waiting work load to hers. Without delay she relentlessly pushed for international mission programs, overseas publishing work, the establishment of a college on the Pacific Coast and a more determined effort by the steadily growing Seventh-day Adventist Church to acquaint people with the fulfillment of prophecy.

Accompanying his mother on a trip to Europe in 1885, William White was witness to the accuracy of her memorable publishing vision of 1875, in which she had been shown the printing presses in operation long before the publishing companies had been established.

"In Basel, Ellen White was permitted to see for the first time with her natural eyes, one of the printing presses that had been shown to her in vision ten years before," he writes. "We arrived in the city late in the evening, and the next morning were shown the various departments of the new publishing house at 48 Weirweg.

"'This place looks natural,' remarked Mrs. White to B. L. Whitney, as we entered the pressroom. 'I have seen these presses before.' Soon the presses stopped, and the young men who had been feeding them were introduced to her. She shook hands with them, and turning to Elder Whitney, she said, 'Where is the other one?'

"Elder Whitney, desiring to ascertain just how much Mrs. White knew about the affairs of the office, inquired, 'What other one, Sister White?'

"She answered, 'There is an older man who works in this room, and I have a message for him.'

"Elder Whitney replied, 'Brother Albert Deichy, foreman of the room, is in the city this morning on business. You will see him here tomorrow.' " [23]

"A few months later," White continued, "we visited Christiania (Oslo) Norway, and when we entered the new publishing house, mother remarked, 'This place seems very familiar to me. I have seen this before.'

"When we reached the pressroom, she said, 'I have seen these presses before. This is one of the places shown me years ago where publications were being issued in countries outside the United States.'

"Then, returning with Elder Matteson to his editorial room, she gave him much counsel about his work, thus indicating her familiarity with the work of this office." [24]

Yet one more country still awaited her scrutinizing look. Writes her son:

"Six years later, in December, 1891, Mrs. White, accompanied by several members of her family and G. B. Starr, arrived in Australia, where she lived and labored nearly nine years. We reached Melbourne the first week of 1892, and when she entered the publishing house in North Fitzroy, she spoke of the building, its different parts, and its uses as though she was fully acquainted with the place.

"When we came to the pressroom, she said, 'I have seen this place before. I have seen these persons, and I know the conditions existing among the workers in this department. There is a lack of unity here, a lack of harmony.'

"Soon after this, she wrote words of counsel to the workers

in the office, and especially to those in the pressroom, which, when heeded, brought about important changes." [25]

Her words and advice were vital to the growing religious movement, and soon, guided by her visions, publishing companies, hospitals, schools and missionary stations began to sprout up all over the world. So extensive was her influence that today the Seventh-day Adventist Church operates the second-largest Protestant-church-affiliated school system in the United States, backed by nine fully accredited senior colleges and two major universities. Of the forty-six publishing companies that grew as the result of her drive, three are in the continental United States. A truly impressive chain of Book & Bible Houses and approximately four thousand salesmen sell their religious literature in the hundred languages into which the books are translated.

If ever a prediction reached complete and accurate fulfillment, this one most certainly did.

The many facets of Ellen White's life impressed her friends and acquaintances in diverse ways. As a homemaker, she was tenderly remembered by her family and those who worked for her; as a writer, she was greatly admired by her contemporaries. But there was more to Ellen White. In her role of what she often referred to as "a messenger of God," she was in constant demand as a speaker and personal counselor. The vault of her Estate containing all of her memoirs, book manuscripts, diaries and personal letters is a treasure house of information. From the yellowing pages of her letters and others penned by those who knew her intimately emerge recollections that portray her as a simple woman burdened with sorrow, fighting discouragement, struggling with disease and possessed with a deep love for flowers and animals and an overpowering concern for people. Other letters picture her as someone firm in convictions, gentle in manner and humble when speaking of her role as God's messenger.

A loving sidelight of Ellen White as a grandmother emerges from Grace White Jacques, the daughter of Ellen's son Willie. Reflecting back on those happy days in the early part of this century, she recalled:

"Whenever we came to see grandmother during the week, we ran up the dark, narrow backstairs to her writing room, instead of using the wide, formal stairs as we did on Sabbath. She would be writing on her lapboard before the bay window. As soon as she would see us enter, she would lay down her pen and greet each one of us with a kiss.

"Sometimes she took my younger brother, Arthur, who was quite a bit younger than I, upon her lap and coddled him with her dainty, loving hands. He would try to count the buttons on the front of her dress, but invariably his number system was not the same as ours. She would then laugh and give him a big hug.

"Grandmother laughed at humorous things," she continued. "She was always able to laugh and enjoy the happy things of life. Outside of her house we were normal, active children, but once inside we did not have to be told to be quiet, for we were filled with much love and respect for her. She had the wonderful ability of always being able to put people at ease."

Showing the understanding Ellen White had for those events that might cause embarrassment to some people, she recalled her mother's anxiety when she found out she was pregnant.

"My mother was forty years old when she gave birth to my youngest brother, Francis. Realizing that she was rather old to be having children, she wondered what grandmother would say. Her fears did not last long, for grandmother told her when she saw the baby that she had been praying that she would live long enough to see another one of my mother's children."

Others, too, often talked about her understanding and

delightful sense of humor. Mrs. Bertha Spear Boger, of Greenville, Tennessee, once spoke of a humorous incident that occurred when she attended a religious service in which Ellen White occupied the rostrum.

"Elder W. C. White was, as usual, on the rostrum with his mother. The meeting had been opened and his mother was in the midst of a good sermon.

"No doubt he had arisen early and felt weary, for with his responsibilities at rest, he relaxed into a good nap. Noticing this, his mother stopped and offered an apology thus— 'When Willie was a baby I used to take him into the pulpit and let him sleep in a basket beneath the pulpit, and he has never gotten over the habit!' Then amid the keen appreciation of the audience, she proceeded as if there had been no break in her thought."

With her grandson Arthur White as guide, we diligently combed through the pages of history and saw the *real* Ellen emerge: dignified, helpful and sincere up until the moment of death.

Concerning her involvement with the principles as revealed to her in the health-reform vision of June 6, 1863, Ellen had been a heavy meat eater for many years and cared relatively little for other types of food. As most of her contemporaries, she felt that meat was necessary to maintain good health.

But the vision changed all that. Compressed into minutes, seemingly endless volumes of health-related principles were shown her, advocating the advantages of a diet void of flesh meat and stimulating food. As uncommon as those concepts were in her day, she not only accepted them but adjusted her own life-style accordingly.

"No more meat from now on!" was the order that reached the cook, and it was promptly carried out.

Awhile later when the family met for breakfast, they found everything nourishing waiting for them—except meat.

Ellen took one look at the table and disgustedly turned around. "Not hungry," she decided, but when she returned at noontime, the same basic meal awaited her. Not until the next day did she decide to join in and eat, for by that time she was famished, and the simple food had began to appear appetizing.

"I placed my arms across my stomach, and said 'I will not taste a morsel. I will eat simple food, or I will not eat at all. . . .' I said to my stomach, 'You may wait until you can eat bread.'" [26]

Starting health reform in her home was only one of the many ways she showed her affection and concern toward her husband and her children; however, these reform ideas were not just limited to her family. Her diary reveals that at times she entertained no less than thirty-five guests for dinner, and all were exposed to vegetarianism. None went away hungry.

Wrote Ellen in 1870:

"I have a well set table on all occasions. I make no change for visitors, whether believers or unbelievers. I intend never to be surprised by an unreadiness to entertain at my table from one to half a dozen extra who may chance to come in. I have enough simple, healthful food ready to satisfy hunger and nourish the system. If any want more than this, they are at liberty to find it elsewhere. No butter or flesh meats of any kind come on my table. Cake is seldom found there. I generally have an ample supply of fruits, good bread, and vegetables. Our table is always well patronized, and all who partake of the food do well, and improve upon it. All sit down with no epicurean appetite, and eat with a relish the bounties supplied by our Creator." [27]

While she pursued these principles till her death at age eighty-seven, and benefitted from them, at times in her travels, conditions demanded some temporary compromise.

Hospitable as she was, there was no denying that the constant influx of visitors and dinner guests posed many a problem—some of them affecting Ellen personally.

In a letter to an acquaintance, written November 12, 1873, she admitted this.

"I have arisen at half past five o'clock in the morning," she wrote, "helped Lucinda wash dishes, have written until dark, then done necessary sewing, sitting up until near midnight; I have done the washings for the family after my day's writing was done. I have frequently been so weary as to stagger like an intoxicated person, but praise the Lord I have been sustained."

Entrusted with the upbringing of her boys—two lived to maturity—and pursuing her religious work meant fusing two full-time endeavors into one life, but it never caused her to neglect her family. Explained Arthur White:

"Her home discipline was firm, but administered with love and kindness. She used simple but effective inducements to keep them in good behavior. Seldom—very seldom—did she use corporal punishment and then only after a quiet talk and earnest prayer."

"I never allowed my children to think that they could plague me in their childhood," wrote the woman who in later years authored the books *Education* and *Child Guidance*. "Never did I allow myself to say a harsh word. . . . When my spirit was stirred, and when I felt anything like being provoked, I would say, 'Children, we shall let this rest now, we shall not say anything more about it now. Before you retire, we shall talk it over.' Having all this time to reflect, by evening they had cooled off, and I could handle them very nicely." [28]

When in the course of work, she and James were forced to leave the children with help employed in the home or with friends for weeks at a time, Ellen's letters to her sons more than verified her attachment and concern for their well being. On September 6, 1859, writing to her twelve-year-old son Henry, she counseled:

"We hope you are well and happy. Be a good, steady boy. If you only fear God and love Him, our happiness will be complete. You can be a noble boy. Love, truthfulness and honesty—these are sacred treasures. Do not lay them aside for a moment. You may be tempted and often tried, but, my dear boy, it is at such a time these lovely treasures shine, and are highly prized. Cling closely to these precious traits, whatever you may be called to suffer. Let truthfulness and honesty ever live in your heart. Never through fear of punishment, sacrifice these noble traits. The Lord will help you to do right. I believe it is your purpose to do right and to please your parents. . . . I must close. Do right because you love to. Preserve these letters I write to you, and read them often; and if you should be left without a mother's care, they will be a help to you.

"Here is a peppermint for Willie."

Her feelings toward her family ran strong, but to her outsiders were just as important. In a number of personal letters, she briefly mentioned some of the ways in which she had tried to relieve the need of families living in neighboring villages.

"We purchase wood of our brethren who are farmers, and we try to give their sons and daughters employment," she wrote while living in Australia and working on her books during the financial depression of 1894, "but we need a large charitable fund upon which to draw to keep families from starvation. . . . I divided my household stores of provisions with families of this sort, sometimes going eleven miles to relieve their necessities." [29] Another letter revealed how sometimes all other work was laid aside in the White home when others required help.

"Last evening we had a Dorcas society in our home," she

wrote, referring to the ladies' welfare auxiliary of the church, "and my workers who help in the preparation of my articles for the papers, and do the cooking and the sewing, five of them, sat up until midnight, cutting out clothing. They made three pairs of pants for the children of one family. Two sewing machines were running until midnight. I think there was never a happier set of workers than were these girls last evening." [30] That these occasions were quite frequent shows in another letter she wrote.

"We do not have to hunt up cases," she confided to a friend, "they hunt us up. These things are forced upon our notice; we cannot be Christians and pass them by and say, 'Be ye warmed and clothed,' and do not those things that will warm and clothe them. The Lord Jesus says, 'The poor ye have always with you.' They are always with you. They are God's legacy to us." [31]

But there was ample to do, for her continuous revelations kept her pen in constant motion.

"Early in my public labors I was bidden by the Lord, 'Write, write the things that are revealed to you,'" she said in an article published in 1906. "At the time this message came to me, I could not hold my hand steady. My physical condition made it impossible for me to write. But again came the word, 'Write the things that are revealed to you.' I obeyed; and as the result it was not long before I could write page after page with comparative ease. Who told me what to write? Who steadied my right hand and made it possible for me to use a pen?—It was the Lord." [32]

"'Your work,' He instructed me, 'is to bear My word. Strange things will arise, and in your youth I set you apart to bear the message to the erring ones, to carry the word before unbelievers, and with pen and voice to reprove from the Word actions that are not right. Exhort from the Word. . . .

"'Be not afraid of man, for My shield shall protect you.

It is not you that speaketh: it is the Lord that giveth the message of warning and reproof. Never deviate from the truth *under any circumstances*. Give the light I shall give you. The messages for these last days shall be written in books, and shall stand immortalized.' " [33]

From the very moment the power to write surged into her hand in 1845 and remained there to the end of her life, she did all of her writing by hand. When in later days she was assisted by secretaries for the copying and preparation of material to be published, she still insisted in doing her writing in that manner, all alone and undisturbed.

"The words I employ in writing what I have seen," she once stated, "are my own, unless they be those spoken to me by an angel, which I always enclose in marks of quotation." [34] The visions enlightened her *mind*; she then in turn transposed those mental impressions into words—and she took her task seriously.

"It is told that at one conference," Arthur White commented, "she was so pressed with her writings that she found it necessary to work while attending a series of meetings. One morning, seated at a small table in the auditorium where a meeting was being held, she wrote steadily while the speaker, J. N. Andrews, lectured. At the noon intermission she was asked her opinion on Elder Andrews' qualifications as a public speaker. 'I wish I could tell you,' she replied earnestly, still preoccupied with her work, 'but it has been so long since I heard him that I really can't express an opinion.' Her concentration had been so intense that she had not realized that he had been the speaker that morning."

On other occasions, while visiting acquaintances, she was observed leaving her host and retreating to a secluded bedroom to continue her writing. Many times she did her writing in the early hours of the morning, but once started, she often had a difficult time in stopping before a certain segment of spiritual importance had been entrusted to paper.

Concerning her hectic work schedule, she wrote in a letter in 1906:

"The evening after the Sabbath I retired, and rested well without ache or pain until half past ten. I was unable to sleep. I had received instruction, and I seldom lie in bed after such instruction comes. There was a company assembled in————, and instruction was given by One in our midst that I was to repeat and repeat with pen and voice. I left my bed, and wrote for five hours as fast as my pen could trace the lines. Then I rested on the bed for an hour, and slept part of the time.

"I placed the matter in the hands of my copyist, and on Monday morning it was waiting for me, placed inside my office door on Sunday evening. There were four articles ready for me to read over and make any corrections needed. The matter is now prepared, and some of it will go in the mail today.

"This is the line of work that I am carrying on. I do most of my writing while the other members of the family are asleep."[35] Another time, early one morning while in Australia, she wrote, "I sit here on my bed, this cold July morning trying to write to you. I have woolen mitts on my hands, leaving my fingers free to write. I place my lamp on one side at my left hand, rather than behind me, and then the light shines on my paper in just the right way. . . . It is a little past two o'clock. I continue to be an early riser and I write every day."[36] *This she wrote at the age of 72!* Even sickness could not diminish her perseverance. Disabled with rheumatic fever for almost a year during the early part of her sojourn in Australia, she nevertheless insisted on remaining active.

"With the writings that shall go in this mail I have, since leaving America, written twenty-hundred pages of letter paper," she wrote. "I could not have done all this writing if the Lord had not strengthened and blessed me in large measure. My arm and shoulder have been full of suffering, hard to bear, but the hand has been able to hold the pen and trace words that have come to me from the Spirit of the Lord." [37]

"You will excuse the poor writing, for I am obliged to change my position about every hour to be able to be made any way comfortable to write at all. I send in this mail sixty pages of letter paper written by my own hand." Then speaking about how she was able to write at all, she continued, "First my hair-cloth chair is bolstered up with pillows, then they have a frame, a box batted with pillows which I rest my limbs upon and a rubber pillow under them. My table is drawn up close to me, and I thus write with my paper on a cardboard in my lap.

"Yesterday I was enabled to sit two hours thus arranged. . . . Then I must change position. She [the nurse] then gets me on the spring bed and bolsters me up with pillows. I may be able to sit some over one hour and thus it is a change, but I am thankful I can write at all." [38]

A study of her books reveals that they can be classified into six completely separate areas. A good number of them deal with admonition, counsel and warning, and contain material originally given to the Church, individuals or specific church leaders. Other writings are concerned more specifically with the history of mankind, with many "behind-the-scene" descriptions as only Ellen White could give them. There are also books filled with her prophecies, presenting detailed information as to the sequence and significance of future events. Still another area well-covered in her writings is the inspirational aspect of living a Christian life. Health-related counsel forms another major segment of her work. Her autobiographical material—heavily focusing on her religious activities—comprises the last group.

George Wharton James, writer, lecturer and contempo-

rary of Ellen White, stated, when writing about her in his
book *California—Romantic and Beautiful* (pp. 319, 320):

"This remarkable woman, also, though almost entirely
self-educated, has written and published more books and in
more languages, which circulate to a greater extent than the
written works of any woman in history."

Arthur White, in summing up the impressive statistics relating to his grandmother's work, has arrived at some remarkable figures.

"Today [1972] there are 24,375 pages in the current E. G.
White books," he pointed out. "Taking these with the earlier
editions which are now out of print, we have a total of
25,685 pages. We may add to this the more than 4,500 articles which have appeared in our various denominational
journals. These reduced to book pages would give us another 20,000 pages. In addition to this there are many
thousands of pages of manuscript matter which, because of
its local or personal character, was not published. We point
to these books as the fruit of a lifework, and yet no great
claims were made by the writer, for she says: [39]

" 'Sister White is not the originator of these books. They
contain the instruction that during her lifework God has
been giving her. They contain the precious, comforting light
that God has graciously given His servant to be given to
the world. From their pages this light is to shine into the
hearts of men and women, leading them to the Saviour.' " [40]

Held in high esteem by the Church she helped organize
are the nine volumes known as *Testimonies for the Church*
consisting of 5,274 pages of advice, visions and counsel dealing with institutional development, church organization,
home and foreign mission endeavors, social and health re-
forms, etc. They show her deep involvement with the birth
of the Seventh-day Adventist Church and the correctness of
her early visions in relationship to the development of his-

tory. Undoubtedly her popularity and the wide circulation of her books bear a direct relationship to the timeliness of her visions.

She had always been cognizant of the personal implications of her life's work from its very inception because of the ridicule, coldness, envy, sarcasm and unbelief that were sometimes leveled at her from her first vision on. She knew instinctively that loneliness, sleepless nights and constant work would tax her health as nothing else could, but she accepted the challenge, though somewhat reluctantly in the beginning.

"When this work was first given me, I begged the Lord to lay the burden on someone else," she said humbly and sincerely. "The work was so large and broad and deep that I feared I could not do it. But by His Holy Spirit the Lord has enabled me to perform the work which He gave me to do." [41]

The waning years of her life were busy ones. During the last fifteen years, while residing at St. Helena, California, she completed ten major books, among which such authoritative volumes as *Story of Prophets and Kings, Education, Ministry of Healing* and *Acts of the Apostles* occupy a predominant place. Yet, the more time that elapsed, the stronger the realization came to her that she might not live until the Second Coming of Christ. It didn't worry her, though understandably it must have been a disappointment since she had been looking forward to witnessing this celestial event ever since becoming associated with William Miller's group in 1844.

How weary she had finally become was evident in her reaction to what transpired in her upstairs bedroom sometime during the night of March 2, 1907. She had been occupied the whole afternoon of that day in a discussion with church officials on church-related matters, and, when the visit ended, was completely worn out. Tired and exhausted and fully aware of every one of her seventy-nine years, Ellen White closed the door to her bedroom and lay down.

"I was suffering from rheumatism in my left side and could get no rest because of the pain," she recalled, referring back to the awesome happening of that night. "I turned from side to side, trying to find ease from the suffering. There was a pain in my heart that portended no good for me."

"At last I fell asleep.

"About half past nine I attempted to turn myself, and as I did so, I became aware that my body was entirely free from pain. As I turned from side to side, and moved my hands, I experienced an extraordinary freedom and lightness that I cannot describe. The room was filled with light, a most beautiful, soft, azure light, and I seemed to be in the arms of heavenly beings.

"This peculiar light I have experienced in the past in times of special blessing, but this time it was more distinct, more impressive, and I felt such peace, peace so full and abundant no words can express it. I raised myself into a sitting posture, and I saw that I was surrounded by a bright cloud, white as snow, the edges of which were tinged with a deep pink. The softest, sweetest music was filling the air, and I recognized the music as the singing of the angels.

"Then a Voice spoke to me, saying,

" 'Fear not; I am your Saviour. Holy angels are all about you.'

"Then this is heaven," I said, "and now I can be at rest. I shall have no more messages to bear, no more misrepresentations to endure. Everything will be easy now, and I shall enjoy peace and rest. Oh, what inexpressible peace fills my soul! Is this indeed heaven? Am I one of God's little children? and shall I always have this peace?"

"The Voice replied, 'Your work is not yet done.'

"Again I fell asleep, and when I awoke I heard music,

and I wanted to sing. Then someone passed my door, and I wondered if that person saw the light. After a time the light passed away, but the peace remained." [42]

For eight more years following that vision she continued her work, but on February 13, 1915, on entering her study from the hallway, she apparently tripped and fell. When she was rushed to the hospital, her X rays revealed an intracapsular fracture of the left femur. She suffered little in the remaining months, but it was obvious that there was little prospect of recovery, primarily due to her advanced age.

She realized that the end was near. A few weeks prior to her death, she called her son Willie.

"I am very weak," she confided to him. "I am sure that this is my last sickness. I am not worried at the thought of dying. I feel comforted all the time, that the Lord is near me. . . . I do not worry about the work I have done. I have done the best I could. I do not think that I shall be lingering long. I do not expect much suffering. I am thankful that we have the comforts of life in time of sickness.

"Do not worry. I go only a little before the others." [43]

Relaxed, she spent the final few weeks of her life in the comfortable office room on the second floor of Elmshaven, her St. Helena home. It was a spacious, light, airy room, with a bay window through which the continuous rays of the warm California sun bathed large portions of the room with a mellow light. Realizing that this was without doubt her last illness, caring hands brought a hospital bed into the room, and once the first weeks of illness were behind her, she was often lifted out of bed and placed in her old familiar chair so that she could watch the ever-changing beauty of spring and summer that spread over the Napa Valley.

Many times during those weeks, anxious friends would drop by and visit briefly as she sat there, gazing at the early blossoms and the budding roses, usually with some of the books she had written resting on her lap.

"I appreciate these books as I never did before," she once remarked. "They are truth, and they are righteousness, and they are an everlasting testimony that God is true." [44]

A peaceful calm prevailed over Elmshaven during the days prior to July 16. Death was rapidly closing in, and everyone knew it.

Beckoning her son over to her bedside, Ellen lovingly fastened her eyes on him one more time and whispered softly,

"I know in whom I have believed. . . . God is Love. . . . He giveth His beloved sleep. . . ."

And on July 16, 1915, at 3:40 P.M., Ellen White died.

Chapter 3

The Enlightened Prophet

THE QUESTION AS to whether or not we believe there is a place for prophets in our already "enlightened" society really depends upon the value we put on supernaturalism in human life. From time immemorial, the idea of supernatural or supernormal powers interfering with or controlling the affairs of man has always been a rather frightening concept. To those who admit the existence of supernatural manifestations, a belief in the existence of a Higher Power is inevitable.

"Only a Higher Power can know the past and the future," they reason, trying to find an acceptable explanation for their own ignorance in this field, "and the least we can do is to be realistic about it whether we appreciate its interference or not." The critics who don't share this point of view but nevertheless continue to probe its manifestations with undying fascination—without wanting to partake of the force behind it—usually end up admitting that "something" exists "somewhere" beyond the physical and visual boundaries of man. It really boils down to the simple fact that to the majority of people evidences of supernaturalism are phenomena to be reckoned with, both in temporal and spiritual affairs.

It is this broad acceptance of the unexplainable that has created a spiritually dangerous problem. Not willing and not sufficiently interested to study the various occult phenomena and learn how to differentiate between constructive and destructive forces, man has allowed psychic phenomena in all its forms to flourish and grow. H. M. S. Richards, Jr., speaker of the "Voice of Prophecy" radio program, commented on this in a recent broadcast.

"We are not speaking of mere legendary tales of ghosts and goblins, of black cats, of old women riding broomsticks through the air," he pointed out. "We are speaking of dark powers which control the minds and bodies of people today and have done so since the earliest records of history. We recall the art of the magicians of Egypt who were buried with Pharaoh's host in the Red Sea; the incantations of Balaam which brought about his own destruction; the sorcerers and necromancers of Nineveh and Babylon who perished with the nations they had deluded; the experience of Saul, the first king of Israel, who went from a necromancer's midnight séance to a suicide's grave; numerous rulers, from Croesus of old to various modern kings and rulers, who, we are told, still consult unseen powers. History's long and often sorrowful records are full of such manifestations in the Christian era. Lucian, the Greek writer born about 120 A.D. wrote pages on the subject in his book concerning the Gods of Syria. In the fourth century, the heathen philosopher Lamlichus writes of evil spirits who simulate the presence of God and wish to be worshipped themselves." [1]

It all demonstrates that the "now" emphasis on "psychic

phenomena" is nothing new. Every generation has recognized its importance.

Throughout the ages, history and religion have been closely intertwined with the development of witchcraft and sorcery, but no one book contains so much authoritative material on the subject as does the compilation of religious and prophetic books commonly known as the Bible. It is the only prophetic handbook which contains substantiated history as well as authenticated prophecy. The entire compilation of sacred writings is so saturated with prophetic utterings that no less than 3,856 texts of the Old Testament are prophetic in nature and one out of every twenty-eight verses in the New Testament is prophetic!

Realizing how much of the Bible is pure prophecy, it is rather difficult to comprehend that while today's psychics do claim to have the same gift of prophecy as did the Biblical prophets and use the Bible's writings to substantiate their claims, not one psychic seems to have borrowed their predictions from Biblical prophecy. But while they boast to be prophets, they nevertheless borrow from other psychics—seers whose accuracies are spoken of in percentages.

Somehow they have missed the greatest handbook of all.

For an in-depth study of projected history, the Bible is the handbook par excellence, more so since it is declared to have been written by the originator of prophecy.

"Remember all that happened long ago; for I am God, there is no other, I am God, and there is no one like me; I reveal the end from the beginning, from ancient times I reveal what is to be; I say, 'My purpose shall take effect, I will accomplish all that I please.' " [2]

According to the prophetic guidebook, communication between the Higher Powers and man had its inception in the Garden of Eden. In fact, the first book of the Bible, historical and prophetic in scope, talks about face-to-face communication, *direct God-to-man contact,* between the

Creator and His creation. But the fall of Adam and Eve forced a dramatic change in this dialogue. Using man's unfaithfulness to his Creator as reason for ceasing this direct approach, intermediaries, *prophets,* were appointed as needed to supplement fading memories of the messages given through the original channel of communication.

"During the first twenty-five hundred years of human history," writes Ellen G. White in the introduction to her masterpiece, *"The Great Controversy,"* "there was no written revelation. Those who had been taught of God, communicated their knowledge to others, and it was handed down from father to son through successive generations." [3]

During the early period of human history, direct communication was a living reality to such historical figures as Adam, Enoch, Abraham, Job, Jacob and others living in the patriarchal age. Developing simultaneously, however, were psychic manifestations that had started in Eden with a Voice speaking through the mouth of a serpent, adding an element of intrigue and treason into the Biblical treasure of history and prophecy. But it did more—it brought to the surface the true character of the battle between good and evil—two opposing forces fighting for the control of the minds of man.

The years during which the prophetic handbook was written are generally regarded as a historic time-span when prophetic and psychic phenomena experienced a high point, but it is often forgotten that female prophets played a role almost as important as that of their male counterparts. True, most of the ancient prophecies were transmitted through prophets such as Samuel, Amos, Daniel, Ezekiel and others, but Biblical history also lists women among the great prophets of old. There was Miriam, the elder sister of Moses the Lawgiver, who was a prophet, and there was Deborah, who was a judge of ancient Israel. Huldah, a prophet in the time of King Josiah; Noadiah, a woman who prophesied in the time of Nehemiah; and Anna, a prophet who lived during the days of King Herod, were all of sufficient importance to be listed in the prophetic guidebook. Both men and women have always been used as channels of communication, and the fact that the overwhelming majority of prophetic writings that survived the ages were penned by men does not alter this fact.

It is interesting to note that the same books which record the timely warnings of the patriarchal prophets also contain prophecies for a time in projected history when prophecy and prophets (both male and female) will again occupy a predominant place in religious life.

"Thereafter the day shall come when I will pour out my spirit on all mankind; your sons and your daughters shall prophesy, your old men shall dream dreams and your young men see visions" (Joel 2:28). Taken separately from all other indications of a similar nature, this seems to indicate a time when everyone will have a chance to become a prophet of God. The prophet Isaiah, however, added something in Isaiah 8:20:

"To the law and to the testimony: if they speak not according to this word, it is because there is no light in them," he stated, clearly indicating that there would be those who would prophesy without being inspired by the right source! John of Patmos, the prophet who authored the Book of Revelation, was even more specific when he pointed out that these true prophets would have "the testimony of Jesus" which is "the Spirit of Prophecy" (Rev. 19:10).

So the idea of false and true prophets appearing simultaneously is *not* new. In fact, this development was not only predicted by those prophets ranking as history's great, but was also foretold by the Son of God nineteen hundred years ago.

"Impostors will come claiming to be messiahs or prophets, and they will produce great signs and wonders to mislead even God's chosen, if such a thing were possible. See, I have forewarned you" (Matt. 24:24). Combine this text with, those previously quoted, and it becomes obvious that a fulfilled prediction does not necessarily transform a psychic into a prophet. It is strict adherence to the ten tests for a true prophet, together with having the testimony of Jesus, that constitute the absolute criterion.

The prophetic guidebook, in speaking of prophets and their function as relay points between God and man, gives adequate information on the various ways utilized in the olden days to apprise men of God's will. A meticulous dissection of Biblical prophecy indicates that only three methods of contact were employed and approved of. It may surprise today's psychic devotees to learn that the favorite methods used by our modern-day seers—clairvoyance, astrology, palmistry, crystal gazing, contacting the spirits of the dead, wizardry and witchcraft—are not found among them. Direct "God-to-man" contact was the most elementary of them all. According to the Book of Genesis it began that way in Eden and continued throughout the early history of mankind. With the introduction of prophets using *visions of the night* and *dreams, a new* element was brought into the rapidly growing field of extrasensory communication, thereby completing the God-ordained network for keeping up a dialogue with wandering man. Since we're living in an age when the Spirit of Prophecy is still active, then we must assume that a true prophet not only follows and adheres to the basic guidelines already given as fundamental elements of the "prophetic communications system," but that he also follows the age-old *methods* set aside for *receiving* these prophetic impulses, either through direct *God-to-man contact*, through *visions* or through *dreams.*

Merely claiming to be a prophet is just not good enough.

In trying to place Ellen White's gift of prophecy in its true perspective, the circumstances surrounding the visions received by her invariably constitute a major point of interest. Although they cannot be regarded as tests on the same level as the ten tests of a true prophet (Chapter One), they are nevertheless indicative of the authenticity of the manifestation.

Arthur L. White has categorized the manner in which his grandmother received her visions in three distinct groups:

1. Visions given in public and accompanied by marked physical phenomena.
2. Visions given during a period of prayer or writing, unaccompanied by physical phenomena.
3. Visions given during the quiet hours of the night, often referred to as "prophetic dreams."

"It has been supposed by some that in Mrs. White's experiences she wrote while in vision," he pointed out, "but this is not true. Some have concluded that when she wrote she was recording words which she heard repeated to her by an angel. This, too, is erroneous, except in rare instances when short, direct quotations are given of what the attending angel said. Some have been of the opinion that there was a mechanical force which guided the pen which she held in her hand. Such a view is also entirely out of harmony with the facts.

"The revelation consisted of the *enlightening of the mind,* and then, when not in vision, it was the task of the prophet—with the aid of the Spirit of God of course—to pass on to others instruction, admonition and information of a divine origin which she had received. A wide range of subjects was covered in the visions.

"At times, the events of the past, present and future were opened up to Ellen White in a most dramatic way, giving her the impression that she was actually witnessing in rapid succession a vivid reenactment of the scenes of history."

As Ellen White explains:

"Through the illumination of the Holy Spirit, the scenes

of the long-continued conflict between good and evil have been opened to the writer of these pages. *From time to time I have been permitted to behold the working, in different ages, of the great controversy between Christ . . . and Satan.*

"As the Spirit of God has opened to my mind the great truths of His Word and the scenes of the past and the future, I have been bidden to make known to others that which has thus been revealed." [4]

Based on the many descriptions Ellen White has given of her visions, D. A. Delafield, a co-worker of Arthur White and one of the associate secretaries involved in the operation of the Ellen G. White Estate, often compares certain phases of her gift to motion-picture projection, an allegory not unlike that used by the famed psychic Peter Hurkos.

"The Holy Spirit flashed upon the mind of the prophet the revelation of truth, sometimes figurative, sometimes literal—while the prophet was rapt in holy vision—and she saw herself viewing the most dramatic scenes," he stated. "To [her] these scenes were as real as any color film dealing with a historical event, or any travelogue that we might view projected on the screen. But in the prophetic vision, God was the divine projectionist! The prophet's mind was merely the silver screen." [5]

To Ellen Harmon, the introduction to the Spirit of Prophecy came at the young age of seventeen, shortly after she, with other members of her family, had left the Methodist Church and had accepted William Miller's preaching concerning the Second Advent of Christ. To all of his followers, the last few months preceding October 22, 1844—the day when Miller expected the Second Coming of Christ to take place—were months of soul-searching but also a period of jubilation and exaltation. Because of a too hasty interpretation of the "Second Coming prophecies," thousands spent those final days with the positive conviction that October 22 had been selected by the heavenly powers as the divine target date. Opposition to Miller's teachings increased sharply. The Advent believers at this time were still scattered throughout the various denominations, and the pressure brought to bear upon them from the nonbelieving clergy became immense. In many instances the converts to the teachings of Miller were not even allowed to express their feelings in their own church, and many church leaders joined in the ridicule and the attack, jeering at those who were expecting the end of the world.

When finally the sun rose above the horizon on that fateful day, more than fifty thousand faithful believers fervently scanned the skies, prayerfully, patiently, awaiting the signs of the return of Christ. But with each passing hour, the warm and comfortable feeling of confidence withered, until it eventually gave way to a disappointment beyond description. And when the sun slowly sank behind the hills, and the hours ticked slowly by till midnight, it became obvious that something had indeed gone wrong. Christ had *not* returned, and the agony was almost too severe to endure.

"Our fondest hopes and expectations were blasted, and such a spirit of weeping came over us as I never experienced before," Hiram Edson, one of the movement's pioneers, wrote in his memoirs. "It seemed that the loss of all earthly friends could have been no comparison. We wept, and wept, till the day dawned." [6]

"To suffer so keen a disappointment was exquisite pain in itself, but to that were added the jeers and ridicule of the scoffers. The Millerites knew they were in an alien hostile world. They shrank from mingling with others. They knew not how to answer the taunting question, 'Why didn't you go up?' Though one of them silenced an inquirer by asking sternly in return, 'And if I *had* gone up, where would you have gone?' Miller, himself, in a personal letter, a few weeks afterward, told a fellow believer of what had happened at Low Hampton in connection with the great day.

He spoke of it as 'a solemn time when even the wicked scoffers stood mute.' But, said he:

" 'It passed. And the next day it seemed as though all the demons from the bottomless pit were let loose upon us. The same ones, and many more who were crying for mercy two days before, were now mixed with the rabble and mocking, scoffing and threatening in a most blasphemous manner.' "[7]

It was a tragic day indeed. They were subjected to endless sarcasm, violent opposition from the pulpit and the press, and many of them had already sold their entire earthly belongings, counting on the accurate fulfillment of the end-time prophecy. Yet when the expected moment of triumph arrived, it turned out to be a flash of disaster, forcing the Millerite movement to reexamine its very foundations.

That their basic premise had been wrong, no one was ready to admit.

"So far as the time element was concerned, the major prophecy on which William Miller and the movement rested, was that found in Daniel 8:14. 'Unto two thousand and three hundred days; then shall the sanctuary be cleansed.' They rightly believed, as the great majority of Protestant prophetic interpreters before them had believed, that in symbolic prophecy a day stands for a year, and that therefore this particular prophecy dealt with a period of two thousand and three hundred years. They also believed that this time period began 457 B.C." [8] and ended in 1844.

Ellen Harmon, newly converted with her parents to the Millerite cause, suffered much the same traumatic ordeal as the other believers—yet to her, the October disappointment meant more, for even though she was only sixteen years old, time seemed to be running out for her.

Commented J. N. Loughborough, a contemporary of Ellen:

"Miss Harmon was at that time in a very critical condition of health. For a number of weeks she had scarcely been able to speak above a whisper. One physician had decided that her trouble was dropsical consumption. He said her right lung was decayed and the left one considerably diseased, and that her heart was affected. He said he did not think she could live but a very short time at most, and was liable to drop away at any time. It was with great difficulty that she could breathe when lying down. At night she obtained rest only by being bolstered up in the bed in an almost sitting posture. Frequent spells of coughing and hemorrhages from the lungs had reduced her physical strength." [9]

Following one of these torture-filled nights, Ellen decided to visit some of her fellow believers across the estuary in South Portland, Maine. It was on a dark wintry morning in December, 1844, a short six or seven weeks after the spiritual disaster had hit the Millerites. She left the house, crossed the bridge and walked the cobblestone path leading to the side door of the two-story grayish building at Ocean and C Street and climbed the narrow stairway to the upstairs apartment belonging to Mrs. Haines, a close friend. Arriving in time for morning worship, she knelt down together with Mrs. Haines and three other friends—and experienced her first vision.

"The Holy Ghost fell upon me," she said later while commenting on this vision, "and I seemed to be rising higher and higher, far above the dark world. I turned to look for the Advent people in the world but I could not find them, when a voice said to me, 'Look again, and look a little higher.' At this I raised my eyes and saw a straight and narrow path, cast up high above the world. On this path the Advent people were traveling to the city which was at the farther end of the path. . . . Soon our eyes were drawn to the east, for a small black cloud had appeared about half as large as a man's hand, which we all knew was the sign of the Son of man. We all in solemn silence faced the cloud as it drew nearer and became lighter, glorious and still more glorious, till it was a great white cloud, while around it were ten thousand angels singing a most lovely song; and upon it sat the Son of man. His hair was white and curly and lay on His shoulders; and upon His head were many crowns. His feet had the appearance of fire; in His right hand was a sharp sickle; in His left a silver trumpet. His eyes were as a flame of fire, which searched His children through and through. Then all faces gathered paleness, and those that God had rejected gathered blackness. Then we all cried out,

" 'Who shall be able to stand? Is my robe spotless?'

"Then the angels ceased to sing, and there was some time of awful silence, when Jesus spoke.

" 'Those who have clean hands and pure hearts shall be able to stand; My grace is sufficient for you.'

"At this our faces lighted up, and joy filled every heart. And the angels struck a note higher and sang again, while the cloud drew still nearer the earth.

"Then Jesus' silver trumpet sounded, as He descended on the cloud, wrapped in flames of fire. He gazed at the graves of the sleeping saints, then raised His eyes and hands to heaven and cried, 'Awake! Awake! Awake! ye that sleep in the dust, and arise.' Then there was a mighty earthquake. The graves opened, and the dead came up clothed with immortality.

". . . Then an angel bore me gently down to this dark world. Sometimes I think I can stay here no longer; all things of earth look so dreary. I feel very lonely here, for I have seen a better land. Oh that I had wings like a dove, then I would fly away and be at rest!" [10]

Years later, while addressing an audience in Australia, she related some of the feelings that came to her during that memorable moment on that bleak day in December.

"They thought that I was dead," she said softly to the

hushed congregation. For while in vision her breathing had ceased, "and there they watched and cried and prayed so long, but to me it was heaven, it was life, and then the world was spread out before me and I saw darkness like the pall of death.

"What did it mean? I could see no light. Then I saw a little glimmer of light and then another, and these lights increased and grew brighter and multiplied and grew stronger and stronger until they were the light of the world. These were the believers in Jesus Christ. . . ."

By now every eye in the audience was moist and fastened intently on the frail-looking woman who seemed to be so close to eternity. Not a sound could be heard except the gentle voice of Ellen White.

"I never thought that I would come to the world again," she continued. "When my breath came again to my body, I could not hear anything. Everything was dark. The light and glory that my eyes had rested upon had eclipsed the light and thus it was for many hours. Then gradually I began to recognize the light, and I asked where I was.

" 'You are right here in my house,' said the owner of the house.

" 'What? Here? I here? Do you not know about it?' Then it all came back to me. 'Is this to be my home? Have I come here again?' Oh the weight and the burden which came upon my soul." [11]

A medium? A psychic? A mere clairvoyant? It seems rather doubtful, for from the moment of her very first vision, the concern she expressed was over humanity's struggle for perfection and not over the outcome of a horse race, the circumstances surrounding political assassinations, Russian MIRV's or the winner of a presidential race. It is no wonder that those who had an opportunity to observe her while in vision would do just that, with the closest scrutiny, often demanding the medical doctors be admitted to examine this strange phenomena. The circumstances surrounding the visions were not always the same nor were the conditions of the visions themselves. However, no matter what the situation was, interested viewers were never prevented from a detailed observation of the visions. From the very beginning, the utmost cooperation was extended to those present to examine Ellen White—as stated by many of her contemporaries.

Numerous eyewitness accounts covering every aspect of her being in vision are among the thousands of documents filed away in the archives of the Ellen G. White Estate.

Martha Amadon, a close associate of Mrs. White, witnessed many of her visions and stated afterward what she had seen.

"As one who has frequently observed her in vision, knowing the company of people usually present, all deeply observant and believers in her exercises, I have often wondered why a more vivid description of the scenes which transpired has not been given.

"In vision her eyes were open. There was no breath . . . but there were graceful movements of the shoulders, arms and hands expressive of what she saw. It was impossible for anyone else to move her hands or arms. She often uttered words singly, and sometimes sentences which expressed to those about her the nature of the view she was having, either of heaven or of earth.

"Her first word in vision was 'Glory,' sounding at first close by and then dying away in the distance, seemingly far away. This was sometimes repeated.

"There was never an excitement among those present during a vision; nothing caused fear. It was a solemn quiet scene, sometimes lasting an hour. . . .

"When the vision was ended, and she lost sight of the heavenly light, as it were, coming back to the earth once more, she would exclaim with a long-drawn sigh, as she took her first natural breath, 'D-a-r-k!' She was then limp and strengthless." [12]

Another witness, M. G. Kellog, M.D., volunteered the following statement after having seen Mrs. White in vision in Michigan on May 29, 1853:

"Sister White was in vision about twenty minutes or half an hour. As she went into vision, every one present seemed to feel the power and presence of God, and some of us did indeed feel the Spirit of God resting upon us mightily. We were engaged in prayer and social meeting Sabbath morning at about nine o'clock. Brother White, my father and Sister White had prayed and I was praying at the time. There had been no excitement, no demonstrations. We did plead earnestly with God, however, that He would bless the meeting with His presence, and that He would bless the work in Michigan.

"As Sister White gave that triumphant shout of 'Glory! G-l-o-r-y! G-l-o-r-y!' which you have heard her give so often as she goes into vision, Brother White arose and informed the audience that his wife was in vision. After stating the manner of her visions, and that she did not breathe while in vision, he invited anyone who wished to do so to come forward and examine her. Dr. Drummond, a physician who was also a First-day-Adventist preacher, who before he saw her in vision had declared her visions to be of mesmeric origin, and that he could *give* her a vision, stepped forward, and after a thorough examination, turned very pale, and remarked, 'She doesn't breathe.'

"I am quite certain that she did not breathe at that time while in vision, nor in any of several others which she has had when I was present. The coming out of vision was as marked as her going into it. The first indication we had that the vision was ended was in her beginning to breathe. She drew her first breath deep, long, and full, in a manner showing that her lungs had been entirely empty of air. After drawing the first breath, several minutes passed before she drew the second, which filled the lungs precisely as did the first; then a pause of two minutes, and a third inhalation, after which the breathing became natural." [13]

Throughout the eyewitness accounts of medical men and trained observers, the same impression that she was without breath is continually emphasized. Humanly speaking, it is utterly impossible to retain both mental and physical capacities while deprived of oxygen; but then, no one yet has ever been able to ascertain the limits of supernatural power, and the possibility that the same power which controlled the prophetic impulses also governed the prophet's physical actions while in vision must be considered.

A classic example of this is found in Daniel 10:5-19, where the old-time prophet Daniel relates his encounter with a mysterious being that appeared to him in vision. Without going into minute detail, the separate segments of his reaction to this should be stated here, inasmuch as they exhibit an amazing similarity to those experienced by Ellen White.

In sequence, this is what occurred:

1. A glorious being appeared to Daniel.
2. He lost his strength and fell in a deep sleep (a trance) with his face turned toward the ground.
3. He heard the voice of the being speaking to him even though in this state.
4. When the being touched him, the prophet arose to his hands and knees—perhaps in vision, but possibly also physically.
5. He was at first unable to speak, but this changed when the being touched his lips.
6. He did not breathe—there was no breath in him.
7. He was strengthened.

T. Housel Jemison, in *A Prophet Among You,* writes in

connection with this, "There is no evidence in the Bible that all of these phenomena always accompanied the vision of every prophet. In fact, they probably did not. Therefore they cannot be used as a basic test of a prophet's experience. However, the presence of some of these characteristics do serve as strong evidence that his communications are of supernatural origin."

Researchers have noticed a striking resemblance between most of these points and Ellen White's state while in vision as the files testify, since most of her daytime visions were witnessed by others, and sometimes in large numbers. Only the visions that reached her during the secret hours of the night were hers and hers alone.

"All through her experience and more particularly in the latter years of her life," Arthur White commented, "the visions were more frequently given during the hours of the night while her mind was at rest and entirely severed from the circumstances and influences that accompany the activities of a busy life." Contradicting those who hold the position that *all* dreams have hidden meanings, Ellen White once commented:

"There are many dreams arising from the common things of life, with which the Spirit of God has nothing to do. There are also false dreams as well as false visions, which are inspired by the spirit of Satan. But dreams from the Lord are classed in the Word of God with visions, and are as truly the fruits of the Spirit of Prophecy as visions. Such dreams, taking into account the persons who have them and the circumstances under which they are given, contain their own proofs of their genuineness." [14]

"It does not seem possible to draw any very precise distinction between the prophetic 'dream' and the prophetic 'vision,'" comments the *M'Clintock and Strong Cyclopædia* on page 646. In the case of Abraham (Gen. 15:1) and of

Daniel (Dan. 7:1), they also seemed to have completely fused with one another.

David Arnold, a contemporary of Ellen White, lists three causes for dreams, allowing only *one* cause, the power of the Holy Ghost, as the one responsible for transmission of divine communications.

"Dreams are produced from three sources," he maintains. "First, by the power of the Holy Ghost moving upon the mental faculties, stamping upon the perceptions and memory by figures or otherwise the intelligence God designs to give. Such was the dream of Pharaoh of the seven fat and lean kine by which God communicated the knowledge of the approaching famine; also Nebuchadnezzar's notable dream of the Metallic Image.

"Second, by the power of Satan; as in the dreams of which Job speaks in Chapter 7:14. 'Then thou scarest me with dreams, and terrifiest me through visions.'

"Third, through a multiplicity of business. During the labors, cares, and excitements of the day the mental organs become surcharged with thoughts and do not sink to rest as soon as the external organs; consequently the thoughts are more or less active and real as the faculties one by one sink away to rest. To this source may be charged a great share of the entire mass of dreams." [15]

To this, modern science has had very little to add. Most psychologists still adhere to this basic understanding.

On one occasion William C. White asked his mother a question that had evidently been bothering him for quite some time.

"Mother, you often speak of matters being revealed to you in the night season," he queried hesitantly. "You speak of dreams in which light comes to you. We all have dreams. . . . How do you know that God is speaking to you in the dreams of which you so frequently speak?"

There is no doubt that Ellen was a patient mother, for in her own amicable manner she gave Willie the answer that put his troubled mind at rest.

"Because the same angel messenger stands by my side instructing me in the visions of the night, as stands beside me instructing me in the visions of the day," she answered.[16] Perhaps this explanation describes the one criterion that can be used in separating ordinary dreams from prophetic dreams, inasmuch as angelic messengers are practically always an integral part of a prophetic dream.

Ofter during her lifetime, vicious attacks were directed toward her, not only questioning the authenticity of the visions themselves, but also the ways in which they were received. To most conscientious religionists of the middle 1800's, Spiritualism appeared as a pronounced danger. To the laymen, however, anything unusual, any unexplainable phenomenon, was immediately classified as Spiritism, and that the religious validity of Ellen White's gift was questioned against this background is understandable.

Most of the criticisms that were levied against her attempted to associate her gift with mesmerism, a hypnotic induction held to involve animal magnetism. It originated with the Austrian physician F. A. Mesmer, and one of its advocates in the United States, Frenchman Charles Poyen, helped considerably to popularize the mesmeric or hypnotic trance in America by touring the New England states with a female subject whom he repeatedly mesmerized. It was one of his pupils, incidentally, a man named Quimby, who eventually brought physical "healing" to Mary Baker Eddy and saw his theories become part of the underlying principles of Christian Science. Ellen White's entrance on the world scene came at a time when mesmerism had just reached its highest peak of popularity; consequently, when Ellen first referred to her visions, the cry "mesmerism" echoed through the halls. Still others, as noted, attributed it to Spiritism. She tried to counter some of her critics by submitting herself to a noted physician who, as a celebrated mesmerizer, informed her that she would be an easy subject to mesmerize and that he would give her a vision while she was under his control. For more than half an hour he attempted to force his will upon her, resorting to many different methods, but ended admitting defeat. Yet criticism continued relentlessly. Disheartened, she at one time began to question her own experience. Not long afterward, she sensed that she was about to receive a vision, but with her doubt being fanned by the sharp tongues of her critics, she resisted.

At that very instant, she was struck dumb, and for a few moments was lost to everything around her. In the vision that followed, it was made clear to her that never again should she question the power behind the gift and that her speech would be restored to her within twenty-four hours. Realizing the immensity of what had just happened, she repented; however, it was not until a full day had passed that the ability to speak returned.

Various reports persisted, however, as to the cause of the visions. In the early days, one Dr. Brown, a spiritualist physician of Parkville, Michigan, stated freely that, according to the reports coming to him concerning Mrs. White, she was experiencing a form of spiritualistic mediumship. He hoped he might have the opportunity of examining her while she was in vision, and declared that he could control her visions.

The occasion presented itself on January 12, 1861, when Mrs. White spoke at a meeting in Parkville. At the close of the service, she was taken in vision. Responding to her husband's invitation, Dr. Brown was invited in and was given permission to examine her. An eyewitness to this examination subsequently related what had happened.

"Before he had half completed his examination, he turned

deathly pale, and shook like an aspen leaf. Elder White said, 'Will the doctor report her condition?' He replied, 'She does not breathe,' and rapidly made his way to the door. Those at the door who knew of his boasting, said, 'Go back, and do as you said you would; bring that woman out of the vision.' In great agitation he grasped the knob of the door, but was not permitted to open it until inquiry was made by those near the door, 'Doctor, what is it?' He replied, *'God only knows; let me out of this house!'* " [17]

It was left to George I. Butler, a contemporary of Ellen White and a religious co-worker of James White, to put into words what so many of those who knew Ellen White believed.

In *The Review and Herald* of June 9, 1874, he summarized all that had been presented to the critics by her supporters.

"All we ask is that people shall be reasonable," he implored in his article. "We are prepared to support by hundreds of living truthful witnesses all that we shall claim, so far as facts are concerned, of the manifestation itself, for this thing has not been done in a corner. For nearly thirty years past these visions have been given with greater or less frequency, and have been witnessed by many, often times by unbelievers as well as those believing them. They generally, but not always, occur in the midst of earnest seasons of religious interest while the Spirit of God is especially present, if those can tell who are in attendance. The time Mrs. White is in this condition has varied from fifteen minutes to one hundred and eighty. During this time the heart and pulse continue to beat, the eyes are always wide open, and seem to be gazing at some far distant object, and are never fixed on any person or thing in the room. They are always directed upward. They exhibit a pleasant expression. There is no ghastly look or any resemblance of fainting. The brightest light may be suddenly brought near her eyes, or feints made as if to thrust something into the eyes, and there is never the slightest wink or change of expression on that account; and it is sometimes hours and even days after she comes out of this condition before she recovers her natural sight. She says it seems to her that she comes back into a dark world, yet her eyesight is in nowise injured by her visions.

"While she is in vision," he continued, "her breathing entirely ceases. No breath ever escapes her nostrils or lips when in this condition. This has been proved by many witnesses, among them physicians of skill, and themselves unbelievers in the visions, on some occasions being appointed by a public congregation for the purpose. It has been proved many times by tightly holding the nostrils and mouth with the hand and by putting a looking glass before them so close that any escape of the moisture of the breath would be detected. In this condition she often speaks words and short sentences, yet not the slightest breath escapes. When she goes into this condition, there is no appearance of swooning or faintness, her face retains its natural color, and the blood circulates as usual. Often she loses her strength temporarily and reclines or sits; but at other times she stands up. She moves her arms gracefully, and often her face is lighted up with radiance as though the glory of Heaven rested upon her. She is utterly unconscious of everything going on around her, while she is in vision, having no knowledge whatever of what is said and done in her presence. A person may pinch her flesh, and do things which would cause great and sudden pain in her ordinary condition, and she will not notice it by the slightest tremor.

"There are none of the disgusting grimaces or contortions which usually attend spiritualist mediums, but calm, dignified, and impressive, her very appearance strikes the beholder with reverence and solemnity. There is nothing fanatical in her appearance. When she comes out of this condition she speaks and writes from time to time what she has seen while in vision; and the supernatural character of these visions is seen even more clearly in what she thus reveals than in her appearance and condition while in vision, for many things have thus been related which it was impossible for her to know in any other way.

"Peculiar circumstances in the lives of individuals, whom she never before had seen in the flesh, and secrets hidden from the nearest acquaintances, have been made known by her when she had no personal knowledge of the parties other than by vision. Often she has been in an audience where she was wholly unacquainted with the individuals composing it, when she would get up and point out person after person whom she had never seen before, in the flesh, and tell them what they had done, and reprove their sins. I might mention many other items of like nature, but space forbids. These things can be proved by any amount of testimony, and we confidently affirm that they are of such character that they could not be accomplished by deception." [18]

Chapter 4

Science Catches Up with a Prophet

WITH THE INTRODUCTION of the Emancipation Proclamation on January 1, 1863, the new year was destined to be highlighted with triumph and tragedy. Flashing cannons illuminated the dusty battlefields from Chancellorsville to Missionary Ridge by way of the blood-soaked trenches of Gettysburg. With alarming ferocity Death roamed indiscriminately through the once peaceful valleys; where battle-hardened soldiers resisted his menacing grip, he turned and scourged the prison camps.

But while North and South continued this senseless slaughter and stained the soil with battle, a Higher Hand began to shape a series of events that would guide Ellen White to a lowly farmer's cottage in Otsego, Michigan, there to meet with Destiny's answer to a threatening gulf of suffering and disease.

Emerging from the Millerites in the 1840's, the Adventists had passed through a trying time, yet now, almost nineteen years after the anticlimactic days of 1844, urged on in their quest for Bible-based truths, their ranks had solidified, and the disappointment of those early days had given way to a purposeful movement. It was as part of this that R. J. Lawrence and M. E. Cornell, two of the group's early advocates, had decided to conduct a series of tent meetings in Otsego. Delighted with their decision, James and Ellen White hitched their buggy and, together with some close friends, left their home on Champion Street in Battle Creek for the thirty-or-so-mile ride to attend the weekend meetings. Two miles outside of Otsego, they stopped to spend the night with close friends, the Aaron Hilliards.

It was a quiet evening. Tired and worn, the visitors sat down for a simple meal with their hosts, and when, after supper, the Hilliards and their friends knelt down for a moment of religious meditation, a sudden shout of GLORY ... glory ... glory! rang triumphantly through the crowded room, slowly losing its intensity as its echoes faded out with the rays of the dying sun.

Rising from their knees, everyone's eyes were intensely focused on the slightly built thirty-five-year-old woman from Battle Creek, who with devoted reverence had knelt down beside her husband James, gently resting her right hand on his shoulder. With eyes wide open, she stared into the distance, occasionally smiling as if in recognition of a familiar face, then again reflecting moments of deep, dedicated concentration. For a full forty-five minutes she remained there, communicating with an unseen Power. As if held by the order of an invisible force, everyone waited tensely for Ellen to "return." Nothing seemed able to disturb the unexplainable majesty that had suddenly filled the room, shielding Ellen from all earthly influence. Then as quietly as it had come, it left. With her face relaxed, Ellen commenced to draw her first breath, indicating that the vision was finally ended, and as though losing sight of a glorious heavenly light, after forty-five minutes of silence, she whispered her first words.

"Dark . . ." she whispered faintly, as a little child in mortal fear, "dark . . ." and while she was groping for understanding the reality of the world once more closed in on her.

We will never know the exact sequence of events that was opened up to her, but the very next day, Ellen White began to write down a portion of what had been revealed to her in what soon became known as the Otsego vision. Prior to June, 1863, her visions had dealt with a logical succession of subjects. In the early days after October, 1844, much of what was channeled through her had focused primarily on the stabilization of the Advent Movement followed by visions dealing directly with Christ's Second Coming. Advice on organizational matters, correcting religious error and visions concerning human relationships were subsequently given; however, with all of the known world living—or rather *surviving*—in an age where subhuman treatment was erroneously regarded as medical aid, the time was ripe for health-related counsel and inspired medical insight. The forty-five-minute Otsego vision had pertained to just that!

It could not have been introduced at a more appropriate moment in history. Misguided medical practice had reached a peak of intense controversy due to the arrogance and ignorance of its practitioners and the ungrounded importance the profession attached to its two favorite methods of treatment: that of bleeding (often to death!) and the overreliance on drugs and opiates—much to the disadvantage of the diseased citizenry. The middle 1800's were indeed a period when ill-founded theory and deep-rooted superstition still formed the basis for many of the actions of the medical profession. Dr. John Janvier Black, in writing his memoirs at the turn of the century, commented:

"Learned professors had their own ideas and opinions,

and these ideas and opinions were generally derived from someone equally as emphatic who had preceded them, probably amplified from time to time as light gradually began to show itself on the medical horizon. Yet most of their ideas and opinions had not fact, scientific or otherwise, for their basis, but an absolutely empirical origin; in other words true science had not yet dawned upon medical practice and medical thought." [1] To this, Dr. J. H. Kellogg in 1876 added, "Twenty years ago when a man had a fever, the doctors thought that he had too much vitality—too much life—and so they bled him, and purged him, and poisoned him with calomel, blue mass, and sundry other poisons, for the purpose of taking away from him a part of his vitality— his life—in other words, *killing him a little!*" [2] It is no wonder that one of George Washington's last deathbed wishes was to be allowed to die without any further interruptions from his physicians. The three extensive bleedings he had been subjected to, not to mention the liberal doses of calomel he was forced to swallow, created in him an intense desire to die—if only to get away from his "heal-masters." As in the case of so many of his contemporaries, he eventually became the victim of the treatment methods of two different schools of thought who battled incessantly for years to defend their methods but without ever reaching a conclusion.

Hard and rough was the language used by many so-called experts, but no one stated the vitriolic controversy as precisely as Drs. Gallup (advocate of bleeding) and Tully (whose preference was poison). Scoffed Gallup, "It is probable that, for forty years past, opium and its preparations have done seven times the injury they have rendered benefit on the great scale of the world," a remark for which Dr. Tully had a fitting answer.

"The lancet is a minute instrument of mighty mischief," he replied diplomatically. Then he got to the heart of the matter. "The King of Great Britain loses every year more

subjects by this means [knife] than the battle and campaign
of Waterloo cost him, with all their glories." [3]

The reason for the fight was soberingly obvious. Nothing,
but *nothing* was really known about the underlying causes of
disease, and all doctors could do was to concentrate on discovering better and more effective ways to suppress the
symptoms of an ailment, either by poisoning the patient
with opiate or mercury concoctions or simply bleeding him
until the fever subsided. Combinations of calomel, prussic
acid, opium and antimony were highly valued as cure-alls
for most ordinary sicknesses. Many a doctor even recommended heavy cigar smoking as a remedy for lung infections,
providing "that the patient should frequently draw in the
breath freely, so that the internal surface of the air vessels
may be exposed to the action of the vapor." [4]

It seemed that ignorance was the most widespread disease
of all, and it infiltrated every segment of society without
regard to persons. Smothered to death in disease-ridden
rooms, covered by germ-infested blankets, windows shut
tight so as to keep out all the clean outside air, shades
drawn to prevent the germ-killing sunlight from reaching
the patient, a starvation diet of bread and water (highly
recommended for patients of all ages) and slowly being bled
to death or poisoned into a deep senseless stupor, a great
number of patients barely had a chance to survive. Those
who stubbornly refused to die usually attempted to lengthen
their lives via home remedies prescribed in *The Family
Medicine Chest Dispensatory;* however, this really meant
going from bad to worse.

Medicine as a profession was so chaotic, and the supporting medical knowledge so primitive, that epidemic after
epidemic continuously killed off many of those who somehow managed to outlast the doctors' care. The ones who
survived the knife of the bleeder or the poisonous prescrip-
tions of the healer had a more than even chance of dying

of cholera, typhoid, smallpox or any one of a number of other infectious diseases. The thousands who died of tuberculosis in the middle 1800's put us on a level with England, where from 1851 through 1855, 50,000 died of this dreaded lung disease. The fact that 30,000 scarlet fever victims boosted the death statistics in England in the 1860's barely created a stir. It has been estimated that most of the 340,000 men who died during the Civil War of wounds and disease were victims of just plain medical ignorance. A full 75 percent of them could have been saved if the most elementary principles of hygiene and first aid as we know them today had been applied.

Addressing the women of America, Mrs. E. P. Miller, M.D., once pointed out, "Could each and all of the diseased within your ranks, with one fell swoop, be set aside, how many do you think would remain? So few, I trust, that it would be scarcely worth the while to count, for upon those on whom no definite disease is praying, nervousness and debility have so strong a hold that life seems scarce worth the effort you are compelled to make in order to keep even your slight hold upon it." [5]

Plagued by illness and bodily discomfort since childhood and belonging to the "diseased generation," Ellen's thoughts had often been drawn to the hope of finding a better way of living, but until that memorable day of June 6, 1863, the subject remained almost a closed book.

The vision of Otsego changed all that. Within the short time of forty-five minutes, her alert mind, open to the influence of the infinite God, was exposed to highly advanced, and for that period, revolutionary, new information dealing with nutrition, health principles and disease treatment, as well as a wealth of pure scientific data—unknown to men of her day. With eyes staring intently into the innermost secrets of the human body through the medium of revelation, she became enlightened as to the causes of disease and received instructions to relay it to those around her.

While the most important thrust of her health message was contained in the 1863 vision, not all of it was released immediately. Tracts containing parts of the revealed information were periodically published, and as time went on, more visions enlarging upon certain health-related areas were given. It is interesting to note, however, that all new material presented by Ellen White as the result of the visions shocked many members of the scientific community with its logic and fundamental soundness, even though most of it was not proved scientifically until years later. In fact, some of it still requires scientific confirmation even today. Her keen foreknowledge of the basis of scientific thought, *now being proved,* has provided a powerful reason for an ever-increasing number of people to turn to the writings of Ellen G. White for the answers to mysterious questions regarding health and medicine. Ellen White had only three years of formal education; she was not a trained scientist, nor a theologian nor a nutritionist; yet much of her inspired insight in these fields, penned more than one hundred years ago, is still regarded as highly advanced and extremely signficant.

"The why and wherefores of this I know not," she professed humbly in 1901, when referring to a point she made in the field of nutrition, "but I give you the instruction as it is given me." [6]

Commented Dr. Jackson A. Saxon, a well-known author and practicing physician in the Washington, D.C., area:

"The Spirit of Prophecy is medically up-to-date. Before starting medicine I was well acquainted with the health ideas found in the writings of Mrs. White. Since finishing medical school I have been in practice for nineteen years. I have not had to change one medical idea that I have

gotten from the writings of Mrs. White, but all my medical
books have had to be replaced with up-to-date versions
based on more modern medical research. As medical science
advanced, I find these guides [referring to her books, ed.]
do not become outdated, but are still ahead of modern
medical research on many health subjects." [7] The late Clive
McCay, Ph.D., a former professor of nutrition at Cornell
University, Ithaca, New York, conveyed the same conviction when, in a speech before a large gathering in Memphis,
Tennessee, in March, 1958, he made the following statement:

"The writings of Ellen G. White . . . provide a guide to
nutrition that comprehends the whole body. . . . When one
reads such works by Mrs. White as *Ministry of Healing* or
Counsels on Diet and Foods, he is impressed by the correctness of her teachings in the light of modern nutritional
science. One can only speculate how much better health the
average American might enjoy, even though he knew almost
nothing of modern science, if he but followed the teachings
of Mrs. White." [8]

A great deal of what Ellen "saw" as being the underlying
causes of many of the nation's illnesses were either disregarded or disbelieved by the medical "experts" of her time.
Science was still too primitive even to grasp a minute portion of what was revealed to her, and the scalpel and arsenic
compounds remained the faithful standbys of the medical
world. Psychic phenomena, prophetic guidance, extrasensory influences were all concepts generally regarded as
fakery, and when Ellen approached the public with her
"revealed insight" on the causative factors in cancer *as far
back as 1863*, naming faulty diet, unwholesome habits and
drugs as causes, her critics laughed and ridiculed her for
her unorthodox views. But forced on by the memories of
her first health-reform vision, she continued to set forth her
views.

The Cancer Threat

Cancer undoubtedly plagued her suffering contemporaries under many different names, as diseases were not always diagnosed correctly; however to Ellen White, there was no mystery concerning its cause. Guided by the Spirit of Prophecy, she pointedly warned of the dangers of cancer and its causative agents in many of her books, lectures and brochures.

In 1902, referring to the modified eating habits of Seventh-day Adventists, she cautioned, "Animals are becoming more and more diseased, and it will not be long until animal food will be discarded by many besides Seventh-day Adventists." [9] It was her diagnosis of meat as a cancer carrier (1905) that proved her far ahead of medical science.

"People are continually eating flesh that is filled with tuberculous and cancerous germs," she stated, looking back on what she had observed while in vision. "Tuberculosis, cancer, and other fatal diseases are thus communicated." [10]

No doubt many who listened to her warnings shook their heads in pity, for how was it possible that a woman with only a third-grade education could possess knowledge far beyond the scope of the scientists of her day? Cancer transmitted by way of a "cancerous germ"? A connection between eating meat and cancer? It all sounded just too incredible to believe; however, now, nearly seventy years after the publication of her book *Ministry of Healing*, science is discovering the very points mentioned by her, and many scientists now have to admit that the information revealed to her in vision was indeed precise.

On June 16, 1971, most of the newspapers across the nation carried a story headlined, "New York Epidemic of Cancer Cited," describing an outbreak of contagious Hodgkin's disease, a type of cancer of the lymph glands.

"A team of scientists has reported what it terms the

world's first 'epidemic' of Hodgkin's disease," the papers reported, discussing thirteen cases of the rare cancer that spread from the members of a high school graduating class.

"The outbreak suggests an infectious disease condition with a carrier state and a long (eight to nine year) incubation period," concluded the scientists in the June, 1971 issue of the well-respected British medical publication *Lancet*. However, one of the authors, Dr. Peter Greenwals, said that the chance of catching Hodgkin's disease through contact with someone who has it is very slight. "It has a low rate of infectivity," he stated.

"Since Hodgkin's disease skipped some members of the class of 1954 [Albany High School, New York], while attacking their close relatives and friends, the investigators concluded it can lie dormant in a carrier state." [11]

In Ellen White's day, the term *virus* was not universally recognized, and her description of "cancerous germs" was as close as she could describe them. Yet the very idea was not generally accepted or recognized until 1911, when virologist Francis P. Raus ground up some cancerous tissue from the breast of a Plymouth Rock hen and, after removing all cancer cells from the extract, injected the remaining fluid into other hens.

"They all developed cancer," he reported afterward. It was not until forty-five years later, in the year 1956, that his work was officially backed by a fellow researcher. *Newsweek* Magazine of June 18, 1956, carried the following story in support of his work, entitled "Viruses and Activating Factors in Cancer." It read:

"In Detroit last week, at a meeting of the third National Cancer Conference, Dr. Wendell Stanley, University of California virologist and Nobel Prize winner, went so far as to state without qualification that he believes, 'viruses cause most of all human cancers. . . . It is known that viruses can lurk in the human body for years, even a lifetime; some cause trouble, some do not. . . . In some cases,' Dr. Stanley theorized, 'the cancer viruses might become active through circumstances such as aging, dietary indiscretions, hormonal imbalance, chemicals, radiation, or a combination of stresses, and malignancies may follow.' " For those who knew and trusted Mrs. White's visions, it was *the* major breakthrough they had been waiting for, and once the first man had officially admitted the existence of the cancer virus—the "cancerous germ" of Ellen White and its probable role in human cancer—other researchers soon followed, now no longer hesitant in announcing their convictions.

"During the past decade, the concept of viral etiology of cancer and allied diseases has gained considerable momentum," reported Dr. Ludwick Gross in the December, 1956, issue of the *Journal of the American Medical Association.* "Experimental data began to accumulate pointing more and more to the possibility that many, if not all, malignant tumors may be caused by viruses. Thus, a large number of malignant tumors of different morphology and in different species of animals could be transmitted from one host to others by filtered extracts." [12] Dr. Robert J. Huebner, chief of the Laboratory of Infectious Diseases at the National Institute of Health at Bethesda, Maryland, added, "There isn't the slightest doubt in our minds that human cancers are caused by viruses. To this extent, they are simply infectious diseases." [13] He based his theory on the belief that the cancer virus lies dormant in the body until certain conditions—hormones, age or irritating chemicals—give it a chance to cause a malignancy.

So *Ellen White was right* when, ninety-three years before the dramatic breakthrough announced by Dr. Stanley, she identified the "cancerous germ" as the cause of cancer and furthermore had isolated the conditions that could trigger the "germ" to become activated. However, the statement she made concerning the fact that cancer can be transmitted through the eating of cancer-infested animal flesh is still the subject of hot debate. Can animal cancers indeed be transferred to humans and vice versa? Can the cancer virus pass the species barrier?

Indications are that it most assuredly can, for an unfortunate transmission of the disease was reported by Purdue University in 1964, when a cancer research worker, Dr. Davis, "caught" cancer while experimenting with a virus. It was the first such case ever reported.[14] The idea of an absolute species barrier was discredited when a British pathologist transmitted human cancer to laboratory animals that very same year.[15]

More recently, (December 6, 1971), a new case of cancer transfer was reported in the nation's newspapers, describing a successful experiment conducted at the University of Southern California. Headed by Dr. Murrey B. Gardness, a team of pathologists transferred cells of a muscular cancer from a seven-year-old girl into embryonic kittens being carried by three cats. After birth, one stillborn and three live kittens from the three cat litters were found to have muscle cancers. One of the three diseased live kittens had a solid tumor in the brain, which the Los Angeles scientists chose for their most exhaustive study.

"The tumor in the cat's brain," reported Dr. Robert J. Huebner, "looked the same as it did in the child." More interesting, however, is that the cancers contained human chromosomes.

"These chromosomes were quite visible after growth," said Dr. Huebner. "There was no mistaking them." (The Washington Post, December 6, 1971).

That today's cancerous animals are being prepared for human consumption in the nation's slaughterhouses and that cancerous chickens are sold freely in the supermarkets (after the removal of the obvious cancers!) are facts that have made headlines in every major paper across the country. Taking the growing scientific confirmation of most of Ellen White's medical insights as basis, there is little doubt —if any—that the nonexistence of a species barrier to the cancer virus will soon be officially recognized.

Yet, not only was she concerned about the consumption of animal flesh, she was also aware as far back as 1864 that —as Dr. Stanley discovered "officially" in 1956—the cancer cell acts only when triggered, and can lie dormant for many years. Said she, speaking about cancer in the aged, "Cancerous humor, which would lay dormant in the system [throughout] their lifetime, is inflamed, and commences its eating, destructive work." [16]

But she wasn't through yet. Still referring to her visions, she proceeded to give dire warnings against the usage of the popular drugs of her day, linking them to cancerous growths.

"The third case was again presented before me," she stated in 1865, while speaking about a vision in which she had been shown the deadly results of mercurial preparations. "The intelligent gentlemen before-mentioned looked sadly upon the sufferer, and said, 'This is the influence of mercurial preparations. . . . This is the effect of calomel. . . . It inflames the joints, and often sends rottenness into the bones. It frequently manifests itself in tumors, ulcers and cancers, years after it has been introduced into the system." [17]

But what about cigarette smoking, you may ask? Isn't that one of the major causes of lung cancer? Didn't she say anything concerning that?

Ellen White certainly did. Throughout her crusade for better health, the use of tobacco was frequently attacked. Persistently she warned against its usage, but to little avail.

Sounding her first alarm in 1864, she cautioned:

"Tobacco is a poison of the most deceitful and malignant kind, having an exciting, then a paralyzing influence upon the nerves of the body. It is all the more dangerous because

its effects upon the system are so slow, and at first scarcely
perceivable. Multitudes have fallen victim to its poisonous
influence. They have surely murdered themselves by this
slow poison."[18] Can you imagine the ridicule to which she
was exposed when she publicly made these statements at a
time when the medical world regarded tobacco and cigar
smoke as an effective cure for lung diseases? "In whatever
form it is used," she repeated her warning in 1876, "it tells
upon the constitution; it is all the more dangerous because
its effects are slow and at first hardly perceptible. . . . It
is more subtle, and its effects are difficult to eradicate from
the system. . . . Those who acquire and indulge the un-
natural appetite for tobacco, do this at the expense of
health. They are destroying nervous energy, lessening vital
forces, and sacrificing mental strength" (1905).[19] And science supports her all the way. In *Smoke Signals*, July–
August, 1962, Dr. Alton Ochsner reiterated scientific evidence backing Mrs. White's statement that the effects of
tobacco are indeed slow but deadly.

"Lung cancer is a disease that began primarily in the mid-
thirties," he explained. "The reason is that twenty years
previously men began to smoke cigarettes heavily in the
United States, beginning during World War I. It takes about
twenty years for the cancer-producing effect of cigarette
smoking to become evident. Prior to the mid-thirties, cancer
of the lung was an extremely rare disease in both sexes, but
affected both sexes with equal frequency.

"This is a disease which is preventable," he concluded.
"It doesn't develop naturally. It is caused by smoking."[20]
The warning was blunt enough, yet to many researchers
the end result of the accumulated studies was nothing new.
As early as 1957, a committee of seven scientists appointed
by the American Cancer Society, the American Heart As-
sociation, the National Cancer Institute and the National
Heart Institute concluded after an intensive study that the

"sum total of scientific evidence established beyond a reasonable doubt that cigarette smoking is a causative factor in the rapidly increasing incidence of human epidermoid-carcinoma of the lung."

Science discovered the facts nearly a century after the Spirit of Prophecy had revealed this danger to Ellen White. But when she talked about it, not many listened. . . .

Students of Ellen White's prophecies are now awaiting one more bit of scientific confirmation—this time of a statement made by her in 1864, linking masturbation to cancer.

"If the practice [masturbation] is continued from the ages of fifteen and upward, nature will protest against the abuse she has suffered and continues to suffer," she gravely warned, "and will make them pay the penalty for the transgression of her laws, especially from the ages of thirty to forty-five, by numerous pains in the system and various diseases, such as affection of the liver and lungs, neuralgia, rheumatism, affection of the spine, diseased kidneys, and cancerous humors. Some of nature's finest machinery gives way, leaving a heavier task for the remaining to perform, which disorders nature's fine arrangements; and there is often a sudden breaking down of the constitution and death is the result." [21] Hormonal imbalance is suggested here—one of the actuating factors projected by Dr. Stanley in his epoch-making statement in 1956.

Taking the astounding accuracy of her prophecies as a guide, may we not expect that the time will come when science will confirm this, too?

Alcohol Damages the Brain—Permanently

Nowadays there is much discussion concerning the possible damaging effects of the various hallucinatory drugs currently available—but for some reason the population has never yet been fully informed as to the true nature of one of the world's greatest curses—alcohol. And it is in this area that so much damage is being done.

A report released in 1969 [22] may well turn out to be the beginning of a new movement to reintroduce a form of prohibition, for the damaging results of the consumption of alcohol—*any* amount of alcohol—are now public record.

"Every time a person takes a few drinks of an alcoholic beverage—even a few beers or cocktails at a social function —he permanently damages his brain, and probably his heart and liver also."

This is the frightening conclusion of an important new medical discovery made by a team of scientists headed by Dr. Melvin H. Knisely, professor of anatomy at the Medical University of South Carolina in Charleston. It was published in *Listen* Magazine, December, 1969.

"For years it had been known that alcoholics suffer serious brain damage, but most doctors dismissed this simply as one of the end effects after years of hard drinking, along with liver damage, kidney malfunction and heart disease often seen in alcoholics at autopsy. Dr. Knisely has now demonstrated that this brain damage is not merely an end effect, but occurs progressively from the first cells destroyed by the very first drink a person takes, and that the damage accumulates relentlessly with every drink he takes thereafter at any time.

"The brains of skid row drunks are usually worthless for use in teaching the structure of the normal brain to medical students," the report concluded.

As startling as these facts may have been when they were first released, the dangers of alcohol were forecast by Ellen White in an address on April 1, 1905, and published in her book *Temperance*.

"The use of liquor or tobacco destroys the sensitive nerves of the brain, and benumbs the sensibilities," [23] she warned.

"The man who has formed the habit of using intoxicants," she stated in *Ministry of Healing*, published the same year, "is in a desperate situation, his will power is weakened. So far as any power in himself is concerned, his appetite is uncontrollable. He cannot be reasoned with or persuaded to deny himself." [24] ". . . reason is paralyzed, the intellect is benumbed, the animal passions are excited, and then follow crimes of the most debasing character." [25]

It would seem courageous of Mrs. White to make such declarations at a time when medical science was not cognizant of the physiological or mental effect of alcohol, were it not for the fact that her statements were based on supernatural revelations, not pseudoscience. The health-reform vision of 1863 had wrought a pronounced change in the work of Ellen White. Untiringly she advocated total abstinence from tobacco and alcohol, not founding her objections on its degrading social effect, but more on the actual physical damage resulting from its usage long before researchers ever showed an interest in it.

What she stated first in 1905 that "it destroys the sensitive nerves of the brain" is now in 1972 officially being recognized as sound medical reasoning backed by fact. "Dr. Knisely's discovery is that the circulating red blood cells become agglutinated when alcohol is imbibed," Glenn D. Everett writes in *Listen*, December, 1969, "and that this seriously interferes with blood circulation through the small arteries, capillaries and veins. 'Agglutination' means that the red blood cells become sticky and adhere together in wads until the blood becomes literally a 'sludge.' As sludge resists passage of the blood through the capillaries, anoxia (absence of oxygen) occurs in nearby tissues." [26] That's where the trouble begins. The neurons, the thinking nerve cells of the brain, require a tremendous amount of oxygen for an efficient operation, and as the sludge blocks the oxygen flow to the neurons, they cease their normal brain functioning.

If the blockage persists for as little as fifteen minutes, the brain cell dies. Since brain cells do not multiply, even the most moderate social drinker hastens the process of mental degeneration by killing off untold numbers of brain cells every time he takes a drink. Furthermore, in support of Ellen White's statement that "reason is paralyzed" and "his will power is weakened," the late Dr. C. B. Courville wrote that alcohol damages every part of the nervous system. He pointed out that the cerebral cortex, that part of the brain responsible for thinking, is badly damaged by alcohol; the cerebellum, concerned with the coordination of various muscle groups—voluntary and involuntary—can also suffer serious damage, for nerve cells in both the cerebral cortex and the cerebellum die as a result of alcohol consumption.[27]

Ellen White, however, went a step further and also listed some of the reasons why so many have an insatiable craving for alcohol in her book *Ministry of Healing* and other health-related volumes.

Using her inspired writings as basis, U. D. Register, Ph.D., associate professor of biochemistry of the School of Health of Loma Linda University, a Seventh-day Adventist institution near Redlands, California, and a team of co-workers conducted a series of fascinating experiments, aimed at finding scientific confirmation for Spirit of Prophecy statements. In the final analysis it proved that experimental rats which were fed meals common to many Americans developed an abnormal taste for alcohol when coffee and spices were added to their diet.

Presenting the results of their research project at the fifty-first annual meeting of the Federation of American Societies for Experimental Biology in Chicago (1967), Dr. Register pointed out that "persons who drink a lot of coffee, live on nutritionally poor diets and use a lot of spices may be driving themselves to alcoholic drink.

"In the University laboratory, where rats were fed pellets of a popular U.S. diet consisting of doughnuts and coffee for breakfast, sweet rolls and coffee for the 10 A.M. and 3 P.M. breaks, hot dogs with mustard and relish, a soft drink with apple pie and coffee for lunch, spaghetti and meatballs, French bread, green beans, chopped salad, chocolate cake and coffee for dinner and were given a choice of water or a solution of ten percent alchohol to drink," he explained, "the rats chose to drink about five times more alcohol than a group of rats on a milk-vegetable control diet.

"In one study, when a typical American breakfast of scrambled eggs, orange juice, toast, bacon and butter was added to their diet, the voluntary consumption of alcohol decreased by almost 50 percent in the rats. The animals decreased their alcohol intake to low levels or completely gave up the drinking habit when they were fed nutritionally balanced meals.

"When spices and coffee were added at the same time, however, there was a four-fold rise in consumption, a synergistic effect which dramatically demonstrated the animal's increased alcohol hunger." [28]

Said Ellen White in 1905:

"By the use of rich, unhealthful food the digestive organs are weakened and a desire is created for food that is still more stimulating. Thus the appetite is educated to crave continually something stronger. The demand for stimulants becomes more frequent and more difficult to resist. The system becomes more or less filled with poison and the more debilitated it becomes, the greater is the desire for these things. One step in the wrong direction prepares the way for another. Many who would not be guilty of placing on their table wine or liquor of any kind will load their table with food which creates such a thirst for strong drink that to resist the temptation is almost impossible. Wrong habits of eating and drinking destroy the health and prepare the way for drunkenness." [29]

It took science exactly sixty-two years to catch up.

Mental and Physical Prenatal Influence

If one hundred years ago a scientist had proposed the ridiculous idea that an unborn child was subject to the activities of the mother, his colleagues would have branded him as severely unbalanced. Even as late as thirty years ago, the very idea of prenatal influence was disregarded. It was not until 1954 that documented evidence was presented, reversing the trend.

It was Dr. Ashley Montagu, writing in *Ladies' Home Journal*, who exploded the myth. In an article entitled "There Is Prenatal Influence" he rejoiced:

"For years scientists have believed that your unborn baby lives an insulated existence protected from all external influences, but this is not true. It is exciting news that you can control the development of your child."

It was indeed great and important news to those who cared, but to the ones who were acquainted with Ellen White's visions, it merely sparked a smile, for eighty-nine years prior to the appearance of the thrilling "news" in the magazine, Ellen, while still living in Michigan in 1865, recalled what she had seen in her health-reform vision, and wrote:

"The irritability, nervousness, and despondency manifested by the mother will mark the character of her child.

"In past generations, if mothers had informed themselves in regard to the laws of their being, they would have understood that their constitutional strength, as well as the tone of their morals, and their mental faculties, would in a great measure be represented in their offspring." [30]

And again, still highly concerned with the daily violations of the laws of nature as revealed to her, she sternly continued her warnings.

"Everywhere you may go," she related in 1865, "you will see deformity, disease, and imbecility, which in very many cases can be traced directly back to the drug-poisons, administered by the hand of a doctor as a remedy for some of life's ills. [31]

"The idea that women, because of their special condition, may let the appetite run riot is a mistake based on custom but not on sound sense. . . . If ever there is a need for simplicity in diet and special care as to the quality of the food eaten, it is in this important period. Women who possess principle, and who are well instructed, will not depart from simplicity of diet at this time of all others. . . .

"If she chooses to eat as she pleases and what she may fancy, irrespective of consequences, she will bear the penalty, but not alone. Her innocent child must suffer because of her indiscretion." [32]

Never did she abandon for one moment the opportunity to instill in the minds of the mothers of her day and those to come a greater responsibility toward the unborn child. She sounded her first warnings in 1865 and 1870, but after having received other health-reform visions, she continued her admonitions in 1890.

"As the result of parental intemperance," she wrote, "children often lack physical strength and mental and moral power.

To a great degree parents are responsible not only for the violent passions and perverted appetites of their children, but for the infirmities of the thousands born deaf, blind, diseased or idiotic." [33]

Just supposing you found yourself back in the days of the middle and late 1800's, and there you hear of a woman with practically no formal education sounding off on health-related topics, so revolutionary and so "unscientific," would you have believed her? Most likely you wouldn't have, and that was exactly the reaction of a great many of her contemporaries. Drugs responsible for deformities? Diet to blame for evil tendencies and infirmities in their offspring? Irritability of the mother responsible for the defects of the still unborn child? It all sounded too fantastic and remained so until 1954, the year of Dr. Montagu's discovery. And just as with the case of Dr. Knisley's announcement linking alcohol with permanent brain damage, so it was with that of Dr. Montagu. Within months following his confirmation of the vision-given concepts of Ellen White, other researchers prepared their findings for publication, all emphatically supporting the Spirit of Prophecy.

Leland H. Scott further substantiated Mrs. White's 1890 statement by saying that "there is a growing evidence that chemical irregularities in the mother's blood brought about by endocrine imbalance, dietary deficiencies, or ill health, may have serious effects. Maternal malnutrition," he continued, "often results in the unborn child being deprived of essential vitamins or nutrients necessary for its normal growth and health. Childhood abnormalities, such as rickets, nervous instability, epilepsy, and cerebral palsy, have been found to result from serious malnutrition in the mother at certain points during the period of pregnancy.

"As previously stated, the emotional status of the mother cannot be transmitted directly to the unborn child. Severe emotional tensions continuing over long periods can nevertheless affect the chemical balance of the mother's blood, and by placental transmission affect the level of fetal activity. There is some evidence that these effects may carry over into infancy in the form of adjustment difficulties." [34]

Dr. Montagu in his *Ladies' Home Journal* article was in full agreement with this.

"Mothers undergoing periods of severe emotional stress during pregnancy frequently have infants which exhibit evidences of irritable and hyperactive nervous systems.

"As recently as June, 1953," he wrote, "Dr. William Kroger, gynecologist of the Chicago Medical School, told the AMA that 'disturbing maternal emotions and behavior may produce a neurotic fetus with a predisposition for a wide variety of psychosomatic diseases.'" To this commented Jane E. Brody, "Everything you do . . . every place you go . . . all the food you eat . . . and every pill you pop into your mouth affects the child you carry."

Other scientists more specifically support Ellen White in her statement that drugs can and often will cause deformity. Dr. Jesse D. Rising of the University of Kansas said in 1958 that "a doctor treating a woman during pregnancy with anesthetics, X ray, ACTH or cortisone-type hormones, may subject the fetus to oxygen shortage or some other threat. The result: physicians now face the horrible possibility of responsibility for many developmental defects." He listed babies born with one eye, abnormal hearts, cleft palate or mongolism and Siamese twins.

"The thoughtful physician," he concluded in his statement, "will not think of abandoning these useful and often life-saving drugs, but he will not lightly prescribe them, and will exert every effort to understand the harmful effects that may result from their use." [35] Thomas M. Rivers, M.D., blames large doses of alcohol as another cause of malformations. [36]

Is prenatal influence a possibility? There is not a scientist alive today who does not consider it a fact—yet again, the realization of this truth came to the surface exactly eighty-nine years after the Spirit of Prophecy first pointed out the connection between the living habits of the mother and the condition of the unborn child. If science had only listened, the thalidomide tragedy of the early 1960's might never have taken place.

Heart Disease—Meat, Fat and Sugar—the Killers

Since 1960 a most disturbing threat to the nation's health has been brought to light. While the threat was practically unknown in the early years of this century, it has now become the nation's number-one killer and claims about half of all the deaths that occur annually in the United States. Known as coronary heart disease, it strikes indiscriminately; at least that was the opinion of many researchers until new facts released in the 1960's indicated that it was closely related to the saturated fats contained in the average American diet. Dr. W. A. Thomas, who was extremely puzzled by this phenomenon, conducted extensive research on the dietary habits of people in various nations and found that "a vegetarian diet can prevent 90 per cent of our thrombo-embolic diseases, (clots in veins and arteries) and 97 per cent of our coronary occlusion." [37]

Due to the fact that the major element lacking in the diet of a vegetarian is animal fat, it was immediately suspect as a cause for coronary heart disease, more so since approximately 42 percent of all the food calories the average American consumes consists of fat, 85 percent of which is saturated or hydrogenated fat. Saturated fats in their natural state are found mostly in animal food products, thereby making the case for vegetarianism quite strong.

Ellen White "knew" this as far back as 1868.

"You have flesh but it is not good material," she exclaimed in that year. "You are worse off for this amount of flesh. If you should come down to a more spare diet, which would take from you twenty-five or thirty pounds of your gross flesh, you would be much less liable to disease. The eating of flesh meats has made a poor quality of blood and flesh. Your systems are in a state of inflammation, prepared to take on disease. You are liable to acute attacks of disease and to sudden death, because you do not possess the strength of constitution to rally and resist disease. There will come a time when the strength and health you have flattered yourself you possessed will prove to be weakness." [38]

"Both the blood [in the meat, ed.] and the fat of animals are consumed as a luxury," she continued, "but the Lord gave special directions that these should not be eaten. Why? Because their use would make a diseased current of blood in the human system. The disregard for the Lord's special directions has brought a variety of difficulties and disease upon human beings. . . . If they introduce into their systems that which cannot make good flesh and blood, they must endure the results of their disregard of God's word." [39]

When she sounded these warnings more than one hundred years ago, very few were ready to accept her counsel; however, with the decided increase in cardiovascular trouble, scientists initiated a frantic search for the culprit and discovered that a high cholesterol content of the blood was always present in persons suffering from heart attacks.

Loma Linda University has conducted a series of major health studies among the members of the Seventh-day Adventist Church in Southern California, aimed at determining whether their dietary habits (vegetarianism and total abstinence from alcohol and tobacco) had any significant influence on their proneness to disease. Truly astounding results were reported by Dr. Richard T. Walden of Loma Linda at the termination of the testing program.

"In contrast with the average American," the findings indicated, "an analysis of the dietary habits of the Seventh-day Adventists who entered upon this study revealed that their intake of fats constituted about 25 percent of their total diet (as compared to 42 percent for non-Adventists), and of this fat only about 65 percent was of the hard variety (as compared to 85 percent for non-Adventists). Further comparisons made indicated that these Seventh-day Adventist men and women on their usual diet had a 15 to 20 percent lower blood cholesterol on the average than did non-Seventh-day Adventists in the study.

". . . These studies in blood cholesterol are of additional interest when considered with the report three years ago on the frequency of hospital admissions for a variety of cancers and coronary artery diseases. That report indicated that Seventh-day Adventists apparently had a 40 percent less frequent occurrence of coronary artery disease than non-Adventists in the same hospital, that this effect was most marked in men, who are usually more at risk than women for the disease, and that the disease began 12 to 15 years later in life on the average Adventist men than among their non-Adventist fellows." [40]

Duke University, a non-Adventist institution, agrees wholeheartedly with Loma Linda's results.

"The large number of cardiovascular disease cases recorded in some sections of the Southeastern United States may be due to cooking and eating traditionally," suggested Dr. Siegfried Heyden of Duke University Medical Center at Durham, North Carolina.

"Many foods prepared in the Carolinas and Georgia are unusually high in fat and sugar content," he observed. "Pork and ham are popular meats; salt pork and bacon drippings are widely used in cooking. All these items have high cholesterol contents." [41] And with that statement, he introduced another element into the case of Food versus Disease—*sugar*.

It has often been queried whether there may be a link between the alarming increase of cancer and cardiovascular disease and the growing tendency to consume more and more meat (animal fat) and sugar—and statistics do indeed indicate the possibility of just such a connection.

Let's take a look at the rise in sugar consumption between the early 1800's and today and see what has occurred.

"In 1822, the average sugar consumption was two-and-a-half teaspoons a day," reports *These Times* on page 18 of the February, 1971 issue. "In 1870 the average person was eating ten teaspoons of sugar a day. At that time [1905] the sugar intake was approximately seventy pounds per capita or an average of twenty teaspoons of sugar each day. Now the average intake is well over 120 pounds each year, and represents over thirty-three teaspoons of sugar per person each day."

What has been the result?

Professor John Yudkin of the University of London is convinced that sugar in particular may be the etiological factor in atherosclerosis or heart-vessel disease. He believes that there is a more definite association between sugar intake and sudden death from heart disease than fat intake and heart disease.[42] This danger was clearly foreseen by Ellen, for in 1860 she wrote, "I frequently sit down to the tables of the brethren and sisters, and see that they use a great amount of milk and sugar. These clog the system, irritate the digestive organs, and affect the brain. Anything that hinders the active motion of the living machinery, affects the brain very directly. And from the light given me, sugar, when largely used, is more injurious than meat."[43]

"The free use of sugar in any form tends to clog the system," she repeated in 1890, "and is not unfrequently the cause of disease."[44] "Far too much sugar is ordinarily used in food. Cakes, sweet puddings, pastries, jellies, jams, are active causes of indigestion. Especially harmful are the custards and puddings in which milk, eggs, and sugar are the chief ingredients."[45]

If this was the case in 1890 when the average person

consumed less than twelve teaspoons per day, how much greater can this danger to health be in our time when the average intake is thirty-three teaspoons per day!

The *Journal of Nutrition,* October, 1970, page 257, in reporting on a series of tests aimed at establishing the effects of sugar in the American diet, noted that "when the sugar in the American diet, (17% of total calories) was replaced by fruits, vegetables and legumes, the following was observed, 'It is concluded that sucrose and milk sugar tend to produce higher serum cholesterol values than equal calories of carbohydrate contained in fruits, leafy vegetables and legumes.'"

Equally as important is the close relationship discovered between the activity of the white cells in fighting bacteria and the level of blood sugar. A study conducted in 1964 concluded that the higher the sugar intake, the smaller the body's defenses are against bacterial disease. Inasmuch as cancer is caused by a minute bacteria—a virus—could there not be a definite connection between high sugar intake and cancer? Not only did Ellen White consistently warn against anything more than a moderate use of sugar, but also the use of all refined carbohydrates in the diet. A moderate use of fats, we today classify as unsaturated, less sugar and more bulk was her advice. And again, as should be expected, science is confirming how right she really was. In the January 16, 1971, issue of *The Washington Post,* an article headlined "Refined Carbohydrates Linked to Increase in Cancer of Colon" stated:

"A leading English medical researcher blames refined carbohydrates diet of western and westernized nations—especially sugar and white flour—for the recent increase in cases of cancer of the colon. The same foods," the article continued, "are also responsible for such diseases of the gastrointestinal tracts as hemorrhoids, diabetes, appendicitis and ulcerative colitis."

The expert Dr. Denis P. Burkitt (discoverer of the lymph gland cancer known as Burkitt's lymphoma) has also formed this conclusion after a diligent study into the dietary habits of nations around the world. He pointed out that in areas where residents eat more roughage and fewer carbohydrates, the incidence of cancer of the colon is negligible.

"The major alteration in diet which has taken place has been the replacement of unrefined carbohydrates such as cereals, maize products and brown bread in favor of refined carbohydrates, which largely means white flour and sugar," he pointed out. "While Americans increased their intake of fats by 7 percent between 1909 and 1963, the consumption of sugar went up 218 percent.

"In view of the (available) evidence", Burkitt concluded, "it seems justifiable to issue a warning against the removal of so much of the unabsorbable fiber from our food and the associated over-ingestion of refined carbohydrates." It is conceiveable that within a short period of time, additional tests now being conducted will indicate that sugar is an important factor in producing both heart disease *and* cancer, thereby scientifically authenticating Ellen White's inspired insight.

The Killing of Our Planet

"At the rate he is going, man could consume and pollute his way to oblivion by the end of the twentieth century." That is the gloomy prediction voiced by a leading ecologist, Dr. Kenneth E. F. Watt of the University of California. Basing his pessimistic statement on the alarming rate at which our modern technological society is consuming the planet's limited natural resources, the overpopulation, the continuing pollution of earth and atmosphere and gross neglect of what remains, he feels that man is preparing our planet for total extinction. The prediction is rather foreboding and frightening, but even worse is the fact that most responsible scientists agree with the possibility that this is exactly what may happen.

When Ellen White lived from 1827 to 1915, the threat of pollution was unheard of, and the farfetched idea that man would someday be accused of killing his own planet would have been considered ludicrous. Now, in 1972, a mere fifty-seven years after her death, man is running scared and has every reason to do so.

The whys and wherefores should be obvious even to the most casual observer.

Man's unchecked compulsion to reproduce himself and to create an abundance of better things with which to make life easier are at the root of it all. Livable space, food and water are rapidly running out. A short twenty-eight years from now we will—or at least we can expect to—reach the year 2000, but what will await us humans if the three and a half billion population of today has increased to the expected seven billion? Today, waterlogged Holland is in a panic, for its water resources are rapidly dwindling, and there is every possibility that the tiny country behind the dikes may face a serious shortage of drinkable water by the year 1975. The Swiss lakes are polluted; the waters of the Rhine are almost too dangerous to touch. Death and disease attack us via the orchards of the nation, and while the smog of Los Angeles is slowly killing the majestic ponderosa pines of the San Bernardino National Forest, the already outlawed DDT, airborne throughout the world on the unpredictable winds of nature, is poisoning the milk of nursing mothers through the food they consume. In fact, in some areas DDT concentration has reached the danger level of two to six times the amount considered safe in milk for commercial use.

The current situation is bad, but that is only part of it. With ever-increasing indifference, new factories are being forced onto the already tired ground, adding more water

William Miller (1782-1849) was among the early and great influences on Ellen G. White (then Ellen G. Harmon) and her family. Miller led in the heralding of the second advent of Christ which he believed would take place in 1843-1844. More than one hundred thousand followed his leadership, young Ellen and her parents among them.

James White (1821-1881) left teaching for the evangelistic platform when he was twenty-one years old. Four years later, he married Ellen G. Harmon and together they crisscrossed the country, dividing their time between traveling and preaching, with White in the beginning earning their living in the forest, on the railroad and in the hayfield.

THE PRESENT TRUTH.

PUBLISHED SEMI-MONTHLY—BY JAMES WHITE.

Vol. I.	MIDDLETOWN, CONN, JULY, 1849.	No. 1.

"The secret of the Lord is with them that fear him; and he will shew them his covenant."—Ps. xxv. 14.

"WHEREFORE, I will not be negligent to put you always in remembrance of these things, though ye know them, and be established in the PRESENT TRUTH." 2 Pet. i: 12.

It is through the truth that souls are sanctified, and made ready to enter the everlasting kingdom. Obedience to the truth will kill us to this world, that we may be made alive, by faith in Jesus. "Sanctify them through thy truth; thy word is truth;" John xvii: 17. This was the prayer of Jesus. "I have no greater joy than to hear that my children walk in truth," 3 John iv.

Error, darkness and fetters the mind, but the truth brings with it freedom, and gives light and life. True charity, or LOVE, "rejoiceth in the truth;" Cor. xiii: 6. "Thy law is the truth." Ps. cxix: 142.

David describing the day of slaughter, when the pestilence shall walk in darkness, and destruction waste at noon-day, so that, "a thousand shall fall at thy side and ten thousand at thy right hand," says—

"He shall cover thee with his feathers, and under his wings shalt thou trust; his TRUTH shall be thy SHIELD and BUCKLER." Ps. xci: 4.

The storm is coming. War, famine and pestilence are already in the field of slaughter. Now is the time, the only time to seek a shelter in the truth of the living God.

In Peter's time there was present truth, or truth applicable to that present time. The Church have ever had a present truth. The present truth now, is that which shows present duty, and the right position for us who are about to witness the time of trouble, such as never was. Present truth must be oft repeated, even to those who are established in it. This was needful in the apostles day, and it certainly is no less important for us, who are living just before the close of time.

For months I have felt burdened with the duty of writing, and publishing the present truth for the scattered flock; but the way has not been opened for me to commence the work until now. I tremble at the word of the Lord, and the importance of this time. What is done to spread the truth must be done quickly. The four Angels are holding the angry nations in check but a few days, until the saints are sealed; then the nations will rush, like the rushing of many waters. Then it will be too late to spread before precious souls, the present saving, living truths of the Holy Bible. My spirit is drawn out after the scattered remnant. May God help them to receive the truth, and be established in it. May they haste to take shelter beneath the "covering of the Almighty God," is my prayer.

The Weekly Sabbath Instituted at Creation, and not at Sinai.

"And on the seventh day God ended his work which he had made; and he rested on the seventh day from all his work which he had made. And God blessed the seventh day, and sanctified it: because that in it he had rested from all his work which God created and made." Gen ii: 2, 3.

Here God instituted the weekly rest or Sabbath. It was the seventh day. He BLESSED and SANCTIFIED that day of the week, and no other; therefore the seventh day, and no other day of the week is holy, sanctified time.

God has given the reason why he blessed and sanctified the seventh day. "Because that in it he had rested from all his work which God had created and made." He rested, and set the example for man. He blessed and set apart the seventh day for man to rest from his labor, and follow the example of his Creator. The Lord of the Sabbath said, Mark ii: 27, "The Sabbath was made for man." Not for the Jew only, but for MAN, in its broadest sense; meaning all mankind. The word man in this text, means the same as it does in the following texts. "Man that is born of woman is of few days and full of trouble." Job xiv: 1. "Man lieth down and riseth not, till the heavens be no more." Job xiv: 12.

No one will say that man here means

The first issue of The Present Truth, *the first denominational magazine founded by James White in 1849, and published as a semi-monthly. This became the weekly* Review and Herald *and was edited by James White until his death in 1881.*

The title page of Ellen G. White's first book, published in 1851, which she called Christian Experience and Views. *It was followed by other books printed in more than 100 languages, with millions of copies distributed.*

Ellen G. White at age 37, with a page from one of her diaries which she kept in 1868. Mrs. White wrote continuously, transcribing her visions to notebooks, diaries, and books. Altogether, more than 100,000 pages—nearly all in longhand—were the result of her labor.

An artist's rendering of Mrs. White's first vision at the home of friends in South Portland, Maine, in December of 1844. This vision was subsequently published as a broadside and distributed under the title "To The Little Remnant Scattered Abroad."

TO THE LITTLE REMNANT SCATTERED ABROAD.

The Hilliard house at Otsego, Michigan, where in 1863 the health reform vision was given to Mrs. White. This subsequently led her to speak out against tobacco as a malignant poison, and against health problems which are today's recurring concerns.

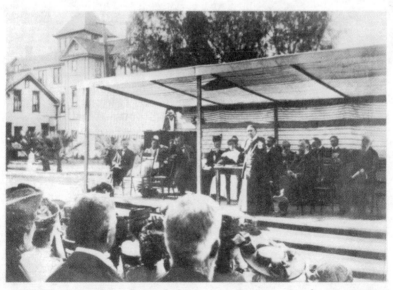

Mrs. White speaking at the dedication of the Loma Linda Sanitarium in 1906. Her effectiveness as a speaker, and her ability to project to audiences which sometimes numbered up to twenty thousand, was almost legendary. It is said that at times her voice carried without amplification more than one mile.

San Francisco burns, following the disastrous earthquake of April 18, 1906, in which more than nine hundred died and property was destroyed at the rate of one million dollars every ten minutes. Four years earlier, Ellen G. White had predicted, following a vision, that "Not long hence, these cities will suffer under the judgment of God. San Francisco and Oakland are becoming as Sodom and Gomorrah, and the Lord will visit them in wrath."

Biographical Information Blank

To be preserved by the General Conference as a matter of permanent record.

1. Full name *Ellen Gould White* (DO NOT WRITE INITIALS)   Usual form *Ellen G. White*

2. Date of filling this blank *March 5, 1909*

3. Present address *Sanitarium, near St. Helena, Napa Co., Cal.*

4. Date and place of birth *Gorham, Maine, Nov. 26, 1827*

5. Names and nationality of parents *Robert Harmon, Eunice Harmon, both Americans.*

6. Mother's maiden name *Eunice Gould*

7. Place or places where earlier years were spent *New England, New York, and Michigan, U.S.A.*

8. Educational advantages in public or private schools (give dates) *Attended public school in Portland, Me., until nine yrs. old; spent short time in private school when 12 yrs. old.*

9. Educational advantages in denominational schools (give dates) *None in schools, but the broad education that comes to an evangelist in the work of soul-winning.*

10. What degrees, if any, have you received, and from what school or schools, and when? *None*

11. Date of conversion *Probably in March, 1840*

11. When, where, and by whom baptized? *Latter part of 1840, at Portland, Me., by Methodist minister.*

12. Were your parents, or either of them, Seventh-day Adventists when you were born? *No. S.D.A's did not yet exist.*

14. To what denomination or denominations did your parents belong? *Methodist*

15. To what denomination or denominations did you belong before accepting present truth? *Methodist*

16. By what means particularly were you brought into the truth? *Study of the Bible, listening to gospel preachers, and by revelation*

17. When, where, and in what capacity did you begin laboring in the cause? *In Maine, 1842, laboring for young friends; 1844-45 began public labors, relating visions, etc.*

Ellen G. White's Biographical Information Blank, filled out in 1909, for the General Conference. In speaking of her formal schooling, it is noted that she "attended public school in Portland, Maine, until nine years old; spent short times in private school when twelve years old." Of her educational advantages, it reports, "None in schools, but the broad education that comes to an evangelist in the work of soul-winning."

Ellen G. White in 1899, when she was seventy-two years old, and just before she returned from Australia. Writing about her in the last years of her life, the historian George Wharton James said, "This remarkable woman, though almost entirely self-educated, has written and published more books and in more languages, which circulate to a greater extent, than the written works of any woman of history."

and air pollution to our now desperate plight and killing millions of fish in the process. Lake Erie is already doomed; the clams of the Raritan Bay in New Jersey have been severely infected by untreated sewage; and reports indicate that fluorides from phosphate plants have affected the bones of cattle in the central portion of Florida to such an alarming extent that they can no longer support themselves but sink to their knees.

It is no wonder that President Richard Nixon's science advisor, Dr. Lee A. DuBridge, recently declared:

"Our spacecraft called earth is reaching its capacity." [46] He might just as well have said that man's destructive nature has finally caught up with him, for we have undoubtedly reached a point of no return.

To Ellen White, in her conscious state, a world doomed by its own actions may have been something of which she was simply afraid. The proof that it would actually transpire reached her by way of revelations penetrating the innermost corridors of her mind, impressing every nerve cell in her brain with impulses filled with dire forebodings. Exactly to what extent Ellen's visions enlightened her as to the man-made devastations that would befall our planet Earth, we do not know; but we do know that in visions prior to 1890 she was shown the havoc man would create on this planet.

In a book in which some of her early revelations are given, she declared, "In the future the condition of things in the cities will grow more and more objectionable. . . . From the standpoint of health, the smoke and dust of the cities are very objectionable." [47] "The physical surroundings in the cities are often a peril to health. The constant liability to contact with disease, the prevalance of foul air, impure water, impure food ("poisonous gases" page 262) are some of the many evils to be met." [48]

"Many will now plead to remain in the cities, but the time will come erelong when all who wish to avoid the

sights and sounds of evil will move into the country; for
wickedness and corruption will increase to such a degree
that the very atmosphere of the cities will seem polluted." [49]
"Satan is working in the atmosphere; he is poisoning the
atmosphere, and here we are dependent upon God for our
lives—our present and eternal life." [50]

Jack Shepherd, former senior editor of the now-defunct
Look Magazine, described the present state of affairs quite
realistically when he wrote, "We are fouling our streams,
lakes, marshes. The sea is next. We are burying ourselves
under seven million scrapped cars, 20 million tons of waste
paper, 48 billion discarded cans and 28 billion bottles and
jars a year. A million tons more of garbage pile up each day.
The air we breathe circles the earth 40 times a year, and
America contributes 140 million tons of pollutants. . . . Los
Angeles smog may cause mass deaths by 1975; noise, strain-
ing our lives, doubles in volume every ten years." [51] It is
frightening and even more so when we realize that all he
did was describe the conditions in America alone! Something is happening to our mother earth, and it appears that
mankind has lost all control. Not only is man destroying the
air and water supply on which he thrives, but is also ex-
terminating plant and animal life at an unprecedented rate.
With new and more sophisticated germ, chemical and
atomic warfare weapons at hand, man now has the ability
to destroy himself with a flick of the wrist; self-destruction
is already a thing of the present. Plankton, the basic food
substance of the sea, now blooms a full month later than it
did in 1950, causing an expert to comment, "these changes
could have huge and perhaps catastrophic effects on the
ecology of the sea if they continue." [52] The possibility that
the atmospheric contamination will diminish the solar energy
that reaches the earth from the sun, thereby bringing about
another ice age is getting stronger and stronger. Animal
species, once plentiful, are now on the verge of extinction.

According to experts at the Smithsonian Institution, during the past 150 years, the extermination of mammals has increased by fifty-five times, and all remaining species of mammals will disappear within the next thirty years if the killing is not stopped. Winston Churchill, worried about the march of history, once remarked, "We seem to be moving, drifting, steadily against our will, against the will of every race, and every people, and every class, toward some hideous catastrophe. Everyone wishes to stop it, but they do not know how."

Said John the Revelator in Revelation 11:18, "And the nations were angry, and thy wrath is come, and the time of the dead, that they should be judged, and that thou shouldest give reward unto thy servants the prophets, and to the saints, and them that fear thy name, small and great; and *shouldest destroy them which destroy the earth.*" (ital. ed.)

Here the prophet John declares that God will intervene in history, that the divine rule will begin at a time when the nations of earth are incensed and when man is about to destroy the earth. The reasons which now cause thoughtful scientists concern for the future are the very reasons the Bible gives as evidence that God is about to save man from himself. The significance of this passage, of course, is that it has had no meaning, no specific relevance in the tide of human affairs, until the past twenty or twenty-five years, for only since the end of the World War II has man developed the potential ability to literally destroy the earth. Christian scholars often refer to the text, Genesis 1:26, which states that God has given man dominion over the earth. The Old Testament expert, Walter Brueggemann, interprets this to mean that "man is to have dominion." He feels that man has been given the responsibility for maintenance, order and control of that which was created on earth and to safeguard it. "To subdue and have dominion," he says, "is not a charter for abuse, but rather a command to order, maintain, protect and care for."

Can it be that man's violation of this basic principle is leading him to his own destruction?

Electricity—the Vital Force

Not one single discovery has affected our civilization as much as that of electricity, but it was not until 1929 that the German psychiatrist Hans Berger personally involved every one of us by announcing that we are all individual electrical generators.

With the publication of a number of strange little pictures, disclosing nothing but irregular wavy lines, he tried to convince his skeptical colleagues that he had uncovered the essence of life: the presence of electrical activity in the human brain. In fact, he voiced his conviction that these electrical impulses emanating from the human brain were responsible for all of our actions and reactions, voluntary and involuntary. However, no one took him seriously. His findings, nevertheless, were of great historical significance, and even though for several years his wavy pictures were not considered a scientific discovery and no attempts were made to duplicate or investigate his claims, his discovery could not remain hidden for very long. Now, some forty-three years later, it has grown into a new science called electroencephalography, and hundreds of laboratories the world over are busily recording and evaluating the fluctuating narrow lines drawn on strips of paper.

Five years after 1929, it was Dr. Charles Mayo of the famed Mayo Clinic who first supported Dr. Berger's discovery.

"Minute electrical charges are vital to the functioning of the brain," he stated unreservedly in 1934. Ernst Weber, president of the Polytechnic Institute in Brooklyn, New

York (*This Week,* December 30, 1962), went even a step further in backing Dr. Berger. "All knowledge of the physical world as scientists conceive it today, rests on the electromagnetic theory," he charged. "These wonderful waves exist in the human body, and *are the vital-force of the heart and the nerves.*"

It is these electrical impulses of the brain and the power of the brain to pick up similar impulses emanating from other sources and other *brains* that have given rise to many theories formulated to explain phenomena such as telepathy and clairvoyance. Early in her life Ellen White recognized the value of electrical power; in fact, not only was she foremost in advocating that electrical power was responsible for the operation of the human body, but she also even credited electricity with providing the needed stimuli for the growth process in plants.

Whether God's prophetic impulses reached the innermost segments of her mind via electromagnetic waves—which is plausible since He is the creator of science—is something no one knows, but the possibility does exist, inasmuch as God has control over all. Dr. Weber's statement that these electromagnetic waves are the vital force of the heart and the nerves certainly supports this concept.

As far back as 1869 it was said by Ellen White that,

"The brain nerves which communicate with the entire system are the only medium through which heaven can communicate to man, and affect his inmost life. Whatever disturbs the circulation of the electric currents in the nervous system lessens the strength of the vital powers, and the result is a deadening of the sensibilities of the mind." [53]

"God endowed man with so great a vital force that he has withstood the accumulation of disease brought upon the race in consequence of perverted habits, and has continued for six thousand years," she wrote in 1872. "This fact of itself is evidence to us of the strength and electrical energy that God gave to man at the Creation. It took more than two thousand years of crime and indulgence of base passions to bring bodily disease upon the race to any great extent. If Adam, at his creation, had not been endowed with twenty times as much vital force as men now have, the race, with their present habits of living in violation of natural law, would have become extinct." [54]

In other statements she credits the electrical force of the brain with the ability to help the body resist disease. [55]

Researchers have found that the electrical energy generated by the human brain does indeed tell us a great deal about the activity of the body it stimulates. The energy generated by the human brain has an electrical potential of one hundred microvolts, admittedly small, yet strong enough to form the basis for accurate measurements of the brain's operation. In conjunction with Ellen White's inspired statement that a disturbance in the circulation of the electric currents in the nervous system lessens the strength of the vital powers, thereby resulting in a deadening of the sensibilities of the mind, [56] Wilder Penfield, a Canadian neurosurgeon, has supplied outside electricity to the human brain in an attempt to explore the depths of the human memory bank. With the use of two small electrodes, he discovered two areas on either side of the head, just forward and above the ear, that appear to be the electronic memory bank for all of the experiences encountered by a person during his lifetime.

As Dr. Penfield probed with the electrode, the patients, who had been given a local anesthetic, vividly recalled certain childhood happenings and places and events they had long since forgotten. In fact, incidents that occurred many years ago were suddenly brought to the surface, and smells and emotional crisis were again reexperienced. All work being done in this rapidly expanding field indicates that electricity forms the basis for *all* of life's actions and *all* of life's experiences. *Electronics World* of April, 1970, calls it, "A unique communications grid that binds all life together. Its phenomenon apparently works on a multi-input basis which operates beyond known physical laws."

During the early period of the modern prophetic time (since 1844), the phenomena experienced by psychic mediums were either accepted or rejected; no attempt was made to put the manifestations to the scientific test. Since the emergence of the realization that electrical impulses form the basis for all of the experiences of life, psychic researchers have tried to explain psychic phenomena on the basis of electricity and have done an *almost* convincing job. All psychics now claim that "electronic communications" is elementary and is the path along which they receive their psychic vibrations. They "tap into the communications channel between God and man"; they claim the ability to beam microwave signals, similar to radar, and have them bounce back, filled with the sought-after information. It's electronics, they say, which enables us to "feel" the past, for it is because of man's electricity emanating from him and remaining in the air after his death that we can touch the past and tune into the events of history.

Many well-known and respected laboratories are now investigating these various claims.

If one hundred microvolts of electrical power are present in everyone of us today, and all of our actions are limited to the power of our (limited) electrical resources, then imagine for one moment the ability that man must have once possessed when he operated on the basis of a full two thousand microvolts or "twenty times as much vital force as men now have." [57] Perhaps ESP (extrasensory perception), or, as some psychics call it, EP (Energy Power), is only a poor substitute for one of the senses with which man was originally endowed at the time of his creation. In whatever way the Power of Prophecy reached Ellen White, it operated beyond the known physical laws and on a wavelength of undetermined power. Speaking with knowledge received from what she often called the "author of science," [58] she readily admitted the influence of the God-power, not only in the affairs of human life, but also in *all* life forms.

"There is life in the seed, there is power in the soil," she once commented, referring to the limitless uses of electricity in life. "But unless infinite power is exercised day and night, the seed will yield no return. The showers of rain must refresh the thirsty field; the sun must impart warmth; electricity must be conveyed to the buried seed." [59]

Substantiating Ellen's statement made in 1900, Dr. H. S. Burr of Yale University revealed at a symposium held at the College of William and Mary in Williamsburg, Virginia, on November 22, 1959, "Periodic, predictable electrical rhythms exist not only in humans but in trees and other forms of life." Following this, he added—at that time, a most startling statement—"The vigor and growth rate of plants already have been successfully predicted by measurements of the electricity in cotton seed."

What did Ellen White say in 1900? "Electricity must be conveyed to the buried seed." Surely she could not have stated it more accurately!

From the moment her health-reform messages were published, beginning with pamphlets soon after her 1863 vision and culminating in her books *Ministry of Healing, Counsels on Health* and *Counsels on Diet and Foods,* a tremendous interest has developed in her inspired advice, more so today, since much of our food is found to be contaminated. She advocates a return to the natural diet of man; fruit, vegetables, grains and nuts, augmented by a limited use of dairy products. In other words, a lacto-ovo-vegetarian diet.

In 1906 she cautioned against the use of the X ray, warnings which have now been confirmed by science. She also cautioned against the overuse of salt, and once more science proved her correct. A connection between mental and physical health? Psychosomatic medicine is based on principles first outlined by Ellen White. She knew all about it as far back as 1867 and gave causes and remedies which psychiatrists are now only beginning to accept. The relationship between poor scholarship and diet was first mentioned by her; she blamed coffee and tea for many unexplained illnesses; and she was extremely critical of the use of hypnosis in medical work. In practically every case, her early inspired insight—all based on visions—was eventually backed by scientific discoveries, even though in many instances a number of years after she first brought it to the attention of the general public.

The belief that man as a three-dimensional being—spiritual, physical and mental—needed to become aware of all that could affect his total personality was the paramount issue throughout her entire health-reform counsel.

On August 11, 1960, Paul Harvey, nationally known news analyst, asked in his syndicated column, while writing about Ellen White as a nutritionist "way ahead of her time," "Are there [perhaps] additional recommendations which this remarkable woman urged upon us and which we have, so far, ignored? Two of her teachings haunt the more progressive nutritionists because if she is right about these also, most of us are wrong and have got to 'catch up' to her advanced knowledge of nutrition. Mrs. White wrote, 'All-wheat flour is not best for a continuous diet. A mixture of wheat, oatmeal and rye would be more nutritious.' Also Mrs. White was essentially a vegetarian. She wrote, 'The life that was in the grains and vegetables passes into the eater. We receive it by eating the flesh of the animal. How much better to get it direct.' Do you suppose we'll discover she was right about these things too?"

Chapter 5

Unmasking the Mastermind

IN DEALING WITH psychic phenomena and prophetic impulses, it has to some extent become customary to judge a prophet by his performance. Foretelling future events, delving into the uncharted corridors of time, falls within the realm of "forbidden" knowledge, except when the God-power directs and controls the phenomena. It has frequently been called the more mysterious aspect of the work of a prophet, and because of this, prophets have often been regarded as special confidants of the Almighty. Throughout the ages, many prophetic warnings have been recorded and many more psychic predictions have been made, but the failure of a number of their predictions to attain complete or even partial fulfillment has forced the psychics to retreat behind a purposely created veil of mystery, using their fulfilled predictions to shield them from unwarranted attention.

Let's face it. No one likes to brag about his failures in life, and psychics least of all, since they invariably claim to be the channels for information from God or "the Supreme Intelligence." Nevertheless they are vulnerable because of their lack of absolute accuracy, and they protect themselves with a beautiful-sounding excuse, their Prophetic Accuracy quotient. Using simple third-grade arithmetic, they deduct their failures from their total list of announced predictions, and the result provides them with their supposedly correct rating as a prophet.

Daniel Logan, the psychic medium, is quite content with this method.

"To me, it seems that if the psychic gives clear evidence of a reasonable percentage of accuracy, then he has done something quite extraordinary," he boasts. "Given the circumstances in which the psychic works and the material with which he deals, it seems to me remarkable that I am able to maintain an accuracy of eighty percent." [1] Others, such as Jeane Dixon and David Bubar, also speak of their Prophetic Accuracy Quotient as being somewhere between 70 and 85 percent. However, no Biblical prophet has ever been evaluated on the basis of his hits or misses, even though, each of them, too, had his unfulfilled prophecies. Does this mean perhaps that psychics and prophets are judged with a double standard? Certainly not! The same number of tests for true prophets still applies to all, but there is a distinct difference between a "conditional prophecy" as given in the Bible and a "chance prediction" originating from a psychic's mind.

In the Bible, there is an element of "controlled uncertainty," known as "conditional prophecy", that has to be considered in every case where a prophecy deals with the response of people. God allows for the existence of just this condition in Jeremiah 18:7-9 (New English Bible) where He says:

"At any moment I may threaten to uproot a nation or a kingdom, to pull it down and destroy it. But if the nation which I have threatened turns back from its wicked ways, then I shall think better of the evil I had in mind to bring on it." This clearly indicates that the only possible escape from the wrath forecast in a Biblical prophecy was a turning away from evil. Prophecies have never been made to threaten man's existence; they were, and still are, a means of indicating to man the purpose of the will of God. An investigative study of prophecy definitely shows that when the human element is drawn into the prophecy—when it concerns the behavior of man—the prophecy of promised reward or punishment is invariably conditional. In the instances where a prophetic warning was not fulfilled as announced, it was always because of the fact that the human element had fulfilled the conditions that would enable God to retract the threatened judgment. You could almost say that a prophecy declaring doom, death or destruction was only pronounced over mankind as a desperate final measure. A 180-degree turn to righteousness was the only possible avenue of escape out of the threatening disaster, and each time this road was taken, the prophecy was annulled. It did not fail; it became void. It was retracted by the Author of Prophecy.

With today's psychics, we also are confronted with the problem of unfulfilled predictions, but whereas it was the exception in the Bible, it is practically the rule of thumb today. It is clearly indicated in the prophetic handbook that only a return to righteousness or a turning away from righteousness can change a prophecy; but psychics, while claiming to have received their "psychic vibrations" from the same source, completely disregard this solely recognized condition given for nonfulfillment and substitute for it their own reasons.

A classic example of this is the way in which seeress Jeane Dixon accounts for the failure of many of her predictions.

"When my predictions don't come true," she explained to me in one of our frequent interviews on psychic affairs, "it is because many of them come to me via telepathy or psychic vibrations emanating from a *person*. When someone plans a certain deed or action, I become aware of his plans by tuning in to his psychic channel of communication with the higher powers. I then in turn use this information for making my predictions. If a prediction fails to come true, it is not because I have been wrong, but it is because he, the originator of the thought vibrations, changed his mind, and decided to alter his previously planned course of action. I simply wasn't aware of this." When a *vision* fails, this, too, she feels can be explained without hurting her reputation. She attributes it to either the reception of an incomplete vision or an incorrect interpretation of the symbols as presented to her.[2] All three reasons listed are convincing to her; to prophecy, however, they are totally unacceptable. In the case of the assassination of Robert Kennedy—an event she foretold with great accuracy—she felt that it could have been avoided by either a change in the assassin's plans or if the Senator had taken the time to listen to her repeated warnings.

"I know he could have lengthened his life if he had only listened,"[3] Mrs. Dixon stated. According to her, the same holds true in the case of the brutal slaying of Dr. Martin Luther King. That tragedy also, she says, came to her telepathically and, consequently, did not have to take place. In reality what she is doing is taking the fickleness and mental instability of an assassin and substituting it for the only Biblically recognized condition given for a retraction of a prophecy. She has even more difficulty in explaining her prediction concerning Bishop James A. Pike. She foresaw that he would be highly successful in "another field and lose his frustration in his new vocation."[4] Sadly enough, however, Bishop Pike died when the book in which her prediction was written was already on the press. In his death, there was no assassin involved; no one planned his demise. She also did not interpret the information incorrectly, for she said that she "saw" him lose his frustrations. The prediction simply failed and left her without even a pet theory to account for its discredit to her P.A.Q.

To be a prophet—dealing with unerring guidelines projected by the Author of Prophecy—must be awe-inspiring, for it enables a mere mortal to peek across the threshold of the future and observe God arranging history in advance; but to a psychic, who bases a highly debatable and dubious gift on a variety of hits and misses, each failure leaning heavily on the support of unfounded theories or unsubstantiated statements, the "gift" can only be confusing. It forces him to hide behind a mental smoke screen of doubletalk, desperately hoping at the same time that his next prediction will even up the score. It is the same as a comparison between truth and falsehood, between Good and Evil, for God instituted prophecy as a channel of communication between Him and His warriors in order to convey instructions to conduct this cosmic battle.

The record of Ellen White as a prophet is not one based purely on the fulfillment of prediction, yet even though she never laid boastful claim to being a prophet, she most definitely did the work of one and more. Her medical insight was faultless in every way; her spiritual foresight was just as broad and grand in scope, for her prophetic warnings were strong and far-reaching. From the moment of her very first vision, Ellen White openly claimed that it was the power of God which spoke through her as He had done through other prophets in ages past.

Whether God required her to have reached a certain mental maturity before giving her the most important vision of her entire life, is something we do not know, but it was not until 1858, the year which ushered in her thirty-first birthday, that the wondrous event occurred.

It was the weekend of March 13 and 14 that Ellen and her husband attended a series of religious meetings in Lovett's Grove near Bowling Green, Ohio. The regular meetings were interrupted during the day of the fourteenth when it was decided to conduct a funeral service in the little schoolhouse which also served as a meeting hall. Delighted to have the Whites with them, those present asked James to address the small congregation. No sooner had he concluded his remarks when Ellen stood up, desiring to add a few words of comfort. After her first few words, she faltered . . . and stopped in the middle of a sentence. Then it happened. A moment of pregnant silence followed, when suddenly she shouted triumphantly, as if forcing her way through a dark cloud,

"Glory to God . . . *Glory to God* . . . GLORY TO GOD!" this time not fading out as was the usual case when she was taken into vision, but shouted with increasing emphasis.

Startled, the audience tensed and looked questioningly at both Ellen and her husband. Slowly, James White got up from his chair and ever so quietly walked over to his wife, and while her face took on an expression of intense concentration, with eyes gazing unblinkingly into the distance, he faced the congregation.

"She is in vision . . . my wife is in vision . . ." he whispered softly to the hushed audience. Cognizant of the fact that he was addressing a number of people to whom Ellen's Gift of Prophecy was not known, he reverently explained how, since her seventeenth year, his wife was often called into vision, and that each time this happened, she was completely detached from her surroundings. His claim that her breathing ceased while in this condition caused many of them to press forward and crowd around her.

"Bring a mirror," James asked in a low tone, and while holding it close to her mouth, he carefully pointed out that the total absence of condensation on the glass proved that her breathing had stopped. A second test, this time with a burning candle held only inches from her nose and mouth, was made, but not a flicker of moving air disturbed the tranquillity of the flame. Stunned, aghast by this unusual phenomenon, the onlookers watched as Ellen slowly made her way through them, gracefully moving her arms, occasionally smiling, and more often giving the impression of staring at scenes transpiring beyond mortal vision, watching secrets that were solely intended for her.

For two long hours she remained in vision, sometimes moving, other times just standing, staring, listening, observing with her spiritual eyes what was being revealed to her. Then came her first deep breath which always signified the beginning of her return to consciousness. Another followed . . . and then another. . . . Slightly bewildered, she glanced at the anxious faces about her, and as the memory of her vision became clear, she realized once again that she had been taken into Supreme confidence.

Writing of this vision two years later, she said:

"In the vision at Lovett's Grove, most of the matter which I had seen ten years before concerning the great controversy between Christ and Satan, was repeated, and I was instructed to write it out. I was shown that while I should have to contend with the powers of darkness, for Satan would make strong efforts to hinder me, yet I must put my trust in God, and angels would not leave me in the conflict." [5] Scores of visions had passed before her; however, this time Ellen was transported into an undefinable dimension of time before and beyond that of recorded history and was made witness to the War in Heaven, the rebellion and fall of Lucifer. Watching the tragedy unfold, she stood appalled and shocked at the infidelity of one who was once an exalted angel.

The files of the Ellen G. White Estate contain all of her recollections of that famous vision, with many passages expressing her emotions of sadness and astonishment as her mind's consciousness locked in on the prophetic impulses of God.

"The Lord has shown me that Satan was once an honored angel in heaven," she stated, "next to Christ. His countenance, like those of the other angels, was mild and expressive of happiness. His forehead was high and broad, showing great intelligence. His form was perfect; his bearing noble and majestic. But when God said to His Son, 'Let us make man in our image', Satan was jealous of Jesus. He wished to be consulted concerning the formation of man, and because he was not, he was filled with envy, jealousy and hatred. He desired to receive the highest honors in heaven next to God.

"Until this time," she recalled, "all heaven had been in order, harmony and perfect subjection to the government of God. It was the highest sin to rebel against His order and will. All heaven seemed in commotion. . . . There was contention among the angels. Satan and his sympathizers were striving to reform the government of God. They wished to look into His unsearchable wisdom and ascertain His purpose in exalting Jesus and endowing Him with such unlimited power and command. They rebelled against the authority of the Son. All the heavenly host were summoned to appear before the Father to have each case decided. It was there determined that Satan should be expelled from heaven, with all the angels who had joined him in the rebellion.

"Then there was war in heaven.

"Angels were engaged in the battle; Satan wished to conquer the Son of God and those who were submissive to His will. But the good and true angels prevailed, and Satan, with his followers, was driven from heaven." [6]

"Satan stood in amazement at his new condition. His happiness was gone. He looked upon the angels who, with him, were once so happy, but who had been expelled from heaven with him. Before their fall not a shade of discontent had marred their perfect bliss. Now all seemed changed. Countenances which had reflected the image of their Maker were gloomy and despairing. Strife, discord, and bitter recrimination were among them." [7] "Satan trembled as he viewed his work. He was alone in meditation upon the past, present and his future plans. His mighty frame shook as with a tempest. An angel from heaven was passing. He called him and entreated an interview with Christ. This was granted him. He then related to the Son of God that he repented of his rebellion and wished again the favor of God. He was willing to take the place God had previously assigned him, and be under His wise command.

"Christ wept at Satan's woe, but told him, as the mind of God, that he could never be received into heaven. Heaven must not be placed in jeopardy. All heaven would be marred should he be received back, for sin and rebellion originated with him. The seeds of rebellion were still within him. He had, in his rebellion, no occasion for his course, and he had hopelessly ruined not only him but the host of angels also, who would then have been happy in heaven had he remained steadfast." [8]

"When Satan became fully conscious that there was no possibility of his being brought again into favor with God, his malice and hatred began to manifest. He consulted with his angels, and a plan was laid to still work against God's government. When Adam and Eve were placed in the beautiful garden, Satan was laying plans to destroy them. It was decided that Satan should assume another form and manifest an interest for man. He must insinuate against God's truthfulness and create doubt whether God did mean just what He said; next he must excite their curiosity, and lead them to pry into the unsearchable plans of God—the very sin of which Satan had been guilty—and reason as to the cause of His restrictions in regard to the tree of knowledge." [9]

We are not enlightened as to which part of this vision her mind fused with these segments of recorded history . . . but there is little doubt that when the mirror showed no breath in her and the candle's flame burned solemnly skyward without so much as a flicker, her mind was reaching out into the vastness of the universe, sharing the eternal secrets of Creation.

"God assembled the angelic host to take measures to avert the threatened evil. It was decided in heaven's council for angels to visit Eden and warn Adam that he was in danger from the foe. Two angels sped on their way to visit our first parents. The holy pair received them with joyful innocence . . . and they had many questions relative to many things which they could but indistinctly comprehend.

"The angels graciously and lovingly gave them the information they desired. They also gave them the sad history of Satan's rebellion and fall." [10] "The angels warned them of Satan and cautioned them not to separate from each other in their employment, for they might be brought in contact with the fallen foe. . . .

"Satan commenced his work with Eve, to cause her to disobey. She first erred in wandering from her husband, next in lingering around the forbidden tree, and next in listening to the voice of the tempter, and even daring to doubt what God had said 'in the day that thou eatest thereof thou shalt surely die.' She thought that perhaps the Lord did not mean just what He said, and venturing, she put forth her hand, took of the fruit, and ate. It was pleasing to the eyes and pleasant to the taste. Then she was jealous that God had withheld from them what was really for their good, and she offered the fruit to her husband, thereby tempting him." [11] "She related to him the wise discourse of the serpent and wished to conduct him at once to the tree of knowledge. She told him she had eaten of the fruit, and instead of her feeling any sense of death, she realized a pleasing, exhilarating influence. As soon as Eve had disobeyed she became a powerful medium through which to occasion the fall of her husband." [12]

"I saw a sadness come over the countenance of Adam. He appeared afraid and astonished. A struggle appeared to be going on in his mind. He felt sure that this was the foe against whom they had been warned, and that his wife must die. They must be separated. His love for Eve was strong, and in utter discouragement he resolved to share her fate. He seized the fruit and quickly ate it. Then Satan exulted. . . .

"The news of man's fall spread through heaven. Every harp was hushed. The angels cast their crowns from their heads in sorrow. All heaven was in agitation. A council was held to decide what must be done with the guilty pair. The angels feared that they would put forth the hand, and eat of the tree of life, and become immortal sinners. But God said that He would drive the transgressors from the garden. Angels were immediately commissioned to guard the way of the tree of life. It had been Satan's studied plan that Adam and Eve should disobey God, receive His frown, and then partake of the tree of life, that they might live forever in sin and disobedience, and thus sin be immortalized. But holy angels were sent to drive them out of the garden, and to bar their way to the tree of life. Each of these mighty angels had in his right hand something which had the appearance of a glittering sword.

"Then Satan triumphed. He had made others suffer by his fall. He had been shut out of heaven . . . they out of paradise." [13]

Her vision of the fall of man was devastating, but it was not limited to the introduction of sin and the actual transfer of the sickness that would destroy, for the time being, eternal life for men both in heaven and on earth. Her accompanying angel brought her to the Courts of Heaven and allowed her to share in the sadness that had embraced the angelic witnesses. She was brought close to the Throne of God and saw the remedy being prepared for erring man.

"I saw the lovely Jesus and beheld an expression of sympathy and sorrow upon His countenance. Soon I saw Him approach the exceeding bright light which enshrouded the Father. Said my accompanying angel,

" 'He is in close converse with His Father.'

"The anxiety of the angels seemed to be intense while Jesus was communing with His Father. Three times He was shut in by the glorious light about the Father, and the third time He came out from the Father, His person could be seen. His countenance was calm, free from all perplexity and doubt, and shone with benevolence and loveliness, such as words cannot express." [14]

"He then made known to the angelic host that a way of escape had been made for lost man. He told them that He had been pleading with His Father, and had offered to give His life as a ransom, to take the sentence of death upon Himself, that through Him man might find pardon; that through the merits of His blood, and obedience to the law of God, they could have the favor of God, and be brought into the beautiful garden, and eat of the fruit of the tree of life.

"At first the angels could not rejoice; for their Commander concealed nothing from them, but opened before them the plan of salvation. Jesus told them that He would stand between the wrath of His Father and guilty man, that He would bear iniquity and scorn, and but few would receive Him as the Son of God. Nearly all would hate and reject Him. He would leave all glory in heaven, appear upon earth as a man, humble Himself as a man, become acquainted by His own experience with the various temptations with which man would be beset, that He might know how to succor those who should be tempted; and that finally, after His mission as a teacher would be accomplished, He would be delivered into the hands of men, and endure almost every cruelty and suffering that Satan and his angels could inspire wicked men to inflict; that He would die the cruelest of deaths, hung between the heavens and the earth, as a guilty sinner; that He would suffer dreadful hours of agony, which even angels could not look upon, but would veil their faces from the sight. Not merely agony of body would He suffer, but mental agony, that with which bodily suffering could in no wise be compared. The weight of the sins of the whole world would be upon Him. He told them He would die and rise again the third day, and would ascend to His Father to intercede for wayward, guilty man." [15]

Was this perhaps the moment when an infinite sadness covered the face of the young woman? None of the witnesses in that quiet public schoolroom could penetrate the sacred communion she was having with the heavens, yet her constantly changing expressions of sorrow, understanding, anguish and those deep smiles of ineffable joy must have been a portrayal of the complex emotions that flashed through her as she watched the dramatic scenes unfold.

"The angels prostrated themselves before Him," she continued her recollection. "They offered their lives. Jesus said to them that He would by His death save many, that the life of an angel could not pay the debt. His life alone could be accepted by His Father as a ransom for man. Jesus also told them that they would have a part to act, to be with Him and at different times strengthen Him; that He would take man's fallen nature, and His strength would not be even equal with theirs; that they would be witnesses of His humiliation and great sufferings; and that as they would witness His sufferings, and the hatred of men toward Him, they would be stirred with the deepest emotion, and through their love for Him would wish to rescue and deliver Him from His murderers; but that they must not interfere to prevent anything they should behold; and that they should act a part in His resurrection; that the plan of salvation was devised, and His Father had accepted the plan.

"With a holy sadness Jesus comforted and cheered the angels and informed them that hereafter those whom He should redeem would be with Him, and that by His death He should ransom many and destroy him who had the power of death. And His Father would give Him the king-dom and the greatness of the kingdom under the whole heaven, and He would possess it forever and ever. Satan and sinners would be destroyed, nevermore to disturb heaven or the purified new earth. . . .

"Then joy, inexpressible joy, filled heaven. And the heav-enly host sang a song of praise and adoration. They touched their harps and sang a note higher than they had done be-fore, for the great mercy and condescension of God in yielding up His dearly Beloved to die for a race of rebels. . . .

"Said the angel [with her] 'Think ye that the Father yielded up His dearly beloved Son without a struggle? No, no. It was even a struggle with the God of heaven, whether to let guilty man perish, or to give His beloved Son to die for him.' Angels were so interested for man's salvation that there could be found among them those who would yield their glory and give their life for perishing man. 'But,' said my accompanying angel, 'that would avail nothing. The transgression was so great that an angel's life would not pay the debt. Nothing but the death and intercessions of His Son would pay the debt and save lost man from hopeless sorrow and misery. . . .'

"I was shown Satan as he once was, a happy, exalted angel. Then I was shown him as he now is. He still bears a

kingly form. His features are still noble, for he is an angel
fallen. But the expression of his countenance is full of anxiety, care, unhappiness, malice, hate, mischief, deceit, and
every evil. That brow which was once so noble, I particularly noticed. His forehead commenced from his eyes to
recede. I saw that he had so long bent himself to evil that
every good quality was debased, and every evil trait was
developed. His eyes were cunning, sly, and showed great
penetration. His frame was large, but the flesh hung loosely
about his hands and face. As I beheld him, his chin was
resting upon his left hand. He appeared to be in deep
thought. A smile was upon his countenance, which made me
tremble, it was so full of evil and satanic slyness."[16]

In rapid sequence, the crowning events of Biblical history
passed before Ellen's mind. In quiet amazement she observed the ancient patriarchs and consecrated prophets lead
the people of Israel; she saw Moses receive the Ten Commandments on the Mount of Sinai and recoiled in horror as
she heard the singing of the apostate Israelites and watched
them dedicate the golden calf. On and on her perception
went, and her mental anguish became more consuming as
she personally witnessed the birth of Christ, only to see it
end on a cross, seemingly ignored by Heaven. Via the apo-
stolic times, she gazed with abhorrence at the massacres of
the early Christians, then proudly viewed the work of the
reformers. She was slowly brought back to her own times,
watching current history evolve; then transported again—
this time into the future—to the events leading up to the
Second Coming of Christ, and was grieved by the heart-
tearing scenes of the final judgment of man.

It was indeed a prophetic vision unequaled in both scope
and magnitude.

She had been taken into full confidence . . . now it was
up to her to act.

The following day, homeward bound on the train, Ellen

discussed with James her vision at length and formulated her plans for the writing of the book covering the great conflict as it was shown to her. Her health was reasonably good at the time, and there seemed to be nothing that would prevent her from carrying out this new challenge. It was Ellen who suggested, while passing through Jackson, Michigan, en route to their home in Battle Creek, to make a stop at the home of Daniel Palmer, an old friend.

Scarcely had they arrived at the Palmers, when Ellen underwent a frightening sensation.

". . . my tongue refused to utter what I wished to say, and seemed large and numb," she recalled. "A strange cold sensation struck my heart, passed over my head and down my right side. For a time I was insensible, but was aroused by the voice of earnest prayer. I tried to use my left limbs, but they were perfectly useless." [17]

Suffering from a severe stroke, she lost all hope of recovery. However, with her slowly returning strength and renewed faith in her mission, she began to rally and immediately started writing the manuscript, relaying her experiences while in vision at Lovett's Grove. In June, as she was in the completion stage of her book, she received light concerning what she had undergone at the Palmers' home.

"I was shown in vision that in the sudden attack at Jackson, Satan intended to take my life, in order to hinder the work I was about to write," she pointed out, "but the angels of God were sent to my rescue." [18] It was not until September of that same year that her work was finished and the 219-page *Spiritual Gifts—The Great Controversy*—was ready for distribution.

Since she witnessed the origin of the struggle for eternal survival, it is no wonder that most of the writings of Ellen White dealt with fundamentally the same subject: that of guiding people out of this degrading dilemma that originated in heaven. . . . Whereas her vision of 1863 can safely be regarded as the most important health-reform vision she had ever received, the 1858 revelation has often been called the most *comprehensive* vision, covering both the fall of man and the great plan of escape. Of all her two thousand revelations, none are comparable in overall significance to this one. Yet, this does not diminish the timely relevance of the surrounding visions. They had their own specific purposes to fulfill. Many times during these intermittent contacts with the God-power, she received additional light on subjects touched upon only briefly in the outline visions of 1858 and 1863. In the case of her health principles, these shorter, more detailed spurts of prophetic knowledge were always of a highly informative nature. They showed her the importance of proper nutrition and the causes of diseases, and outlined the steps necessary to check them and to prevent their spreading. Her major spiritual vision in 1858, however, was framed within the boundaries of historical events, venturing out as far as the Second Coming of Christ, with such precise clarity and deep insight that it still baffles researchers today. Mental impressions destined to prepare the world for the Second Coming involved countless minutes of her vision, and all of these prophetic time fragments revealed the intricate planning behind it. Simultaneously, Ellen was also made aware of Satan's carefully devised counterplans for the conquest of man. It was because of this that the angel, who constantly attended her while she was in vision, disclosed to her the minute details, the *identifying marks*, of the movement that was to spearhead the Devil's battle on earth.

Ellen's early years were marked by a national feeling of great spiritual confusion, dramatically manifested both in the birth of the Millerite Movement and in modern Spiritualism—organizations which were diametrically opposed, both in aims and operations. Starting in the home of the Fox sisters in 1848, Spiritualism spread like wildfire, adopting a religious image before its danger to Christianity was recognized. Many looked upon the rappings and spirit manifestations as fraud or illusionary tricks, but by now these have completely evaporated, for the deceptive power of Spiritualism and the Biblical references predicting it suggest strongly that the last days of human history will be wrapped in an extraordinary display of spiritualistic or psychic phenomena. Says the prophet John:

"Then I saw coming from the mouth of the dragon, the mouth of the beast, and the mouth of the false prophet, three foul spirits like frogs. These spirits were devils, with power to work miracles. They were sent out to muster all the kings of the world for the great day of battle of God the sovereign Lord." [19] Jesus also commented on this, having as background His recollections of His original encounter in the first dramatic battle fought between Himself and Satan as observed by Ellen White in 1858.

"For there shall arise false christs, and false prophets, and shall show great signs and wonders; insomuch that, if it were possible, they shall deceive the very elect." [20] "But this prophecy," said Ellen, "was also spoken for the last days. This sign is given as a sign of the second advent. Even now false christs and false prophets are showing signs and wonders to seduce His people." [21]

"And he doeth great wonders," John the Revelator continued, giving more identifying marks of these spirits of devils, "so that he maketh fire come down from heaven on the earth in the sight of men, and deceiveth them that dwell on the earth by the means of those miracles which he had power to do in the sight of the beast." [22] If there is one common operational method that ties all three, the dragon, the beast and the false prophets, together, it is the emergence of the three "spirits of devils" working miracles. In other words, it is this *spirit force*, this *Spiritualist force*, that will be the single factor connecting the three institutions together, and its supernatural phenomena will be the token of its unearthly power. The Book of Revelation clearly indicates that there will be three separate powers, working and acting as *one*, in the persecution of those who stubbornly and resolutely refuse to submit to the power of the Devil prior to the final war on earth.

A considerable amount of Ellen White's work as a prophet was directly involved with shedding more light on this particular segment of Biblical prophecy. Soon after the birth of modern Spiritualism in 1848, in fact, as early as March 24 of the following year, she was shown the power of this manifestation, and from the moment of its inception, she began to list its identifying marks.

"I saw in vision," she wrote warningly, "that the mysterious knockings in New York and other places were the power of Satan, and that such things would be more and more common, clothed in a religious garb, so as to lull the deceived to greater security."[23] "Some of it was from him, and some directly through his agents, but it all proceeded from Satan. It was his work that he accomplished in different ways."[24]

"I saw the rapidity with which this delusion was spreading," she continued. "A train of cars was shown me, going with the speed of lightning. The angel bade me look carefully. I fixed my eyes upon the train. It seemed that the whole world was on board, that there could not be one left. Said the angel,

" 'They are binding in bundles ready to burn.'

"Then he showed me the conductor, who appeared like a stately, fair person, whom all the passengers looked up to and reverenced. I was perplexed and asked my attending angel who it was.

"He said, 'It is Satan. He is the conductor in the form of an angel of light. He has taken the world captive. They are given over to strong delusions, to believe a lie, that they may be damned.' " 25

"I saw that soon it would be considered blasphemy to speak against the rapping, and that it would spread more and more, that Satan's power would increase, and some of his devoted followers would have power to work miracles, and even to bring down fire from heaven in the sight of men. I was shown that by the rapping and mesmerism these modern magicians would yet account for all the miracles wrought by our Lord Jesus Christ, and that many would believe that all the mighty works of the Son of God when on earth were accomplished by this same power." 26

"As Spiritualism more closely imitates the nominal Christianity of the day, it has greater power to deceive and ensnare. Satan himself is converted after the modern order of things. He will appear in the character of an angel of light. Through the agency of Spiritualism, miracles will be wrought, the sick will be healed, and many undeniable wonders will be performed. And as the spirits will profess faith in the Bible and manifest respect for the institutions of the church, their work will be accepted as a manifestation of divine power." 27

"The Protestants of the United States will be foremost in stretching their hands across the gulf to grasp the hand of Spiritualism; they will reach over the abyss to clasp hands with the Roman power; and under the influence of this threefold union, this country will follow in the steps of Rome in trampling on their rights of conscience. . . ." 28

"Side by side with the preaching of the gospel, agencies are at work which are but the medium of lying spirits. Many a man tampers with these merely from curiosity, but seeing evidence of the working of a more than human power, he is lured on and on, until he is controlled by a will stronger than his own. He cannot escape from its mysterious power."29

"The line of distinction between professed Christians and the ungodly is now hardly distinguishable. Church members love what the world loves and are ready to join with them, and Satan determines to unite them in one body and thus strengthen his cause by sweeping all into the ranks of Spiritualism. Papists, who boast of miracles as a certain sign of the true church, will be readily deceived by this wonder-working power; and Protestants, having cast away the shield of truth, will also be deluded. Papists, Protestants and worldlings will alike accept the form of godliness without the power, and they will see in this union a grand movement for the conversion of the world and the ushering in of the long-expected millennium." [30]

"Through Spiritualism, Satan appears as the benefactor of the race, healing the diseases of the people, and professing to present a new and more exalted system of religious faith; but at the same time he works as a destroyer. His temptations are leading multitudes to ruin. Intemperance dethrones reason; sensual indulgence, strife and bloodshed follow. Satan delights in war, for it excites the worst passions of the soul and then sweeps into eternity its victims steeped in vice and blood. It is his object to incite the nations to war against one another, for he can thus divert the minds of the people from the work of preparation to stand in the day of God." [31]

"In accidents, and calamities by sea and by land, in great conflagrations, in fierce tornadoes and terrific hailstorms, in tempests, floods, cyclones, tidal waves, and earthquakes, in every place and in a thousand forms, Satan is exercising his power. He sweeps away the ripening harvest, and famine and distress follow. He imparts to the air a deadly taint, and thousands perish by the pestilence. These visitations are to become more and more frequent and disastrous. Destruction will be upon both man and beast." [32]

It was indeed a devastating indictment, yet it was only a

fragment of that which was shown her of Satan's strategy in her 1858 vision at Lovett's Grove and in other amplifying visions. These visions enabled her to penetrate the shield of secrecy obscuring the miracles that he would be performing in the name of God and revealed to her the immensity of the task of the holy angels in combating the evil influence of Lucifer. Her accompanying angel also spread out before her the satanic delusions mankind would have to face—and faithfully Ellen repeated these in her book *Spiritual Gifts*.

"Through the two great errors, the immortality of the soul and Sunday sacredness," she relayed, "Satan will bring the people under his deception." [33]

"A belief in the spiritual manifestations opens the doors to seducing spirits and doctrines of devils, and thus the influence of evil angels will be felt in the churches." [34] "Love is dwelt upon as the chief attribute of God, but it is degraded to weak sentimentalism, making little distinction between good and evil. God's justice, His denunciations of sin, the requirements of His holy law, are all kept out of sight. The people are taught to regard the Decalogue as a dead letter. Pleasing, bewitching fables captivate the senses and lead men to reject the Bible as the foundation of their fate. Christ is as verily denied as before; but Satan has so blinded the eyes of the people that the deception is not discerned." [35]

"We have reached the perils of the last days," she continued prophetically, "when some, yes, many, shall depart from the faith, giving heed to seducing spirits and doctrines of devils. Be cautious in regard to what you read and how you hear. Take not a particle of interest in spiritualistic theories. Satan is waiting to steal a march upon everyone who allows himself to be deceived by his hypnotism. He begins to exert his power over them just as soon as they begin to investigate his theories." [36]

"Satan has long been preparing for his final effort to deceive the world. The foundation of his work was laid by the assurance given to Eve in Eden, 'Ye shall not surely die.' 'In the day ye eat thereof then shall your eyes be opened, and ye shall be as gods, knowing good and evil' (Gen. 3:4, 5). Little by little he has prepared the way for his masterpiece of deception in the development of spiritualism. He has not yet reached the full accomplishment of his designs; but it will be reached in the last remnant of time." [37]

Her detailed, inspired knowledge of the developing activities of Spiritualism, the earthbound arm of the militant evil spirits, serves a twofold purpose. All uncertainty and doubt should be eradicated from the minds of those who wonder whether the source of her gift of prophecy was possibly satanic, inasmuch as she consistently spoke out and wrote against the mushrooming satanic movement. At the same time, her visions also provided us with the *modus operandi* of Spiritualism—a knowledge vital to us if we want to escape its stranglehold.

In the visions previously quoted—all dating back to the year 1858 or earlier—she was shown a number of unmistakable identifying marks, fourteen of which we will use as separate indictments of Satan's plan for the conquest of humanity. Each one of them will enable us to distinguish and recognize Spiritualism in those places where it has infiltrated into religious and secular society.

This is how the indictment appears:

1. Through Spiritualism, many false christs and false prophets will become public figures.
2. It will appear that the whole world will be "aboard" the spiritualistic movement.
3. It will be considered blasphemy to speak against its manifestations.
4. It will claim that all miracles wrought by Jesus were merely psychic manifestations.

✗ 5. The movement will closely imitate nominal Christianity.
   6. Through its power, miracles will be wrought and the sick will be healed.
   7. Protestants will be foremost in grasping the hand of Spiritualism.
✗ 8. Spiritualism will work side by side with the preaching of the gospel.
✗ 9. It will be regarded as a grand movement for the conversion of the world.
✗ 10. Spiritualism will profess to present a new and more exalted system of religious faith.
   11. It will advocate the immortality of the soul and the Sunday sacredness.
   12. Spiritual manifestations will be accepted into the churches.
✗ 13. The Ten Commandments will be taught to be a "dead letter"; the Bible will no longer be regarded as the foundation of faith.
   14. Seducing spirits will introduce doctrines of devils in the last days.

Taking each point individually, it becomes rather evident, concerning indictment number *one*, that the *prophecy regarding the emergence of false prophets* is in the process of being fulfilled—and has been for quite a few years. At no time in history has there been such an influx of "prophets," clairvoyants and mediums specializing in forecasting the future. Jeane Dixon, Criswell, Louis Heubner, David Bubar, Arthur Ford, Edgar Cayce and Daniel Logan are typical of what has been happening in this respect. With the exception of Arthur Ford and Daniel Logan, none are willing to admit a connection with Spiritualism; in fact, many of the 140,000 psychic fortune-tellers now operating in this country profess to believe the exact opposite of its teaching—but their activities betray them.

The National Spiritualist Association of Churches, however, adopted a list of general definitions in 1914, stating the various ways in which "their" spirit power manifests itself.

"The phenomena of Spiritualism," it says, "consists of Prophecy, Clairvoyance, Gift of Tongues, Laying on of Hands, Healing, Visions, Trance, Apports, Levitation, Raps, Automatic and Independent Writings, Paintings, Voice, Materialization, (Thought) Photography, Psychometry," thereby placing the aforementioned psychic mediums in direct relationship to the teachings of Spiritualism. To the majority of us, psychics are people who have access to a channel of communications that works on a frequency beyond that of the known spectrum, listening to intelligences that shower them with a wealth of information emanating from a dimension unseen by human eyes. This definition will probably suffice as well as all the others, for collectively all those definitions can be boiled down to one simple three-letter abbreviation, "SCS," short for Satanic Communications System, for that's what it's all about. Miracles claimed by mediums using these methods therefore, are operating in direct fulfillment of the Spirit of Prophecy's warning through Ellen White.

It will appear that the whole world will be "aboard" the Spiritualistic movement is point number *two* on the list of identifying marks. At the time it was made, this statement, referring to the growth of the psychic movement, seemed completely out of place. Yet Ellen saw beyond the growing pains of the sect and did not limit her vision merely to observing the first indications surrounding the mysterious knockings in Hydesville, New York. When she made her prediction a short twelve months after the raps, there was nothing to suggest that its spread would be so phenomenal. However, it soon changed.

The eleventh edition of the *Encyclopædia Britannica* states that "Spiritualism spread like an epidemic," and estimates made in 1910 showed that at that time North America *alone* had at least sixteen million recognized Spiritualists, while world membership was listed as sixty million. *A. B. C. of Spiritualism,* published in 1920, states, "A mighty tide of thought and sentiment in favor of the main propositions of Spiritualism is sweeping all over the world. . . . The Teachings of Spiritualism under the organizations, through the press, through Psychic Research . . . will go on and on, conquering and to conquest, until the whole world shall know and rejoice in the great truth: 'There is no death,' and all God's great family are linked in glad communication and fellowship." [38]

Latest membership estimates are so wild and so astronomical that it is fair to assume that even the organized spiritualist movement has difficulty in arriving at a reasonable figure, particularly since there are uncounted millions of believers still maintaining their memberships in Christian churches for one reason or another.

The *third* indictment dealing with the prediction by Ellen White that *soon it would be considered blasphemy to speak against the rappings* (psychic manifestations) found public fulfillment in a section of the *Centennial Book of Modern Spiritualism in America,* 1948 edition. It stated:

"Neither priest nor press should uncharitably speak of, or touch this holy word Spiritualism, only with clean hands and pure hearts; and Spiritualists should honor their blessed gospel of immortality." While this frank admission on the part of the spiritualist movement is merely another piece of the puzzle that helps complete the pattern of deceit and falsehoods, it is the crediting of the *Biblical miracles to psychic phenomena,* point number *four,* that is rapidly becoming one of the greatest identifying marks of the spiritualists. *The Spiritualist Manual,* 1955 edition, makes the allegation that the Bible is in reality nothing but a compilation of Spiritualist phenomena. *The opening of the iron gate for Peter by an angel* (Acts. 12: 7-10); *clairvoyant appearances* (as of Moses and Elias on the Mount and of Christ after the resurrection); *speaking with unknown tongues* (as at Pentecost); *trances* (as of Paul, II Cor. 12:2, 4); *direct spirit writing* (as on the palace walls of Babylon, Dan. 5:5); *levitation,* (as when Philip was caught away, Acts 8:39, 40); *clairvoyance and clairaudience,* (as with the voice heard by Saul the persecutor, Acts 9:4, 7); *healing* (as by Jesus, Peter and Paul); and *dreams and visions* (as with John the Revelator and Daniel) are all considered psychic phenomena and are attributed to the working of the spirit world. *Even all the miracles performed by Jesus while on earth are considered to have been nothing but spiritualist phenomena.* Yet there is more, a great deal more. According to Mrs. White's spiritual insight, *the movement, for example, will try to imitate nominal Christianity* which is the *fifth* indictment. In this case, too, proof is readily available.

"Spiritualism is a religion because it strives to understand, and to comply with the Physical, Mental and Spiritual Laws of Nature, which are the laws of God," states the *Centennial Book* on page 22. Late as this official admission came (1948), the transformation from a loosely knit movement to church organization had begun as early as 1893. In that year, "Spiritualism shifted to a religious basis and declared itself to be a church," LeRoy Edwin Froom noted. "As more and more church people accepted Spiritualism, this religious phase became inevitable."

"Though the first Spiritualist congregation, as an individual church, was established in Sturgis, Michigan, in 1858, it was not until 1893 that action was taken declaring the entire movement to be a church. Thenceforth Spiritualist congregations spread everywhere, with ordained ministers, church manuals, hymnals, yearbooks, et cetera—and even a type of seminary." [39] It is within this organization that *spiritual healing* (point number *six*) operates.

With thousands of "faith healers," "magnetists," "healing

mediums" and "spirit healers" now practicing their deceitful profession, it might be well to see what they say concerning their own work and power.

The *Centennial Book* defines a Spiritualist healer as "one who, either through his own inherent powers, or through his mediumship, is able to impart vital, curative force to pathologic conditions" (page 22). Russell S. Waldorf, first president of the Spiritual Healers' League of the Natural Spiritualist Association, adds, "The energy or vital curative force supplied by a healer is received by him in his capacity as a medium, relayed to him by those doctors in the spirit world who continue their work in their chosen field." [40]

In 1909, the N.S.A. Convention held in Rochester, New York, adopted a fivefold definition of spiritual healing. It states in part that "it is the sense of this convention that Spiritual Healing is a gift possessed by certain Spiritualist mediums, and that this gift exercised by and through the direction and influence of excarnate spiritual beings for the relief, cure and healing of both mental and physical diseases of humankind." [41]

An intriguing case of "spirit healing" was reported from London where a duodenal ulcer was supposedly removed by a being from the spirit world, identifying himself as the spirit of a certain Dr. Reynolds who was said to have died more than a century before. It is the only case on record, according to my knowledge, where a "materialized" spirit worked at a surgical table.

Describing the healing, Ellaine Elmore said, "The hands of the spirit seemed to disappear inside the patient's body. While performing the operation, the materialized spirit declared he would bring 'the ulcer through a temporary hole in the stomach.' After the ulcer was removed, it was sent to a laboratory in Manchester and identified as 'an acute duodenal ulcer.' The medical authority performing the analysis certified it as an acute ulcer and commented on the 'freshness of the tissue and also the fact that there was no trace of modern surgical methods having been used.' " [42] Since its initial introduction, spirit therapy has grown to such fantastic proportions that there are now spiritualistic hospitals, in various parts of the world, staffed with spiritualistic "doctors" and "nurses." How far will it go? Two of the most outspoken psychic seers, Jeane Dixon and David Bubar, are very frank when discussing the value and nature of this development.

Grouping all supernatural manifestations under the general umbrella of psychic phenomena, Jeane Dixon says, "Before the completion of the next decade, popularity of ESP and psychic phenomena will reach an all-time high. No longer will people be inhibited by what others may say about them; they will have reached the age of experimentation in psychic matters and will probe its depths to discover the power of spirituality. Many will find faith in the Lord through ESP." [43]

Her statement is more theoretical than that of David Bubar, who unreservedly predicts that "toward the end of the 1970's, many medical doctors will join the ranks of the faith healers, and as a result new healing methods will be introduced into the medical world. What is now known as 'spiritual healing' and 'faith healing' will be channeled into one of the greatest revolutionary changes in the history of mankind. It will force the entire field of conventional medicine to revert to hitherto unaccepted healing methods." [44] "Because of the psychological and emotional changes now developing within the human body," he continues, "a new awareness of psychic phenomena will come to the surface. People will become more intuitive, more clairvoyant, more clairaudient, and more sensitive in all areas of energy communication." [45]

With great accuracy, Ellen White predicted the miracles and healing powers of Spiritualism, but she did more. Remembering the great controversy vision, she pointed out (indictment number seven) that *"Protestants will be foremost in grasping the hand of Spiritualism."* It was the late Arthur Ford, ordained clergyman and internationally known Spiritualist medium, who became the single most important agent to advance the fulfillment of this prophecy. It began quite innocently, yet from the very moment of its inception, the Spiritual Frontiers Fellowship, brainchild of Arthur Ford, confirmed the validity of Ellen White's vision. Formed in 1956 principally by three men, Albin Bro, missionary and educator, Paul Higgins, a Methodist pastor, and Arthur Ford, it advocated the "encouragement of study within the Churches of psychic phenomena as related to personal immortality, spiritual healing and prayer." [46]

"When we explore the psychic faculties we are not dabbling in something new and strange," commented Arthur Ford at the group's spring conference in 1958. "We are just trying to remind the people in the churches of something that has always been part of the Christian Gospel, but has been neglected for centuries." [47] Comprising more than half of its executive council of twenty-four members are clergymen of the Presbyterian, Methodist, Congregationalist, Episcopalian, Baptist and other churches, but in its principles, the organization is merely a front for the promulgation of spiritualist doctrines. So popular was Arthur Ford among Protestant and Catholic clergy that at one of his 7:00 A.M. breakfast meetings in Greenwood, South Carolina, it was reported that no less than 174 men had turned out to hear him speak on the connection between psychic phenomena and religion. It is highly significant that within the Bible belt stronghold, every local Protestant minister and Roman Catholic priest was present at the breakfast!

Ford's group, however, is not the only organization responsible for the infiltration of spiritualism into the Christian churches. Parapsychology, also known as the "New Frontier of the Spirit World" is making inroads that are almost beyond belief. Dr. J. B. Rhine, director of the Parapsychology Laboratory of Duke University, has been working for more than forty years trying to discover scientific proof for the doctrine of immortality. His studies, as he once stated, "have been encouragingly successful and indicate the presence of an extra-physical or spiritual power in what might be called man's living spirit." Adding to this he said, "The principal aim was to test the world-wide belief in the realm of discarnate spirit personalities." [48]

One of the major trends in the basic philosophy of parapsychology is to regard God as some kind of "Universal Intelligence," responsible for all of life's actions. Man's mind —according to the parapsychologists—is "part" of this Universal Intelligence but is limited in its operation by its surroundings.

One of the aims of parapsychology is to reconcile psychic phenomena with religion, each one supplementing the other. Said Dr. Alson J. Smith, "Parapsychology . . . brings hope— for world peace, hope for more brotherly relations among men, hope for a new unity of religious faith." [49] "Doctrine, dogma, and form or organization all become secondary to the witness and power of the inner, supersensory life. *Parapsychology will help unite Christendom* by emphasizing that super-normal element that all denominations have in common and minimizing those divisive elements that have their roots in time obsession." [50] It is parapsychology's purpose to reinforce Christianity by bringing in the elements of spiritualism as a cohesive element.

Surely the Spirit of Prophecy foresaw just this development.

One will never know exactly how God was able to impress so many details concerning the world's decisive stages on the mind of Ellen White, but all-knowing, God filled every living cell of her memory with the knowledge of events to come and added to it identifiable highlights to show the progress of fulfillment. Spiritualism, Satan's plan of conquest, has already become an accepted form of worship. One of its advocates, Shaw Desmond, is convinced that soon the Christian religion will become the religion of the psychics.

"Religion and Science," he says, "will not only talk, but will walk together." [51] When that happens, he states, "the Atomic World will be riddled with the psychic, steered by the psychic." [52] Believing that the "church itself was born at Pentecost in a rush of wind and flame and spirit-filled utterances," Spiritualism feels that "by a slight change of name, 'medium' for 'prophet', 'clairvoyance' for 'discernment of spirits', 'psychic phenomena' for 'miracles', 'spirit light' for 'tongues of fire' "; they claim the close affinity of the two systems should be apparent to all sincere investigators and students. One of its leading advocates, the Reverend D. Mona Berry asserts, "Modern Spiritualism is a powerful ally of true Christianity, a system of religion which will never die if purged of its unscientific theology, its irrational concepts of God, of man, of life and death in the hereafter." [53] The impact of its infiltration into the Christian churches will more than likely result in the unification of the various denominations. It is the only way in which Spiritualism can reach its aim of becoming the grand movement for world conversion—the realization of which all its leaders are striving for. That grand old man of mystery, the creator of the Sherlock Holmes novels, Sir Arthur Conan Doyle, himself one of the predominant figures in the formative years of the spirit movement, admitted this. "The ultimate merit of that revelation, which came in so humble a shape, will be the simplification of religion, the breaking down of the barriers between the sects, and a universal creed which will combine the ethics of real Christianity with direct spiritual communication," [54] he declared proudly. "Spiritualism will sweep the world, and make it a better place to live. When it rules over all the world, it will banish the blood of Christ. Spiritualism has a mighty mission to fulfill, and spiritualists are missionaries of this new teaching of the so-called 'Christ spirit'." [55]

That the Spiritualists regard their faith as being a more exalted system of religious worship goes practically without saying. A belief in the immortality of the soul—the most basic precept of Spiritualism—and its acceptance in the community of Christian churches is already a known and established fact. All doctrines of this spirit-based religion are actually in stark contradiction to the ground rules of Christianity, inasmuch as they disregard the value of the Ten Commandments and hold no faith in the Bible as the foundation of Christian faith.

In the thirteen points of the indictment discussed thus far, developments have been forecast which are presently being fulfilled. Hiding in a cloak of religious sanctity, this anti-Christian movement is now uncovering itself with quiet determination and has manifested itself in a resurgence of witchcraft and open devil worship (point number *fourteen*).

When Ellen White predicted, "*We have reached the perils of the last days, when some, yes, many shall depart from the faith giving heed to seducing spirits and doctrines of devils,*" countless critics disregarded it and smiled—wondering where it would all end. In her time it was a prophecy; yet today it is history. Anyone doubting whether or not we are really living in the closing days of earth only has to journey to San Francisco and find California Street, and all of his skepticism will surely vanish. There, in all his ugly reality, Satan is revealing himself. Those who know the extent of his boldness shiver when confronted with this latest situation.

"Weird and loathsome," is the way one visitor to the First National Church of Satan described her impressions, and a personal interview I had with the church's High Priest, Anton Szandor LaVey, more than confirmed this feeling.

Seated on a black chair, robed in black and flanked by an ancient skull and an impressive collection of books on ritual magic, LaVey was more than willing to submit to a number of questions, directed at exposing the true nature of this radically new venture of the Prince of Darkness.

He laughed heartily when I asked him the reasons for the existence of his church.

"I believe that we are all Satanists," he pointed out, building a philosophical base for our interview, "at least if not seven days a week then perhaps one or two days a week. Yet, Satan has never been fully understood. The devil in one form or another has always existed but has never been able to stand up literally and speak for himself. His advocates have been practically nonexistent. This has now changed. Satan needs us as a defender if he is to come forth with an air of respectability.

"I was given a particular ordination by an ancient order to call the church of Satan into being, and I felt that the year 1966, the 'Year of the Beast' or the 'Year of Satan,' numerologically speaking, was the year for his emergence. For centuries now, it has been believed that anything that a person does for self-sustenance, enjoyment or pleasure is wrong. All of these so-called sins have been invented by the churches to assure guilt feelings on the part of the sinner. We feel that a sin is not a sin if it is something that is done the natural way and doesn't hurt anyone else."

"If you don't believe in sin, does that mean that there are no rules and doctrines guarding your church?"

LaVey stared at the yellowed skull on the mantelpiece and thought for a moment.

"We do have doctrines," he answered, "but they are quite different from those you believe in.

"A true Satanist believes in God, but as a force, a reckoning device which balances the universe. God is a very powerful action-and-reaction device but is not concerned whether people suffer pain or pleasure; whether they live or die; whether humans or animals are in misery, in torment or in love. God is a force; Satan is the embodiment of all that we are concerned with on this earth.

"The doctrines of our church are as follows:

"Satan represents indulgence instead of abstinence.

"Satan represents vital existence instead of spiritual pipe dreams.

"Satan represents undefiled or unhypocritical wisdom instead of that of hypocritical self-deceit.

"Satan represents kindness to those who deserve kindness instead of love wasted on ingrates.

"Satan represents responsibilities to those responsible instead of concerns for psychic vampires.

"Satan represents man as just another animal, sometimes better but more often worse than those that walk on all fours . . . who, because of this so-called spiritual development, has become the most obnoxious and vicious animal of all.

"Satan, of course, represents all the so-called sins and virtues as they all lead to physical and mental gratification.

"Through Satanism, man's rightful place in nature is refound. We are no longer suffocating weaklings groping in the dust, beseeching God to throw us a crumb of mercy. As sorcerers and sorceresses we are strong. The knowledge of the left-hand path, the way of Satan, has not been lost throughout the ages. With our power and knowledge, we now command our God Satan. A Satanist worships nature in its majesty, and by doing so he sanctifies himself and his natural humanity.

"The Satanic Church advocates and teaches indulgence. As a Satanist you learn how to indulge in the so-called Seven Deadly Sins, as they all lead to physical and mental gratification.

"We have one sin, and that is the sin of self-deceit."

"Someone who belongs to God calls himself a child of God. What—if anything—do you call yourself?"

Spontaneously came the answer, without so much as a second's hesitation.

"To say that I am 'possessed of the Devil' would be incorrect," he replied. "I am in league with the Devil, and as such, I am a child of the Devil. You can compare me to the Pope. He claims to represent Christ; I claim to represent Lucifer. I am proud of this distinction. I transmit my new nature to my followers. When people join my church, they become more evil, because they learn how to become evil in a more effective way. Evil is just and right. Evil spelled backward is live, and to us this life represents Satanism. We believe that only those who fully give themselves to Satan have any chance of returning afterward. . . ."

"Are you in regular contact with your master?"

Anton LaVey nodded emphatically.

"Yes. I can force Satan to do anything that I want, because as long as he dwells within me, within my body, I am forcing myself. I am Satan, Satan is I. I am in regular contact with Satan also through my own actions and certainly through practicing of what I preach.

"Prayer is something I certainly don't believe in. Prayer to a Satanist is a nasty word. Prayer and hope represent apprehension, and apprehension represents not being sure of yourself and of being without confidence in one's God. The true Satanist commands his god or simply states what he wants to have. He faces the west, the traditional abode of the Devil and commands his God."

In answer to my question about the reaction of religious and governmental circles concerning his movement, High Priest LaVey commented:

"We have been officially recognized by the State of California as a church, and as such we are authorized to perform marriages and baptisms in the name of Satan. Our wedding ceremony consists of the invocation or reading a hymn to Satan and a very simple invocation to the Gods of Pleasure. There are no vows like 'I do.' The only vow made is the intent. Just wanting to stay with one another for a reasonable length of time is sufficient grounds for marriage under Satanism.

"The sacrament of baptism too is important in Satanism. A person baptized in the name of Satan embraces the concept of Satanism for life, contrary to the idea of baptism being symbolic of cleansing a person from sin. The basic idea with us is that, through baptism in the name of Satan, we invoke him to induce in the child all the appreciation for all the indulgences and gratifications of life in that life, so he will never make an attempt to stamp these things out.

"We dedicate our children to Satan.

"Interestingly enough, the majority of church leaders I have been in contact with treat us with a rather amused acceptance. I have not noticed any great controversy or reaction from religious sources, probably because their dogma and my dogma are basically very similar. The Devil has been keeping them in business so long that they can't afford to believe that he doesn't exist. They admit his existence, and my church gives them a shot in the arm. It backs their sermons with reality. . . . They need us!"

Since my original interview, the Church of Satan has published *The Satanic Bible*, listing all the Satanic revelations. Among the latter, "The Book of Satan" contains the most blasphemous principles ever transmitted through a human medium. The following ten statements are representative of the Devil's doctrines:

1. Open your eyes that you may see, Oh men of mildewed minds, and listen to me ye bewildered millions!
2. For I stand forth to challenge the wisdom of the world; to interrogate the "laws" of man and of "God"!
3. I request reasons for your golden rule and ask the why

and wherefore of your ten commands.

4. Before none of your printed idols do I bend in acquiescence, and he who saith "thou shalt" to me is my mortal foe!

5. I dip my forefinger in the watery blood of your impotent mad redeemer, and write over his thorn-torn brow: The TRUE prince of evil—the king of the slaves!

6. Behold the crucifix; what does it symbolize? Pallid incompetence hanging on a tree.

7. No creed must be accepted upon authority of a "divine" nature. Religions must be put to the question. No moral dogma must be taken for granted—no standard of measurement deified. There is nothing inherently sacred about moral codes. Like the wooden idols of long ago, they are the work of human hands, and what man has made, man can destroy!

8. Give blow for blow, scorn for scorn, doom for doom— with compound interest liberally added thereunto! Eye for eye, tooth for tooth, aye four-fold, a hundred-fold! Make yourself a terror to your adversary, and when he goeth his way, he will possess much additional wisdom to ruminate over. Thus shall you make yourself respected in all the walks of life, and your spirit—your immortal spirit—shall live, not in an intangible paradise, but in the brains and sinews of those whose respect you have gained.

9. There is no heaven of glory bright, and no hell where sinners roast. Here and now is our day of torment! Here and now is our day of joy! Here and now is our opportunity! Choose ye this day, this hour, for no redeemer liveth!

10. Say unto thine own heart, "I am mine own redeemer."

Need more be said?

There is no doubt that the emergence of this Satanic movement is in direct fulfillment of Ellen White's prediction that "seducing spirits will introduce doctrines of devils in the last days." It is the most important step Satan has undertaken since the introduction of Spiritualism in the 1800's.

Since its formation in 1966, the First National Church of Satan has added at least ten thousand new converts. Some even claim that it has already exceeded the twenty thousand mark. "Pleasuredomes" or Satanic churches have been organized in many countries, and there is hardly a major city in American without a branch of the Satanic Church. One of the main reasons for this tremendous growth is no doubt their Satanic Bible written by High Priest LaVey and the special correspondence courses in Satanism. Over three hundred letters per week arrive at the church's headquarters in San Francisco, inquiring into the aims and doctrines of the Satanic Church, and everyone is treated with the utmost respect and courtesy.

"We are trying to convey the impression that Satan is not the bad guy who causes pain or hardship, but rather that *he is the only deity, the only saviour who cares.*

"It is on this concept that we have built our church."

A more precise fulfillment of prophecy is hard to find!

Chapter 6

A Two-Pronged Controversy

Not so long ago, my phone began ringing with grave insistency. On the other end of the line was the editor of one of the country's major national publications.

He was curious about the Ellen White phenomena and didn't try to hide it.

"If she was *that* good about making medical predictions more than one hundred years ago," he said pointedly, "then she must have been a prophet, but then, shouldn't she also have made some prophecies concerning the end of the world? The *psychics* do. . . ."

And thus with his inquiry, he opened up a new chapter for the book, for not only did Ellen White predict events to be fulfilled, she forecast a whole series of climactic happenings that would transmit waves of controversy and menacing actions pulsating through the entire Christian world. Her spiritual discernment provided her with such deep prophetic insight that it would extend far beyond the scope of this book even to attempt to relate all of her end-time prophecies.

I mentioned this to my editor-friend.

"How about singling out one or two," he countered, "just so I can see how deep she really went!" and with that request, the search began.

Much came to Ellen White on the clear channel of the superconscious, but the one issue that dominated many of her prophetic visions was a two-pronged religious persecution, such as never has been known in the history of the world. If this is true—and there is no reason to question the legitimacy of her visions—then it will dwarf both the persecutions of the early Christians and the concentration camps of World War II into insignificance! . . .

Civil Intolerance of Religious Beliefs

Standing on one side of my desk is an impressive array of reference books dealing with psychic phenomena and the prophetic power of Ellen G. White. Daily, comparisons are being made, charts drawn up and evaluations construed to ascertain what is in store, yet when Ellen White spoke prophetically about the rapidly approaching period of religious intolerance and persecution, all psychic predictions of her would-be "colleagues" fade away.

"How can religious intolerance become a danger in our democratic society?" This has been asked many times over in great bewilderment, yet nothing can arouse a hotter argument or kill a friendship faster and more devastatingly than a disagreement on either politics or religion. To make matters worse, she foresees a problem caused not by just *one* of these issues but by a *combination of the two. She forecasts a fusion of church and state, resulting in a totalitarian regime that will cause the cruelty of Communism to appear as gentle as a lamb's fantasy.*

Viewing the persecution as an integral part of the great controversy between the two heaven-born adversaries, she unhesitantly attributes the strategic moves leading up to the final struggle to Satan.

"As he [Satan] influenced the heathen nations to destroy Israel, so in the near future he will stir up the wicked powers of earth to destroy the people of God. All will be required to render obedience to human edicts in violation of divine law. Those who will be true to God and to duty will be menaced, denounced, and proscribed. They will be 'betrayed both by parents, and brethren and kinsfolk, and friends.'" [1] "Satan will excite indignation against the humble minority who conscientiously refuse to accept popular customs and traditions. Men of position and reputation will join with the lawless and the vile to take counsel against the people of God. Wealth, genius, education will combine to cover them with contempt. Persecuting rulers, ministers, and church members will conspire against them." [2]

If a psychic ever made a prediction like this one, I would seriously be inclined to raise my eyebrows and wonder about the vagueness of it all, for this prediction does not carry a "time element" within it, nor is it specific enough as to the exact nature of the violations—except for saying that it would be because of a transgression of the divine law. If she had stopped at this point, it most certainly would have appeared as nothing more than a well-intended paragraph written by an intensely religious woman. However, in further prophetic revelations, revealed to her in the great controversy vision of 1858 and subsequent visions, the prominent issue of the approaching struggle for religious freedom was shown her.

Being directed by her accompanying angel to a conversation taking place between Satan and his angels, Ellen became more cognizant of what he, the Devil, considered the central theme in his battle for mankind.

"We must watch those who are calling the attention of the people to the Sabbath of Jehovah," she heard him scheme. "They will lead many to see the claims of the law of God. . . . The Sabbath is the great question which is to decide the destiny of souls. We must exalt the Sabbath of *our* creating. We have caused it to be accepted by both worldlings and church-members; now the church must be led to unite with the world in its support. . . . We must excite popular indignation against them. We will enlist great men and worldly-wise men upon our side, and induce those in authority to carry out our purposes. Then the Sabbath which *I* have set up shall be enforced by laws the most severe and exacting . . . we will finally have a law to exterminate all who will not submit to our authority. When death shall be made the penalty of violating *our* Sabbath, then many who are now ranked with commandment keepers will come over to our side." [3]

Sunday and Sunday Laws

Biblically, the concept of Sunday laws is closely intertwined with the emergence of the Antichrist,* either a force which exalts itself against the will and work of God, or a being that will impersonate Christ, both in appearance and in actions. Since the major prophets have always combined 1) the end of the world; 2) the final judgment of men, and 3) the Second Coming of Christ, it is reasonable to believe that the appearance of the Antichrist will transpire before these events occur.

For centuries, even the psychics have foreseen the coming of an Antichrist who will exhibit grand and awesome power,

---

* A term meaning "against Christ" or "in place of Christ." Either to denote powers and influences, or in the ultimate, the Antichrist *par excellence,* the Prince of Evil, Satan himself.

and some even have caught a glimpse of the religious persecution that will precede it. All Biblical indications point toward an eventual fusion of church and state. This amalgamation will place so much pressure on the legislators that, for the first time since 321 A.D., extreme and far-reaching Sunday laws will again be passed by the national legislatures of the major nations. Once this happens in the United States, it may mean the death throes of the Constitution.

To some, a law enforcing Sunday observance and forbidding religious celebrations on the Sabbath may seem as a matter of minor religious significance, as most of the Christian world has attempted to transfer the sacredness of the Seventh Day to the first day anyway; but to Jews, Seventh-day Adventists, Seventh-day Baptists and others, it will mean that the worship on their God-ordained Sabbath will be forbidden by a mere law of man. Since this day was instituted by the Creator as a rest day to commemorate the birth of a world, it is quite understandable that they seriously object to laws aimed at coercing them to violate what the Bible holds most sacred.

What makes it even more vital is that it is an inviolable part of the Ten Commandments and as such cannot be tampered with.

Studying this approaching conflict, it was astonishing to learn that although most Christians observe the First-day Sunday instead of the Seventh-day Sabbath, the majority of their leading theologians agree wholeheartedly that there is *no Biblical foundation* for keeping holy the Sunday. All evidence and authority for the transfer of the day of rest from the seventh to the first rests with the Catholic Church, and it is proud of it.

"From this same Catholic Church you have accepted your Sunday, and that Sunday, as the Lord's day, she has handed down as tradition; and the entire Protestant world has accepted it as tradition; for you have not an iota of

Scripture to establish it. Therefore that which you have accepted as your rule of faith," writes D. B. Ray in *The Papal Controversy*, "inadequate as it of course is, as well as your Sunday, you have accepted the authority of the Roman Catholic Church." [4] "Nowhere in the Bible do we find that Christ or the apostles ordered that the Sabbath be changed from Saturday to Sunday," a Catholic theologian echoed in 1947. "We have the commandment of God given to Moses to keep holy the Sabbath day, that is the seventh day of the week, Saturday. Today most Christians keep Sunday because it has been revealed to us by the church [Roman] outside the Bible." [5]

And the Protestants? They all agree—or nearly all. A few short quotations from theologians belonging to various Protestant denominations will more than prove the point.

"There was and is a commandment to keep holy the Sabbath day, but that Sabbath day was not Sunday," Dr. Edward T. Hiscox, renowned *Baptist* theologian writes. "It will be said, however, and with some show of triumph, that the Sabbath was transferred from the seventh to the first day of the week. . . . Where can the record of such a transaction be found? Not in the New Testament—absolutely not. There is no scriptural evidence of the change of the Sabbath institution from the seventh to the first day of the week." [6]

The *Episcopalians* write in their *Encyclopedia of Religious Knowledge:*

"Sunday (Dies Solis, of the Roman calendar, 'day of the sun' because dedicated to the sun), the first day of the week, was adopted by the early Christians as a day of worship. The 'sun' of latin adoration they interpreted as the 'Sun of Righteousness.' . . . No regulations for its observance are laid down in the New Testament, nor, indeed, is its observance even enjoined." [7]

"Sunday being the day on which the Gentiles solemnly adored that planet and called it Sunday, partly from its influence on that day especially, and partly in respect to its divine body (as they conceived it), the Christians thought fit to keep the same day and the same name of it, that they might not appear causelessly peevish, and by that means hinder the conversion of the Gentiles, and bring a greater prejudice than might be otherwise taken against the gospel." [8]

Strangely enough, even though the *Lutheran Church* keeps the Sunday as the day of rest, Martin Luther would very probably never have approved.

Said he, "They [the Catholics] allege the Sabbath changed into Sunday, the Lord's Day, contrary to the Decalogue, as it appears, neither is there any example more boasted of than the changing of the Sabbath day. Great, they say, is the power and authority of the church, since it dispensed with one of the Ten Commandments." [9] But what do the Methodists, the Presbyterians and the historians think? Are their views also in harmony with the others? Yes. All, without exception, give Romanism and paganism the credit!

The historian Hutton Webster, Ph.D., states, "The early Christians had at first adopted the Jewish seven-day week with its numbered week days, but by the close of the third century A.D. this began to give way to the planetary week; and in the fourth and fifth centuries the pagan designations became generally accepted in the western half of Christendom. The use of the planetary names by Christians attests the growing influence of astrological speculations introduced by converts from paganism. . . . During these same centuries the spread of Oriental solar worships, especially that of Mithra (Persian sun worship), in the Roman world, had already led to the substitution by pagans of dies Solis for dies Saturni, as the first day of the planetary week. . . . Thus gradually a pagan institution was ingrafted on Christianity." [10]

The validity of the seven-day cycle was never questioned,

nor was there ever any actual doubt as to whether the cycle remained the same and is still as sacred as when it was first instituted.

Concerning the legal aspects of Sunday keeping, Chief Justice Clark, speaking for the Supreme Court of North Carolina, said:

"Sunday was first adopted by the Christians in lieu of Saturday long after Christ. The first 'Sunday law' was enacted in the year 321 after Christ, soon after the emperor Constantine had abjured paganism, and apparently for a different reason than the Christian observance of the day. . . . Evidently Constantine was still something of a heathen. As late as the year 409 A.D. two rescripts of the emperors Honorius and Thedosius indicate that Christians then generally observed the Sabbath (Saturday not Sunday).

"The curious may find these set out in full, Codex just., lib. I, tit. IX, Cx 13. Not till the end of the ninth century was Sunday substituted by law for Saturday as the day of rest by a decree of the Emperor Leo. (Leo Consl., 54)."

But—Sunday was still regarded as a *religious* holiday, and as such there was no danger on the horizon of getting it confused with the principles of government. Even the U.S. Constitution guaranteed that. The argument, "How can the state legislate that which clearly belongs within the authority of the church" seemed to be a valid point, *but it all changed on May 29, 1961, when the Supreme Court of the United States ruled by a majority vote that Sunday laws are civil, not religious, in nature and therefore are constitutional! By giving itself the power to regulate religious holidays, the United States Supreme Court took the first step on the road to a fusion between church and state!*

Seventy-six years prior to this misuse of judicial authority, Ellen White foresaw this incredible development, when she warned:

"Political corruption is destroying love of justice and re-

gard for truth; and even in free America, rulers and legislators, in order to secure public favor, will yield to the popular
demand for a law enforcing Sunday observance. Liberty of
conscience, which has cost so great a sacrifice, will no longer
be respected." [11]

A development in 1962 confirmed the validity of her prediction. On the seventh day of June, 1962, by a vote of
twenty-one to fourteen, the Massachusetts legislature approved an amendment to the existing Sunday laws, per-
mitting observers of the seventh day to keep their business
establishments open on Sunday. Commented M. E. Loewen:

"Immediately an editorial appeared in the *Pilot*, the
Catholic archdiocesan paper, fiercely attacking the senators
who voted for the amendment. The names of these senators
were printed, and the promise was made that these men
would be remembered at the next election."

"The editorial continued, 'The senators responded to
pressures that will destroy the Sunday observances in favor
of those—principally Jews and Adventists—who worship on
Saturday.' This indeed was a frank admission that the religious motive was predominant.

"The next Sunday, the Catholics attending services in the
Boston area were urged to contact their senators and urge
reconsideration. It was reported that a vicious attack was
mounted which became almost unbearable in its intensity.

"On Monday morning reconsideration of the amendment
was voted, and after a short discussion the measure was
killed by a vote of thirty-one to eight." [12]

Measures like these, Ellen White saw, would be milestones on the way to complete abolishment of religious
liberty.

"When our nation, in its legislative councils, shall enact
laws to bind the conscience of men in regard to their religious privileges," she prophesied, "enforcing Sunday observance, and bringing oppressive power to bear against

those who keep the seventh-day Sabbath, the Law of God will, to all intent and purposes, be made void in our land; and national apostasy will be followed by national ruin." [13]

There is no doubt that the question of the Sabbath will become one of *the* most important issues which will confront the world. Said Satan, as overheard by Ellen White:

"The world will become mine. I will be the ruler of the earth, the prince of the world. I will so control the minds under my power that God's Sabbath shall be a special object of contempt. A sign? I will make the observance of the seventh day a sign of disloyalty to the authorities of earth. Human laws will be made so stringent that men and women will not dare to observe the seventh-day Sabbath. For fear of wanting food and clothing, they will join with the world in transgressing God's law. The earth will be wholly under my dominion." [14]

After the initial steps leading to the introduction of laws governing the religious observance of the people have been taken, she sees more stringent enactments being instituted aimed at ensuring *absolute* compliance with the new laws. Not satisfied with the mere laws of men, Satan will employ the psychics to a far greater extent than ever before to enforce the principles pushed forward by the accusers.

"Communications from the spirits will declare that God has sent them to convince the rejectors of Sunday of their error, affirming that the laws of the land should be obeyed as the law of God. They will lament the great wickedness in the world, and second the testimony of religious teachers that the degraded state of morals is caused by the desecration of Sunday. Great will be the indignation excited against all who refuse to accept their testimony." [15] That the spirits are already communicating this to their earthbound mediums was evidenced in one of the trance-contacts of Edgar Cayce.

When asked to explain the statement given in Genesis,

"In six days God made the heaven and earth," the spirit contact relayed in part the following answer through the unconscious medium:

". . . This is the origin of our traditional concept that the seventh day is a holy day, to be sanctified as commemorating the day when all preparation was completed for the incoming of the first Son of God, and those of His brother souls that chose to come with Him into the earth. *The Son's day became Sunday in our tradition.*" [16]

But there are more signs attesting to the rapidity with which the religious persecution is approaching, and Ellen White listed them all with unfailing accuracy.

"When Protestantism shall stretch her hand across the gulf to grasp the hand of the Roman power," she prophesied in 1885, "and when she shall reach over the abyss to clasp hands with Spiritualism, when, under the influence of this three-fold union, our country shall repudiate every principle of the Constitution as a Protestant and republican government . . . then we may know that the time has come for the marvelous workings of Satan and that the end is near." [17]

After outlining many of the steps that will ultimately result in a firm alliance between Catholicism, Protestantism and Spiritualism, the visions showed her one of the saddest reoccurring events in human history, men killing men for their religious convictions.

"The decree will go forth," she solemnly predicted, "that they must disregard the Sabbath of the fourth commandment, and honor the first day, or lose their lives." [18] Her vision included more than just the United States in this threat of a worldwide bloodbath, and this she made clear after recollecting the scenes of her great controversy vision.

"When the protection of human law shall be withdrawn from those who honor the law of God," she warned, "there will be, in different lands, a simultaneous movement for their destruction. As the time appointed in the decree draws near, the people will conspire to root out the hated sect. It will be determined to strike in one night a decisive blow, which shall utterly silence the voice of dissent and reproof." [19] And then Ellen enters upon one of the most descriptive sections of her great vision and narrates in the first person plural what she "saw" and "experienced." She relates it as though she was actually there and part of the crowd for which the death decree had been issued.

Many times in the past I have heard critics raise objections to some of the prophetic statements made by Ellen White.

"There is no specific time element attached to many of her predictions," they cry out discouragingly. "She doesn't give us years and dates like the psychics do." Perhaps it is better this way, for inasmuch as her prophecies come directly from the Source of Prophecy and deal with human nature, the factor of "controlled uncertainty" always applies. Ellen White once said that if the body of believers that had developed out of the Millerite Movement had done its work as charged during the decade that followed the great disappointment, the world would already have ended. No, Ellen never voiced specific time predictions, but she did pinpoint specifically the events that would eventuate in the "time of the end," and these constitute a more than adequate guideline.

Bridging the Gulf

When in 1885 she wrote, "The Protestants of the United States will be foremost in stretching their hands across the gulf to grasp the hand of Spiritualism; they will reach over the abyss to clasp hands with the Roman power," she indeed looked ahead to a complete fulfillment. The late Richard Cardinal Cushing, in a pastoral letter, confirmed this belief.

"For the past several centuries there has been either a great silence or a species of embittered argument between us and those who, like us, bear the Christian name. Whether in silence or in recrimination, there has been a great gulf between us. *The gulf we set ourselves to bridge,*" he wrote on March 6, 1960. This development caused Methodist Bishop James K. Matthews, president of the Massachusetts Council of Churches, to comment, "There is now an increasingly clear voice being heard across what might have been termed an abyss of separation . . . the cry, 'Brother,' and that's a cry that has been directed from both sides, and we find that abyss perhaps isn't as broad or as deep as was supposed." [20] Even Pope John XXIII, regarded as one of the most liberal Catholic leaders of this century, pleaded,

"May we hope with a father's love for your return. Honesty demands that we let our separated brethren know that this is our ultimate reason for participating in the ecumenical movement, and that we manifest it in practice by seeking to convert even devout Protestants." [21] Spiritualism has now become an integral element in the Christian churches, but the imminent unity between Protestantism and Catholicism—completing the triangle—was not foreseen by religionists of Ellen's time, even though the similarities were in some respects too obvious to be ignored.

"It is not without reason," Ellen wrote, "that the claim has been put forth in Protestant countries that Catholicism differs less widely from Protestantism than in former times. There has been a change; but the change is not in the papacy. Catholicism indeed resembles much of the Protestantism that now exists, because Protestantism has so greatly degenerated since the days of the Reformers." [22]

That the papacy has not changed at all is clearly reflected in a statement in *Our Sunday Visitor*, where the undeniable facts are once again emphasized.

"Protestantism is just as wrong now as it was in 1517," the article exclaims. "It is the duty incumbent on us as Catholics to 'spread the word' and make America Catholic. . . . Father

Isaac Hecker founded the Paulist Fathers for the express purpose of 'making America Catholic.' They are still at it and doing a fine job of it. It is the goal of every bishop, priest, and religious order in the country. No Catholic can settle, with good conscience, for a policy of appeasement, *or even mere coexistence* with a non-Catholic community." [23] A statement to which Father Gustave Weigel, S.J., added, "For ecumenical work the Catholic can follow only one tactic. He must ask the Protestant to be converted to Catholicism." [24]

These are but two of Ellen White's predictions that we see coming true in our day; however, there are others dealing with the repudiation of the United States Constitution which are even more serious. In order to bring about a fusion between the power of church and state, measures would have to be taken to alter the principles of the Constitution. Being of the opinion that the American Constitution has not as yet been sufficiently tested in history to show its true value, in 1963, a renowned Roman Catholic scholar published his views on this approaching issue.

"I just don't understand the reverence, not to say adoration, which everybody here seems to pay to the 'Amuricun Constitooshun,' said Father Bernard Leeming, S.J., caustically. "I want to hear some American get up and shout: 'Give us justice. Give us decency. And to hell with the American Constitution!'

"After all, the American Constitution, though a most respectable document, was composed at a particular period in history—and that only 180 years or so ago. I have talked with the Lord North whose grandfather tried to suppress the American rebels. The night before I flew from London, I slept in an Augustinian monastery built in 1248. Perhaps for this reason I don't attach so great importance to things only a couple of centuries old." [25]

If this were an isolated case, I would not have brought it

up, but with the controversy now raging over possible state aid to parochial schools and the need of the Roman Catholic Church for a law change to enable it to receive these sorely needed funds in order to keep their school system operational, the question of the true validity of the principles of the United States Constitution has indeed already become a major national issue.

Another interesting end-time prediction, once again supporting Ellen White's theme that Sunday laws will be one of the most important signs signifying the beginning of the termination of the world, was made by her as the result of the 1858 vision and those which followed. Agonized by what she had witnessed, she cautioned:

"Those who honor the Bible Sabbath will be denounced as enemies of law and order, as breaking down the moral restraints of society, causing anarchy and corruption, and calling down the judgments of God upon earth. Their conscientious scruples will be pronounced obstinacy, stubbornness, and contempt of authority. They will be accused of disaffection toward the government." [26] Once more Cardinal Cushing took up the challenge posed by this prophecy and voiced his Church's opinion in no uncertain terms.

"United States Catholics feel as I do—that the one thing that can save Latin America, even in its relations with this country, is the [Roman] Catholic religion. It is the one bond shared by all. . . . Some non-Catholic sects, such as the Jehovah's Witnesses, the Seventh-day Adventists, and other extremists, are doing immeasurable harm by destroying the faith of the poor people. They are simply making the roadway wider, more attractive and more accessible for the army of communists." [27]

It is safe to assume that the motives underlying the cardinal's statement must be other than a fear of Communism, inasmuch as the Seventh-day Adventists, singled out by him as "doing immeasurable harm" in Latin America, are, as their name implies, keepers of the Seventh Day, not the first. That they are "destroying the faith of the poor people" is also contrary to the fact, considering that in their Inter-American Division, they operate 364 elementary schools, 51 secondary schools and 8 colleges, with a total enrollment of nearly 40,000 students. With their 7 major hospitals and 18 clinics, the work of the Seventh-day Adventists in the medical field is also impressive. Is there any doubt that this controversy, already making rapid strides, can be anything *but* a beginning of the fulfillment of Ellen White's prediction?

Coming of the Antichrist

Closely coupled to the forecast of the introduction of stringent Sunday laws are prophecies pointing toward the working of the Antichrist, culminating in a being who will appear on the world scene claiming to be Christ but whose aim will be the religious and moral seduction of mankind.

As a prophetic guidebook, the Bible contains much information on this subject, and although many psychics do not profess a great faith in the Bible, except for finding a text that might tend to prove the reliability of a part of their gift, the question as to the true identity of the Antichrist is clearly answered in the Bible.

From the account of human origin as found in the Book of Genesis, it is certain that the introduction of the Satanic force on earth resulted in an immense problem for mankind from its very outset. The first-century prophet, John, imprisoned on the Isle of Patmos, referred to this after having received his all-encompassing Revelation.

"And there was war in heaven," he writes. "Michael and his angels fought against the dragon; and the dragon fought and his angels, and prevailed not; neither was their place found any more in heaven. And the great dragon was cast out, that old serpent, called the Devil, and Satan, which deceiveth the whole world, he was cast out into the earth, and his angels were cast out with him." [28] That this war is still raging—but now on earth—is the theme of the entire Bible and the message of all the prophets who contributed to it. When Biblical writers refer to the Evil One, there is a free interchange in the Bible of the names of Satan, Devil, Dragon and Serpent. Secular sources list a minimum of seventy-seven different names for Satan still utilized by various devil-worshiping cults around the world, indicative that his influence is widespread.

The Bible prophets record many identifying marks, milestones, which can guide us to the time when the emergence of the Antichrist may be expected. True, it is not known exactly how much time will expire between the appearance of the Antichrist and the Second Coming of Christ; however, when the signs pointing toward the Second Coming are being fulfilled, the introduction of the Antichrist must be imminent.

Earthquakes, revolutions, famines, wars, pestilences, religious persecution and false prophets as mentioned in Chapter 13 of Mark and Chapter 24 of Matthew are indications that the final days are at hand.

"Then, if anyone says to you, 'Look, here is the Messiah', or, 'Look, there he is', do not believe it. Impostors will come claiming to be messiahs or prophets, and they will produce signs and wonders to mislead God's chosen, if such a thing were possible. But you be on your guard; I have forewarned you of it all.

"But in those days, after that distress, *the sun will be darkened, the moon will not give her light; the stars will come falling from the sky, the celestial powers will be shaken.* [italics ed.] Then they will see the Son of Man coming in the clouds with great power and glory, and he will send out the angels and gather his chosen from the four winds, from the farthest bounds of earth to the farthest bounds of heaven." [29]

John the Revelator speaks of the same event as part of the opening of "the sixth seal," but he added a devastating earthquake.

"And I behold when he had opened the sixth seal, and lo, there was a *great earthquake*; and the *sun became black as sackcloth of hair*, and the *moon became as blood*; and the *stars of heaven fell unto the earth*, [italics ed.] even as a fig tree casteth her untimely figs, when she is shaken of a mighty wind." [30] He was undoubtedly inspired by the same source, even though his prophecy was penned ninety-eight years after the birth of Christ. There is now only one celestial event yet unfulfilled after the four great signs marking the "opening of the sixth seal," and that is the Second Coming of Christ, preceded by the sly seductive moves of the Antichrist.

It is the assumption that inasmuch as the four major signs of the sixth seal are grouped together in two short verses, they should follow each other in order and in a relatively short period of time. Historically no other time span fits as accurately as the seventy-eight years between November 1, 1755, and November 13, 1833.

The Great Earthquake

The most striking fulfillment of this first-century prophecy, the *"great earthquake,"* took place on November 1, 1755, when a catastrophe known as the Lisbon Earthquake hit with tremendous force, affecting a vastness of area unequaled in history.

Robert Sears writes:

"The great earthquake of 1755 extended over a tract of at least four millions of square miles. Its effects were even extended to the waters, in many places where the shocks were not perceptible. It pervaded the greater portions of the continents of Europe, Africa and America; but its extreme violence was exercised on the southwestern part of the former." [31]

"In Africa, this earthquake was felt almost as severely as it had been in Europe. A great part of the city of Algiers was destroyed. Many houses were thrown down at Fez and Mequinez, and multitudes were buried beneath their ruins. . . . It is probable . . . that all Africa was shaken by this tremendous convulsion. At the North, it extended to Norway and Sweden; Germany, Holland, France, Great Britain, and Ireland were all more or less agitated by the same great and terrible commotion of the elements." [32] "The city of Lisbon . . . previous to that calamity . . . contained about . . . 150,000 inhabitants. . . . Mr. Barretti says 'that 90,000 persons are supposed to have been lost on that fatal day.' " [33]

"The shock of the earthquake was instantly followed by the fall of every church and convent, almost all the large public buildings and more than one fourth of the houses. In about two hours after the shock, fires broke out in different quarters, and raged with such violence for the space of nearly three days, that the city was completely desolated. . . . The terror of the people was beyond description. Nobody wept; it was beyond tears. They ran hither and thither, delirious with horror and astonishment, beating their faces and breasts, crying, 'Misericordia! The world's at an end!' " [34] "In the course of about six minutes, sixty thousand persons perished. The sea first retired, and laid the bar dr̈ it then rolled in, rising fifty feet above its ordinary level. The mountains . . . were impetuously shaken, as it were, from their very foundations; and some of them opened at their summits, which were split and rent in a wonderful manner, huge masses of them being thrown down into the subjacent valleys." [35] Even in Britain the quake was felt with great intensity.

We will readily admit that there have been other earthquakes with even greater devastation wrought in a localized area, but never before (or since) has one earthquake covered so many millions of square miles.

And the Sun Became Black as Sackcloth . . .

One thing is evident; if the Lisbon earthquake was in actuality the beginning of the series of unordinary events forecast in the prophecy of John, then the second one on the list should be the "blackened sun"—and indeed it was. It happened twenty-five years later and since that time has been known as "the darkest day in history."

Noah Webster reports:

". . . the obscuration began about ten o'clock in the morning, and continued till the middle of the next night, but with differences of degree and duration in different places. . . . The true cause of this remarkable phenomenon is not known." [36]

An eyewitness described the happening as follows:

"In the morning the sun rose clear, but was soon overcast. The clouds became lowery, and from them black and ominous, as they soon appeared, lightning flashed, thunder rolled, and a little rain fell. Toward nine o'clock, the clouds became thinner, and assumed a brassy or coppery appearance, and earth, rocks, trees, buildings, water, and persons were changed by this strange, unearthly light. A few minutes later, a heavy black cloud spread over the entire sky except a narrow rim at the horizon, and it was as dark as it usually is at nine o'clock on a summer evening. . . .

"Fear, anxiety, and awe gradually filled the minds of the people. Women stood at the door, looking out upon the dark landscape; men returned from their labor in the fields; the carpenter left his tools, the blacksmith his forge, the tradesman his counter. Schools were dismissed, and tremblingly the children fled homeward. Travelers put up at the nearest farmhouse. 'What is coming?' queried every lip and heart.

It seemed as if a hurricane was about to dash across the land, or as if it was the day of the consummation of all things.

"Candles were used; and hearth fires shone as brightly as on a moonless evening in autumn. . . . Fowls retired to their roosts and went to sleep, cattle gathered at the pasture bars and lowed, frogs peeped, birds sang their evening songs, and bats flew about. But the human knew that night had not come. . . .

"Dr. Nathanael Whittaker, pastor of the Tabernacle church in Salem, held religious services in the meetinghouse, and preached a sermon in which he maintained that the darkness was supernatural. Congregations came together in many other places. The texts for the extemporaneous sermons were invariably those that seemed to indicate that the darkness was consonant with Scriptural prophecy. . . . The darkness was most dense shortly after eleven o'clock." [37]

More precise information came from Professor Samuel Williams, who, for the historical record, reported:

"The *time* of this extraordinary darkness was May 19, 1780. It came on between the hours of ten and eleven A.M., and continued until the middle of the next night, but with different appearances at different places. . . .

"The *degree* to which the darkness arose was different in different places. In most parts of the country it was so great that people were unable to read common print, determine the time of day by their clocks or watches, dine, or manage their domestic business, without the light of candles. In some places the darkness was so great that persons could not see to read common print in the open air, for several hours together; but I believe this was not generally the case.

"The *extent* of this darkness was very remarkable. Our intelligence in this respect is not so particular as I could wish; but from the accounts that have been received, it seems to have extended all over the New England States.

It was observed as far east as Falmouth (Portland, Maine).
To the westward we hear of its reaching to the furthest
parts of Connecticut, and Albany. To the southward it was
observed all along the seacoasts, and to the north as far as
our settlements extend. It is probable it extended much beyond these limits in some directions, but the exact boundaries cannot be ascertained by any observations that I have
been able to collect.

"With regard to its *duration*, it continued in this place at
least fourteen hours; but it is probable this was not exactly
the same in different parts of the country.

"The *appearance* and *effects* were such as tended to make
the prospect extremely dull and gloomy. Candles were
lighted up in the houses, the birds, having sung their evening songs, disappeared, and became silent; the fowls retired to roost; the cocks were crowing all around, as at break
of day; objects could not be distinguished but at a very
little distance; and everything bore the appearance and
gloom of night." [38]

Still, as the evening of that dreadful day, the nineteenth
of May, was drawing to a close, only two of the events
forecast in Revelation had occurred, and I seriously question
whether casual Bible students at that time considered a
possible connection between these and the prophecy of the
sixth seal. However, to the more than casual observer, the
night of the nineteenth brought the third phenomenon—
all in conformity with the prophetic vision—for it turned out
to be as unusual as the day that had just ended.

The Moon Became as Blood

"The intense darkness of the day was succeeded, an hour
or two before evening, by a partially clear sky, and the sun
appeared, though it was still obscured by the black, heavy
mist." [39] "After sundown, the clouds came again overhead,

and it grew dark very fast. Nor was the darkness of the night less uncommon and terrifying than that of the day; notwithstanding there was almost a full moon, no object was discernible but by the help of some artificial light, which, when seen from the neighboring houses and other places at a distance, appeared through a kind of Egyptian darkness which seemed almost impervious to the rays." [40] "The darkness . . . was probably as gross as ever has been observed since the Almighty fiat gave birth to light," the official records state. "I could not help conceiving at the time, that if a very luminous body in the universe had been shrouded in impenetrable shades, or struck out of existence, the darkness could not have been more complete. A sheet of white paper held within a few inches of the eyes, was equally invisible with the blackest velvet." [41]

The darkness held until approximately one o'clock, and even though the moon occasionally became visible after nine, it did nothing to dissipate the blackness that had covered the sky, for whenever it was seen, it had the appearance of blood.

An eclipse was out of the question according to the records for that year, in view of the fact that the moon had fulled on the previous night. No natural phenomena could account for the quick succession of events.

The prophet John had not specified that all four signs would occur within a few years, yet three of them reached complete and accurate fulfillment within only twenty-five years, and Bible students anxiously awaited the fourth.

It took a generation before it happened, but when it did, it created an awesome spectacle.

The Stars Fell from Heaven

Never before did prophetic power display its authority as impressively as when the stars fell from heaven on November 13, 1833. A reporter for the *New York Journal of*

Commerce later wrote an eyewitness account of the fulfill-ment of the fourth sign.

". . . At the cry, 'Look out of the window,' I sprang from a deep sleep, and with wonder saw the east lighted up with the dawn and meteors. . . . I called to my wife to behold; and while robing, she exclaimed, 'See how the stars fall!' I replied, 'That is the wonder:' and we felt in our hearts that it was a sign of the last days. For truly 'the stars of heaven fell unto the earth, even as a fig tree casteth her untimely figs, when she is shaken of a mighty wind.' Revelation 6:13.

"And how did they fall? Neither myself nor one of the family heard any report; and were I to hunt through nature for a simile, I could not find one so apt to illustrate the appearance of the heavens, as that which St. John uses in the prophecy before quoted. . . . The falling stars did not come, as if from several trees shaken, but from *one*: those which appeared in the east fell toward the east; those which appeared in the north fell toward the north; those which appeared in the west fell toward the west; and those which appeared in the south (for I went out of my residence into the park), fell toward the south; and they fell, not as *ripe* fruit falls. Far from it. But they flew, they were *cast*, like the unripe fruit, which at first refuses to leave the branch; and, when it does break its hold, flies swiftly, *straight* off, descending; and in the multitude falling, some cross the track of others, as they are thrown with more or less force." [42] "It seemed as if the whole starry heavens had congregated at one point near the zenith, and were simul-taneously shooting forth, with the velocity of lightning, to every part of the horizon; and yet they were not exhausted —thousands swiftly followed in the tracks of thousands, as if created for the occasion." [43] "No celestial phenomenon has ever occurred in this country, since its first settlement, which was viewed with such intense admiration by one class in the community, or with so much dread and alarm by another. It's sublimity and awful beauty still linger in many minds. . . . Never did rain fall much thicker than the meteors fell toward the earth; east, west, north, and south, it was the same. In a word, the whole heavens seemed in motion. . . . From two o'clock until broad daylight, the sky being perfectly serene and cloudless, an incessant play of dazzling brilliant luminosities was kept up in the whole heavens." [44] "The whole heavens seemed in motion, and suggested to some the awful grandeur of the image employed in the Apocalypse, upon the opening of the sixth seal, when 'the stars of heaven fell unto the earth.' " [45]

The wonder caused Denison Olmsted to comment:

"The shower pervaded nearly the whole of North America, having appeared in nearly equal splendor from the British possessions on the north, to the West Indian Islands and Mexico on the south, and from sixty-one degrees of longitude east of the American coast, quite to the Pacific Ocean on the west. Throughout this immense region, the duration was nearly the same. The meteors began to attract attention by their unusual frequency and brilliancy, from *nine to twelve o'clock* in the evening; were most striking in their appearance from *two to five*; arrived at their maximum, in many places, about *four o'clock*; and continued until rendered invisible by the light of day." [46]

Thus, with the complete and unconditional fulfillment of the four signs indicating the opening of the "sixth seal," the stage has been set for the Second Coming of Christ preceded by the appearance of the Antichrist. It seems clear to students of prophecy that we are now in the time when we may look for the appearance of the Antichrist in his ultimate manifestation.

Forecast of the Psychics

Examining all the available evidence, the existence of a counterfeit program of prophecy calculated to equal certain well-publicized portions of Biblical prophecies concerning the Second Coming becomes undeniably real. Craving for still more recognition, the major psychics of the world have lost no opportunity to take up the challenge of forecasting the entrance of either the Antichrist or a new "leader" for Christianity, described as a man of majestic bearing and Christlike in appearance.

While many psychics agree in principle about this happening, their predicted details vary greatly. Some, as the years go by, even change the original interpretation of their visions regarding this, the end result being a version diametrically opposed to their first disclosure.

I vividly recall my discussions with seeress Jeane Dixon on the subject of the coming of the Antichrist. Her prediction of the "Child of the East" as printed in the first biography about her by Ruth Montgomery often puzzled me because of what appeared to me its rather naïve interpretation. Her vision, she recollected, was preceded by a strange crackling noise within the light bulbs of the chandelier hanging from her bedroom ceiling, this being an indication to Mrs. Dixon that a vision of extreme importance was about to be relayed to her. For three consecutive nights, the peculiar crackling sound emanated from the chandelier, and as the glowing brilliance of the bulbs slowly decreased, her attention was drawn to a luminous ball of light suspended directly in the middle of each bulb. . . .

It was on the morning following the third "crackling" that Jeane Dixon, stepping to her bedroom window, realized that her vision had finally "arrived."

"As she gazed outside she saw, not the barelimbed trees and city street below, but a bright blue sky above a barren desert. Just above the horizon was the brightest sun that she had ever seen, glowing like a golden ball. Splashing from the orb in every direction were brilliant rays which seemed to be drawing the earth toward it like a magnet. Stepping out of the brightness of the sun's rays, hand in hand, were a Pharaoh and Queen Nefertiti. Cradled in the Queen's other arm was a baby, his ragged, soiled clothing in startling contrast to the gorgeously arrayed royal couple.

" 'The eyes of this child were all-knowing,' Jeane says softly. 'They were full of wisdom and knowledge.'

"A little to one side of Queen Nefertiti, Jeane could glimpse a pyramid. While she watched entranced, the couple advanced toward her and thrust forth the baby, as if offering it to the entire world. Within the ball of the sun, Jeane saw Joseph guiding the tableau like a puppeteer pulling strings. Now, rays of light burst forth from the baby, blending with those of the sun and obliterating the Pharaoh from her sight." [47]

"Jeane shifted her gaze back to the baby. He had by now grown to manhood, and a small cross which formed above him began to expand until it 'dripped over the earth in all directions. Simultaneously, peoples of every race, religion, and color (black, yellow, red, brown and white), each kneeling and lifting his arms in worshipful adoration, surrounded him. They were all as one.' Unlike previous visions, which had gradually faded away from Jeane, this one moved ever nearer until she seemed to be in the very midst of the action, joining in the adoring worship." [48] Later, while commenting on this, Jeane remarked that she knew instinctively that this vision meant that she had come face to face with the "beginning of wisdom."

When asked for an interpretation of her revelation, she explained it in this way to Ruth Montgomery.

" 'A child, born somewhere in the Middle East shortly after 7 A.M. (EST) on February 5, 1962, will revolutionize the world. Before the close of the century he will bring together all mankind in one all-embracing faith. This will be the foundation of a new Christianity, with every sect and creed united through this man who will walk among the people to spread the wisdom of the Almighty Power.

" 'This person, though born of humble peasant origin, is a descendant of Queen Nefertiti and her Pharaoh husband; of this I am sure. There was nothing kingly about his coming—no kings or shepherds to do homage to this new-born baby—but he is the answer to the prayers of a troubled world. Mankind will begin to feel the great force of this man in the early 1980's, and during the subsequent ten years the world as we know it will be reshaped and revamped into one without wars or suffering. His power will grow greatly until 1999, at which time the peoples of this earth will probably discover the full meaning of the vision.' " [49]

So, according to Jeane Dixon, a child born in 1962 will be the "founder of a new Christianity," uniting all sects and creeds and will spread the wisdom of God. Making matters even more serene, he will be the answer to the fervent prayers of the world and will reshape it into one without wars or suffering.

Jeane Dixon thoroughly believes that she has God's Gift of Prophecy and, consequently, felt honored to be able to join the adoring throng in the worship of the child.

Many people have since questioned her whether this child could possibly be the Antichrist, but Mrs. Dixon always maintained the viewpoint that inasmuch as she was only inspired by God, this had to be a "good" vision, and the child would indeed be the "founder of a new Christianity" . . . in actuality a reappearance of Christ.

This she sincerely believed in 1962 and firmly stuck to it until 1969, when she abruptly changed her interpretation and identified the child as the Antichrist, who is now supposedly preparing himself for the great seduction. True, conditional prophecies do exist, but this was not one of them. It denoted a complete turnabout of positions, marking her once more as a mere psychic whose visions and interpretations are far from infallible. Without giving any excuse for the drastic difference between interpretations, she now says:

" 'The circumstances surrounding the birth of the "Child of the East" and the events I have since seen taking place in his life make him appear so Christlike, yet so different, that there is no doubt in my mind that the "child" is the actual person of the Antichrist, the one who will deceive the world in Satan's name.' " [50]

The psychic seer Nostradamus foresaw the coming of the Antichrist; Edgar Cayce predicted the emergence of a religious giant; Criswell also foresees a new Christian leader of great stature who will guide the world to the time when wars will be no more; and Daniel Logan hangs his prediction of a new leader on a confirmation of Jeane Dixon's vision. The latest of the seers to endorse this conjecture is David Bubar, who says:

"I see a great effort being conducted when we near the year 2000 [1999] to duplicate many facets of Creation, and in some ways, man will be able to do so under the guidance of a new spiritual leader, who will emerge and take full control of those who wish to be 'enlightened.' " [51]

If psychics are, as Spiritualism proudly boasts, working with spirit powers and are inspired and controlled by them, then the idea of a "Devil's timetable," a prophetic counterfeit of the last day's events is very believable.

Ellen White, too, saw the last day's events and the appearance of the Antichrist, not through paganistic symbols such as a burning sun, pyramids, pagan royalty or Joseph acting out the role of a puppeteer, but in a way so typical of the elevating manner in which God revealed the future to her.

"Persons will arise pretending to be Christ Himself," she saw, "and claiming the title and worship which belong to the world's Redeemer. They will perform wonderful miracles of healing and will profess to have revelations from heaven contradicting the testimony of the Scriptures." [52] But then "as the crowning act in the great drama of deception, Satan himself will personate Christ. The church has long professed to look to the Saviour's advent as the consummation of her hopes. Now the great deceiver will make it appear that Christ has come. In different parts of the earth, Satan will manifest himself among men as a majestic being of dazzling brightness, resembling the description of the Son of God given by John in the Revelation." [53] (Rev. 1:13-15.)

"The prince of darkness, who has so long bent the powers of his mastermind to the work of deception, skillfully adapts his temptations to men of all classes and conditions. . . . He who could appear clothed with the brightness of the heavenly seraphs before Christ in the wilderness of temptation, comes to men in the most attractive manner as an angel of light. He appeals to the reason by the presentation of elevating themes; he delights the fancy with enrapturing scenes; and he enlists the affections by his eloquent portrayals of love and charity. He excites the imagination to lofty flights, leading men to take so great pride in their own wisdom that in their hearts they despise the Eternal One." [54]

"The glory that surrounds him is unsurpassed by anything that mortal eyes have yet beheld. The shout of triumph rings out upon the air: 'Christ has come! Christ has come!' The people prostrate themselves in adoration before him, while he lifts up his hands and pronounces a blessing upon them, as Christ blessed His disciples when He was upon the earth. His voice is soft and subdued, yet full of melody. In gentle, compassionate tones he presents some of the same gracious, heavenly truths which the Saviour uttered; he heals the diseases of the people, and then, in his assumed character of Christ, he claims to have changed the Sabbath to Sunday, and commands all to hallow the day which he has blessed." [55]

"Antichrist is to perform his marvelous works in our sight," she predicts gravely. "So closely will the counterfeit resemble the true that it will be impossible to distinguish between them except by the Holy Scriptures." [56] Both the Biblical prophets *and* Ellen White forecast an Antichrist who will make a final desperate surge to deceive the world; but the psychics foresee a "spiritual leader" who will introduce a new era of peace and tranquility. Ellen White sees Antichrist as Satan himself, a mysterious being resembling the description of the Son of God. Quite a difference!

There is, however, one more perplexing aspect to their predictions. Psychics without exception fearfully await the year 1999. Nostradamus points toward that year as the termination date of the conflict between good and evil. According to his interpreters, this conflict is to commence in the year 1973, and all psychics are in agreement with him as to the importance of the year 1999.

Has the deception reached such intensity so as actually to predict that earth's last day will occur at a moment when all world-end prophecies will already have been fulfilled in order to lure the spiritually uncommitted into a feeling of false security? Or is it possible that the year 1999 will be the year of the emergence of the Antichrist? It would certainly be consistent with the Devil's vanity that he would predict the time of his own triumphal entry.

It is a secret to be revealed only by the course of history.

Chapter 7

Destiny

AT A MEASURED pace, a black horse-drawn surrey moved slowly over the picturesque gravel paths that snaked quietly along the whispering brooks and gentle flowing hills of California's fertile Napa Valley. The time was early twentieth century, and even though wagons were an everyday sight along the California roadways, this particular one invariably caused the working field hands in the vineyards to stop for a moment to give respectful attention. It was not to the carriage itself that they looked but to the slight, reposeful figure of the aging little woman inside, who smilingly focused her deep blue eyes upon every uplifted face— for she knew many of them, and they knew her.

Ever since she had moved into the area of St. Helena around the turn of the century, the black surrey had soon become part of the growing traditions of Northern California. So great was the love many of the orchard and vineyard owners and workmen had for the "little woman with the white hair" that they felt compelled to show their respect—if only with a smile—for Ellen White's presence in St. Helena and its environs had done more for them than many would like to admit.

The San Francisco earthquake had not changed much in the northern part of the state. Naturally, some had felt the necessity to adjust their life-style and perhaps "take another look" at religion, but many more didn't, and within a short time after the tragedy, all was forgotten again—even the promises made to repent.

Ellen White, having been taken into the Supreme confidence so many times since the great earthquake, knew and understood. However, during the later years of her life, her concern for people became even more intense, more heartfelt, and seeing her days shorten, she held onto life with a desperate tenacity. Being a woman and mother first and a prophet second, she had that innate instinct to care, and the occasional morning rides she began soon after moving into Elmshaven, her St. Helena home, became a regularly recurring event. Once she realized the people's need for love and a friendly word, she made it her business to see them, talk to them and visit with their children, telling them of Jesus' love.

It is questionable whether many of those nameless uplifted faces along the paths knew her by name. To most of them she was simply known as "that little old woman with the white hair who always spoke so lovingly of Jesus." Distributing clothes, stopping by to help someone with an ill child, bringing a food basket, were all part of her "extra" daily activities. She felt they needed her, and this conviction grew stronger as she continued to recall the frightening details that had been shown her concerning the final judgment of man.

Her later years had cast her in a steady routine of travel, lectures, writing and relaxation. Often when the quivering memory of a night-time vision did not end her sleep, her intense desire to share her experiences with others *would*. Grace White Jacques, granddaughter of Ellen, spoke about this when relating those years to Judy Howard, author of the *Youth Instructor* article, "My Special Grandmother."

"During the later years of her life," she recalled, "grandmother began her work in the early morning hours. She retired at seven or eight oclock in the evening. Often visions of the night were given to her, and she would soon rise and begin her work. At other times she was awakened by an angel in the early hours of the morning to write letters or to work on one of her books.

"By the time Miss McEnterfer rose, grandmother often had many pages written. Her helpers would sometimes ask how she awoke so early. She might reply that an angel had touched her shoulder. By eleven o'clock in the morning she had completed a day's work.

"Grandmother thought for a while that she would live till Jesus came the second time. But one night she had a dream in which she came out of a very dark place into a bright light, and grandfather was with her. When he saw her by his side he exclaimed in surprise, 'What, have you been there, too, Ellen?' She understood that to mean that the Lord would let her rest in the grave a little while before His coming. After this vision of the night she was ready to die. Her life had been resigned to do the Lord's will." [1]

It may have been this dream that increased her zeal, for the closer she came to the end of her days, the more of a challenge the contacts with the neighbors and their hired help had become. Health-and-temperance-minded as she was, she felt a deep pity and overwhelming concern for the hundreds of Southern Europeans who were employed in the flourishing orchard and winery business in the hills and the valley surrounding her Elmshaven retreat. Her health-reform visions had clearly pointed out to her the physical and

spiritual dangers synonymous with alcohol and intemperance, and with her memory still keen and alert, quick flashes
of recollection brought to her mind the pertinent facts of
those major visions as she stopped to visit with those working near the roadside. She wasn't always loved for her views,
but she was respected—and lovingly she continued to voice
her warnings.

This she did in the spring of the year and kept on when
the falling leaves had covered the dusty mountain trails
with a soft, rustling, multicolored blanket. Tucked in
securely against the wind, she still rode around on the
same trails during the mild months of the winter, enjoying
the recreation and ever alert, always hoping to find others
to infect with her love for Jesus.

She never gave up.

How much of the former visions actually flashed through
her mind while counseling, no one will ever know, but
there is no doubt that her comprehensive revelation of 1858
and succeeding amplifying visions formed the basis for
most of what she did during her active years, for she always
spoke with awe about the end of the world and the final
judgment that was awaiting mankind.

As in the case with human justice, the Eternal Judge, too,
she had been shown, would call for investigative judgments
of both the righteous and the wicked, followed by executive
judgments. The difference, however, was in the sentencing.
While she had seen the judgment of the righteous terminate
with the Second Coming of Christ and eternal life, the
executive judgment of the wicked was projected to take
place at the expiration of one thousand years of desolation
on earth, ending with eternal death.

In her role as prophet, she had closely observed the
various happenings surrounding this last judicial process,
and the eternal finality of it had shaken her.

Little did the vineyard workers realize that the "little

woman" was a special confidante of the Eternal One. After all that God had revealed to her, it is no wonder that her concern was so deep and all-consuming. She talked about her visions to very few of her casual acquaintances, but her writings more than explained her experiences and emotions as she witnessed the dramatic scenes that constantly unfolded before her. The prophetic impulses were indelibly embedded in her brain and affected all of her actions.

Some of the most moving descriptions of the last days of mankind and the final judgment were penned in the early hours of the morning when the new dawn was still shrouded with haze. Undisturbed, she would sit for hours, lapboard resting on the arms of her comfortable chair, writing down a verbal interpretation of the mental impressions she received, ever sensitive to the recall of the visions. Combining segments from her great controversy visions concentrating on the final days, a touching story of pathos and immeasurable sadness develops—but no one can describe it more accurately than Ellen White herself.

It was during a visit to the home of a fellow Millerite in Exeter, Maine, in mid-February, 1845, a scant two months after her first vision, that she was initiated into the controversial issues of the great galactic struggle between God and His adversary. While intently listening to the simple service, the slightly built seventeen-year-old girl suddenly lost all affinity with her friends, and gently, ever so gently, she closed her eyes . . . and while her breathing ceased, she slowly sank to the floor . . . and within seconds she was in vision.

Vision of Destiny

It was only the third time that she had been called to witness the unearthly scenes, but not before had the cosmic struggle been presented to her in such clear and exacting detail. Afterward she remembered:

"I saw a throne, and on it sat the Father and the Son," she whispered humbly to those around her, and while her eyes still seemed focused on the far-off scenes, she continued:

"I gazed on Jesus' countenance and admired His lovely person. The Father's person I could not behold, for a cloud of glorious light covered Him. I asked Jesus if His Father had a form like Himself. He said He had, but I could not behold it, for said He, 'If you should once behold the glory of His person, you would cease to exist.'

"Before the throne I saw the Advent people, the church and the world. I saw two companies, one bowed down befor the throne, deeply interested, while the other stood uninterested and careless. Those who were bowed before the throne would offer up their prayers and look to Jesus; then He would look to His Father, and appear to be pleading with Him. A light would come from the Father to the Son and from the Son to the praying company. Then I saw an exceeding bright light come from the Father to the Son, and from the Son it waved over the people before the throne. But few would receive this great light. Many came out from under it and immediately resisted it; others were careless and did not cherish the light, and it moved off from them. Some cherished it, and went and bowed down with the little praying company. This company all received the light and rejoiced in it, and their countenances shone with its glory.

"I saw the Father rise from the throne, and in a flaming chariot go into the holy of holies within the veil, and sit down. Then Jesus rose up from the throne, and the most of those who were bowed down arose with Him. I did not see one ray of light pass from Jesus to the careless multitude after He arose, and they were left in perfect darkness. Those who arose when Jesus did, kept their eyes fixed on Him as He left the throne and led them out a little way.

"Then He raised His right arm, and we heard His lovely

voice saying, 'Wait here; I am going to My Father to receive the kingdom; keep your garments spotless, and in a little while I will return from the wedding and receive you to Myself.'" [2] It was a partial vision of the preliminary scenes of the judgment, and it was not until 1858 that she was given a definitive uninterrupted view of what was to follow.

At first referring back to what she had seen in 1845, she completed her initial impressions in later years with the new, complete end-time vision, and emotions of sadness and joy alternated with pity and justified pride as she watched the King make the final preparations.

"Jesus then clothed Himself with precious garments. Around the bottom of His robe was a bell and a pomegranate, a bell and a pomegranate. A breastplate of curious work was suspended from His shoulders. As He moved, this glittered like diamonds, magnifying letters which looked like names written or engraved upon the breastplate. Upon His head was something which had the appearance of a crown. When fully attired, He was surrounded by angels, and in a flaming chariot He passed within the second veil.

"I was then bidden to take notice of the two apartments of the heavenly sanctuary. The curtain, or door, was opened, and I was permitted to enter. In the first apartment I saw the candlestick with seven lamps, the table of shewbread, the altar of incense, and the censer. All the furniture of this apartment looked like purest gold and reflected the image of the one who entered the place. The curtain which separated the two apartments was of different colors and material, with a beautiful border, in which were figures wrought of gold to represent angels. The veil was lifted, and I looked into the second apartment. I saw there an ark which had the appearance of being of the finest gold. As a border around the top of the ark, was most beautiful work representing crowns. In the ark were tables of stone containing the Ten Commandments.

"Two lovely cherubs, one on each end of the ark, stood with their wings outstretched above it, and touching each other above the head of Jesus as He stood before the mercy seat. Their faces were turned toward each other, and they looked downward to the ark, representing all the angelic host looking with interest at the law of God. Between the cherubim was a golden censer, and as the prayers of the saints, offered in faith, came up to Jesus, and He presented them to His father, a cloud of fragrance arose from the incense, looking like smoke of most beautiful colors. Above the place where Jesus stood, before the ark, was exceedingly bright glory that I could not look upon; it appeared like the throne of God.

"As the incense ascended to the Father, the excellent glory came from the throne to Jesus, and from Him it was shed upon those whose prayers had come up like sweet incense. Light poured upon Jesus in rich abundance and overshadowed the mercy seat, and the train of glory filled the temple. I could not long look upon the surpassing brightness. No language can describe it. I was overwhelmed and turned from the majesty and glory of the scene." [3]

Angel With A Fearful Warning

"As the ministration of Jesus closed in the holy place, and He passed into the holiest, and stood before the ark containing the law of God, He sent another mighty angel with a third message to the world. A parchment was placed in the angel's hand, and as he descended to the earth in power and majesty, he proclaimed a fearful warning, with the most terrible threatening ever borne to man. This message was designed to put the children of God upon their guard, by showing them the hour of temptation and anguish that was before them.

"Said the angel, 'They will be brought into close combat with the beast and his image. Their only hope of eternal life is to remain steadfast. Although their lives are at stake, they must hold fast the truth.' The third angel closed his message thus: 'Here is the patience of the saints: here are they that keep the commandments of God, and the faith of Jesus.' As he repeated these words, he pointed to the heavenly sanctuary. The minds of all who embrace this message are directed to the most holy place, where Jesus stands before the ark, making His final intercession for all those for whom mercy still lingers and for those who have ignorantly broken the law of God. This atonement is made for the righteous dead as well as for the righteous living. It includes all who died trusting in Christ, but who, not having received the light upon God's commandments, had sinned ignorantly in transgressing its precepts.

"After Jesus opened the door of the most holy, the light of the Sabbath was seen, and the people of God were tested, as the children of Israel were tested anciently, to see if they would keep God's law. I saw the third angel pointing upward, showing the disappointed ones the way to the holiest of the heavenly sanctuary. As they by faith enter the most holy, they find Jesus, and hope and joy spring up anew. . . .

"It was represented to me that the remnant followed Jesus into the most holy place and beheld the ark and the mercy seat, and were captivated with their glory. Jesus then raised the cover of the ark, and lo! the tables of stone, with the Ten Commandments written upon them. They trace down the lively oracles, but start back with trembling when they see the fourth commandment among the ten holy precepts, with a brighter light shining upon it than upon the other nine, and a halo of glory all around it. They find nothing there informing them that the Sabbath has been abolished, or changed to the first day of the week.

"The commandment reads as when spoken by the voice of God in solemn and awful grandeur upon the mount, while the lightnings flashed and the thunders rolled; it is the same as when written with His own finger on the tables of stone: 'Six days shalt thou labor, and do all thy work: but the seventh day is the Sabbath of the Lord thy God.' They are amazed as they behold the care taken of the ten commandments. They see them placed close by Jehovah, overshadowed and protected by His holiness. They see that they have been trampling upon the fourth commandment of the decalogue, and have observed a day handed down by the heathen and papists, instead of the day sanctified by Jehovah. They humble themselves before God and mourn over their past transgressions.

"I saw the incense in the censer smoke as Jesus offered their confessions and prayers to His Father. And as it ascended, a bright light rested upon Jesus and upon the mercy seat; and the earnest, praying ones, who were troubled because they had discovered themselves to be transgressors of God's law, were blessed, and their countenances lighted up with hope and joy. They joined in the work of the third angel and raised their voices to proclaim the solemn warning. But few at first received it; yet the faithful continued with energy to proclaim the message. Then I saw many embrace the message of the third angel and unite their voices with those who had first given the warning, and they honored God by observing His sanctified rest day." [4]

The Last Warning

"I saw angels hurrying to and fro in heaven, descending to the earth, and again ascending to heaven, preparing for the fulfillment of some important event. Then I saw another mighty angel commissioned to descend to the earth, to unite his voice with the third angel, and give power and force to his message. Great power and glory were imparted to the angel, and as he descended, the earth was lightened with his glory.

"The light which attended this angel penetrated everywhere, as he cried mightily, with a strong voice, 'Babylon the great is fallen, is fallen, and is become the habitation of devils, and the hold of every foul spirit, and a cage of every unclean and hateful bird.' The message of the fall of Babylon, as given by the second angel, is repeated, with the additional mention of the corruptions which have been entering the churches since 1844. The work of this angel comes in at the right time to join in the last great work of the third angel's message as it swells to a loud cry. And the people of God are thus prepared to stand in the hour of temptation, which they are soon to meet. I saw a great light resting upon them, and they united to fearlessly proclaim the third angel's message.

"Angels were sent to aid the mighty angel from heaven, and I heard voices which seemed to sound everywhere, 'Come out of her, My people, that ye be not partakers of her sins, and that ye receive not of her plagues. For her sins have reached unto heaven, and God hath remembered her iniquities.'

Some chose life and took their stand with those who were looking for their Lord and keeping all His commandments. The third message was to do its work; all were to be tested upon it, and the precious ones were to be called out from the religious bodies. A compelling power moved the honest, while the manifestation of the power of God brought a fear and restraint upon their unbelieving relatives and friends, so that they dared not, neither had they the power to, hinder those who felt the work of the Spirit of God upon them.

Mighty miracles were wrought, the sick were healed, and signs and wonders followed the believers. God was in the work, and every saint, fearless of consequences, followed the convictions of his own conscience and united with those who were keeping all the commandments of God; and with power they sounded abroad the third message.

"Servants of God, endowed with power from on high, with

their faces lighted up, and shining with holy consecration, went forth to proclaim the message from heaven. Souls that were scattered all through the religious bodies answered to the call, and the precious were hurried out of the doomed churches, as Lot was hurried out of Sodom before her destruction. God's people were strengthened by the excellent glory which rested upon them in rich abundance and prepared them to endure the hour of temptation. I heard everywhere a multitude of voices saying, 'Here is the patience of the saints: here are they that keep the commandments of God, and the faith of Jesus.'

"I was pointed down to the time when the third angel's message was closing. The power of God had rested upon His people; they had accomplished their work and were prepared for the trying hour before them. They had received the latter rain, or refreshing from the presence of the Lord, and the living testimony had been revived. The last great warning had sounded everywhere, and it had stirred up and enraged the inhabitants of the earth who would not receive the message.

"I saw angels hurrying to and fro in heaven. An angel with a writer's inkhorn by his side returned from the earth and reported to Jesus that his work was done, and the saints were numbered and sealed. Then I saw Jesus, who had been ministering before the ark containing the ten commandments, throw down the censer. He raised His hands, and with a loud voice said, 'It is done.' And all the angelic host laid off their crowns as Jesus made the solemn declaration, 'He that is unjust, let him be unjust still: and he which is filthy, let him be filthy still: and he that is righteous, let him be righteous still: and he that is holy, let him be holy still.'

"Every case had been decided for life or death. While Jesus had been ministering in the sanctuary, the judgment had been going on for the righteous dead, and then for the righteous living. Christ had received His kingdom, having made the atonement for His people and blotted out their sins. The subjects of the kingdom were made up. The marriage of the Lamb was consummated. And the kingdom, and the greatness of the kingdom under the whole heaven, was given to Jesus and the heirs of salvation, and Jesus was to reign as King of kings, and Lord of lords.

"As Jesus moved out to the most holy place, I heard the tinkling of the bells upon His garment; and as He left, a cloud of darkness covered the inhabitants of the earth. There was then no mediator between guilty man and an offended God. While Jesus had been standing between God and guilty man, a restraint was upon the people; but when He stepped out from between man and the Father, the restraint was removed and Satan had entire control of the finally impenitent.

"It was impossible for the plagues to be poured out while Jesus officiated in the sanctuary; but as His work there is finished, and His intercession closes, there is nothing to stay the wrath of God, and it breaks with fury upon the shelterless head of the guilty sinner, who has slighted salvation and hated reproof. In that fearful time, after the close of Jesus' meditation, the saints were living in the sight of a holy God without an intercessor. Every case was decided, every jewel numbered. Jesus tarried a moment in the outer apartment of the heavenly sanctuary, and the sins which had been confessed while He was in the most holy place were placed upon Satan, the originator of sin, who must suffer their punishment.

Plagues and Agony

"Then I saw Jesus lay off His priestly attire and clothe Himself with His most kingly robes. Upon His head were many crowns, a crown within a crown. Surrounded by the angelic host, He left heaven. The plagues were falling upon the inhabitants of the earth. Some were denouncing God and cursing Him. Others rushed to the people of God and begged to be taught how they might escape His judgments. But the saints had nothing for them. The last tear for sinners had been shed, the last agonizing prayer offered, the last burden borne, the last warning given. The sweet voice of mercy was no more to invite them.

"When the saints, and all heaven, were interested for their salvation, they had no interest for themselves. Life and death had been set before them. Many desired life, but made no effort to obtain it. They did not choose life, and now there was no atoning blood to cleanse the guilty, no compassionate Saviour to plead for them, and cry, 'Spare, spare the sinner a little longer.' All heaven had united with Jesus, as they heard the fearful words, 'It is done. It is finished.' The plan of salvation had been accomplished, but few had chosen to accept it. And as mercy's sweet voice died away, fear and horror seized the wicked. With terrible distinctness they heard the words, 'Too late! too late!'

"Those who had not prized God's Word were hurrying to and fro, wandering from sea to sea, and from the north to the east, to seek the Word of the Lord. Said the angel, 'They shall not find it. There is a famine in the land; not a famine of bread, nor a thirst for water, but for hearing the words of the Lord. What would they not give for one word of approval from God! but no, they must hunger and thirst on. Day after day have they slighted salvation, prizing earthly riches and earthly pleasure higher than any heavenly treasure or inducement. They have rejected Jesus and despised His saints. The filthy must remain filthy forever.'

"Many of the wicked were greatly enraged as they suffered the effects of the plagues. It was a scene of fearful agony. Parents were bitterly reproaching their children, and children their parents, brothers their sisters, and sisters their brothers. Loud, wailing cries were heard in every direction, 'It was you who kept me from receiving the truth which would have saved me from this awful hour.' The people turned upon their ministers with bitter hate and reproached them, saying, 'You have not warned us. You told us that all the world was to be converted, and cried, Peace, peace, to quiet every fear that was aroused. You have not told us of this hour; and those who warned us of it you declared to be fanatics and evil men, who would ruin us.' But I saw that the ministers did not escape the wrath of God. Their suffering was ten-fold greater than that of their people.

"I saw the saints leaving the cities and villages, and associating together in companies, and living in the most solitary places. Angels provided them food and water, while the wicked were suffering from hunger and thirst. Then I saw the leading men of the earth consulting together, and Satan and his angels busy around them. I saw a writing, copies of which were scattered in different parts of the land, giving orders that unless the saints should yield their peculiar faith, give up the Sabbath, and observe the first day of the week, the people were at liberty after a certain time to put them to death. But in this hour of trial the saints were calm and composed, trusting in God and leaning upon His promise that a way of escape would be made for them.

"In some places, before the time for the decree to be executed, the wicked rushed upon the saints to slay them; but angels in the form of men of war fought for them. Satan wished to have the privilege of destroying the saints of the Most High; but Jesus bade His angels watch over them. God would be honored by making a covenant with those who had kept His law, in the sight of the heathen round about them; and Jesus would be honored by translating, without their seeing death, the faithful, waiting ones who had so long expected Him.

"Soon I saw the saints suffering great mental anguish. They seemed to be surrounded by the wicked inhabitants of the earth. Every appearance was against them. Some began to fear that God had at last left them to perish by the hand of the wicked. But if their eyes could have been opened, they would have seen themselves surrounded by angels of God. Next came the multitude of the angry wicked, and next a mass of evil angels, hurrying on the wicked to slay the saints. But before they could approach God's people, the wicked must first pass this company of mighty, holy angels. This was impossible. The angels of God were causing them to recede and also causing the evil angels who were pressing around them to fall back.

"It was an hour of fearful, terrible agony to the saints. Day and night they cried unto God for deliverance. To outward appearance, there was no possibility of their escape. The wicked had already begun to triumph, crying out, 'Why doesn't your God deliver you out of our hands? Why don't you go up and save your lives?' But the saints heeded them not. Like Jacob they were wrestling with God. The angels longed to deliver them, but they must wait a little longer; the people of God must drink of the cup and be baptized with the baptism. The angels, faithful to their trust, continued their watch. God would not suffer His name to be reproached among the heathen. The time had nearly come when He was to manifest His mighty power and gloriously deliver His saints. For His name's glory He would deliver every one of those who had patiently waited for Him and whose names were written in the book.

"I was pointed back to faithful Noah. When the rain descended and the flood came, Noah and his family had entered the ark, and God had shut them in. Noah had faithfully warned the inhabitants of the antediluvian world, while they had mocked and derided him. And as the waters descended upon the earth, and one after another was drowning, they beheld that ark, of which they had made so much sport, riding safely upon the waters, preserving the faithful Noah and his family.

"So I saw that the people of God, who had faithfully warned the world of His coming wrath, would be delivered. God would not suffer the wicked to destroy those who were expecting translation and who would not bow to the decree of the beast or receive his mark. I saw that if the wicked were permitted to slay the saints, Satan and all his evil host, and all who hate God, would be gratified. . . . Angels of God shielded the saints. As they cried day and night for deliverance, their cry came up before the Lord.

Second Coming of Christ

"It was at midnight that God chose to deliver His people. As the wicked were mocking around them, suddenly the sun appeared, shining in His strength, and the moon stood still. The wicked looked upon the scene with amazement, while the saints beheld with solemn joy the tokens of their deliverance. Signs and wonders followed in quick succession. Everything seemed turned out of its natural course. The streams ceased to flow. Dark, heavy clouds came up and clashed against each other. But there was one clear place of settled glory, whence came the voice of God like many waters, shaking the heavens and the earth. There was a mighty earthquake. The graves were opened, and those who had died in faith under the third angel's message, keeping the Sabbath, came forth from their dusty beds, glorified, to hear the covenant of peace that God was to make with those who had kept His law.

"The sky opened and shut and was in commotion. The mountains shook like a reed in the wind and cast out ragged rocks all around. The sea boiled like a pot and cast out stones upon the land. And as God spoke the day and the hour of Jesus' coming and delivered the everlasting covenant to His people, He spoke one sentence, and then paused, while the words were rolling through the earth.

"The Israel of God stood with their eyes fixed upward,

listening to the words as they came from the mouth of Jehovah and rolled through the earth like peals of loudest thunder. It was awfully solemn. At the end of every sentence the saints shouted, 'Glory! Hallelujah!' Their countenances were lighted up with the glory of God, and they shone with glory as did the face of Moses when he came down from Sinai. The wicked could not look upon them for the glory. And when the never-ending blessing was pronounced on those who had honored God in keeping His Sabbath holy, there was a mighty shout of victory over the beast and over his image.

"Soon appeared the great white cloud, upon which sat the Son of man. When it first appeared in the distance, this cloud looked very small. The angel said that it was the sign of the Son of man. As it drew nearer the earth, we could behold the excellent glory and majesty of Jesus as He rode forth to conquer. A retinue of holy angels, with bright, glittering crowns upon their heads, escorted Him on His way. No language can describe the glory of the scene. The living cloud of majesty and unsurpassed glory came still nearer, and we could clearly behold the lovely person of Jesus. He did not wear a crown of thorns, but a crown of glory rested upon His holy brow. Upon His vesture and thigh was a name written, King of kings, and Lord of lords. His countenance was as bright as the noonday sun, His eyes were as a flame of fire, and His feet had the appearance of fine brass. His voice sounded like many musical instruments.

"The earth trembled before Him, the heavens departed as a scroll when it is rolled together, and every mountain and island were moved out of their places. 'And the kings of the earth, and the great men, and the rich men, and the chief captains, and the mighty men, and every bondman, and every freeman, hid themselves in the dens and in the rocks of the mountains; and said to the mountains and rocks, Fall on us, and hide us from the face of Him that sitteth on the

throne, and from the wrath of the Lamb: for the great day
of His wrath is come; and who shall be able to stand?' Those
who a short time before would have destroyed God's faithful children from the earth, now witnessed the glory of God
which rested upon them. And amid all their terror they
heard the voices of the saints in joyful strains, saying, 'Lo,
this is our God; we have waited for Him, and He will save
us.'

"The earth mightily shook as the voice of the Son of God
called forth the sleeping saints. They responded to the call
and came forth clothed with glorious immortality, crying,
'Victory, victory, over death and the grave! Oh death, where
is thy sting? Oh grave, where is thy victory?' Then the living saints and the risen ones raised their voices in a long,
transporting shout of victory. Those bodies that had gone
down into the grave bearing the marks of disease and death
came up in immortal health and vigor." [5] "Adam, who stands
among the risen throng, is of lofty height and majestic form,
in stature but little below the Son of God. He presents a
marked contrast to the people of later generations; in this
one respect is shown the great degeneracy of the race." [6]
"The living saints are changed in a moment, in the twinkling
of an eye, and caught up with the risen ones, and together
they meet their Lord in the air. Oh, what a glorious meeting! Friends whom death had separated were united, never
more to part.

"On each side of the cloudy chariot were wings, and beneath it were living wheels; and as the chariot rolled upward, the wheels cried, 'Holy,' and the wings, as they moved,
cried, 'Holy,' and the retinue of holy angels around the
cloud cried, 'Holy, holy, holy, Lord God Almighty!' And the
saints in the cloud cried, 'Glory! Alleluia!' And the chariot
rolled upward to the Holy City. Before entering the city,
the saints were arranged in a perfect square, with Jesus in
the midst. He stood head and shoulders above the saints

and above the angels. His majestic form and lovely countenance could be seen by all in the square.

"Then I saw a very great number of angels bring from the city glorious crowns—a crown for every saint, with his name written thereon. As Jesus called for the crowns, angels presented them to Him, and with His own right hand, the lovely Jesus placed the crowns on the heads of the saints. In the same manner the angels brought the harps, and Jesus presented them also to the saints.

"The commanding angels first struck the note, and then every voice was raised in grateful, happy praise, and every hand skillfully swept over the strings of the harp, sending forth melodious music in rich and perfect strains." [7] "Little children are borne by holy angels to their mothers' arms. . . . With joy unutterable parents see the crown, the robe, the harp, given to their children. The days of hope and fear are ended. Their children have been redeemed." [8] "Some of them had very bright crowns, others not so bright. Some crowns appeared heavy with stars, while others had but few. All were perfectly satisfied with their crowns. And they were all clothed with a glorious white mantle from their shoulders to their feet. Angels were all about us as we marched over the sea of glass to the gate of the city. Jesus raised His mighty, glorious arm, laid hold of the pearly gate, swung it back on its glittering hinges, and said to us, 'You have washed your robes in My blood, stood stiffly for My truth, enter in.'

"We all marched in and felt that we had a perfect right in the city.

"Here we saw the tree of life and the throne of God. Out of the throne came a pure river of water, and on either side of the river was the tree of life. On one side of the river was a trunk of a tree, and a trunk on the other side of the river, both of pure, transparent gold. At first I thought I saw two trees. I looked again, and saw that they were united at the top in one tree. So it was the tree of life on either side of the river of life. Its branches bowed to the place where we stood, and the fruit was glorious; it looked like gold mixed with silver." [9]

"As the ransomed ones are welcomed to the City of God, there rings out upon the air an exultant cry of adoration. The two Adams are about to meet. The Son of God is standing with outstretched arms to receive the father of our race —the being whom He created, who sinned against his Maker, and for whose sins the marks of the crucifixion are borne upon the Saviour's form. As Adam discerns the prints of the cruel nails, he does not fall upon the bosom of his Lord, but in humiliation casts himself at His feet, crying: 'Worthy is the Lamb that was slain!' Tenderly the Saviour lifts him up and bids him look once more upon the Eden home from which he has so long been exiled." [10]

Return to the Garden of Eden

"The Garden of Eden remained upon the earth long after man had become an outcast from its pleasant paths. The fallen race were long permitted to gaze upon the home of innocence, their entrance barred only by the watching angels. At the cherubim-guarded gate of Paradise, the divine glory was revealed. . . . When the tide of iniquity overspread the world, and the wickedness of men determined their destruction by a flood of waters, the hand that had planted Eden withdrew it from the earth." [11]

"After his expulsion from Eden, Adam's life on earth was filled with sorrow. Every dying leaf, every victim of sacrifice, every blight upon the fair face of nature, every stain upon man's purity, was a fresh reminder of his sin. Terrible was the agony of remorse as he beheld iniquity abounding, and, in answer to his warnings, met the reproaches cast upon himself as the cause of sin.

"With patient humility he bore, for nearly a thousand years, the penalty of transgression. Faithfully did he repent of his sin and trust in the merits of the promised Saviour, and he died in the hope of a resurrection.

"The Son of God redeemed man's failure and fall; and now, through the work of the atonement, Adam is reinstated in his first dominion.

"Transported with joy, he beholds the trees that were once his delight—the very trees whose fruit he himself had gathered in the days of his innocence and joy. He sees the vines that his own hands have trained, the very flowers that he once loved to care for. His mind grasps the reality of the scene; he comprehends that this is indeed Eden restored, more lovely now than when he was banished from it.

"The Saviour leads him to the tree of life and plucks the glorious fruit and bids him to eat. He looks about him and beholds a multitude of his family redeemed, standing in the Paradise of God. Then he casts his glittering crown at the feet of Jesus, and, falling upon His breast, embraces the Redeemer. He touches the golden harp, and the vaults of heaven echo the triumphant song, 'Worthy, worthy, worthy is the Lamb that was slain, and lives again!' The family of Adam take up the strain and cast their crowns at the Saviour's feet as they bow before Him in adoration." [12]

"Within the city there was everything to feast the eye. Rich glory they beheld everywhere. Then Jesus looked upon His redeemed saints; their countenances were radiant with glory; and as He fixed His loving eyes upon them, He said, with His rich, musical voice, 'I behold the travail of My soul, and am satisfied. This rich glory is yours to enjoy eternally. Your sorrows are ended. There shall be no more death, neither sorrow nor crying, neither shall there be any more pain.'

"I saw the redeemed host bow and cast their glittering

crowns at the feet of Jesus, and then, as His lovely hand raised them up, they touched their golden harps, and filled all heaven with their rich music and songs to the Lamb.

"I then saw Jesus leading His people to the tree of life, and again we heard His lovely voice, richer than any music that ever fell on mortal ear, saying, 'The leaves of this tree are for the healing of the nations. Eat ye all of it.' Upon the tree of life was most beautiful fruit, of which the saints could partake freely. In the city was a most glorious throne, from which proceeded a pure river of water of life, clear as crystal. On each side of this river was the tree of life, and on the banks of the river were other beautiful trees bearing fruit which was good for food.

"Language is altogether too feeble to attempt a description of heaven. As the scene rises before me, I am lost in amazement. Carried away with the surpassing splendor and excellent glory, I lay down the pen and exclaim, 'Oh, what love! what wondrous love!' The most exalted language fails to describe the glory of heaven or the matchless depths of a Saviour's love.

"My attention was again directed to the earth.

Wilderness on Earth

"The wicked had been destroyed, and their dead bodies were lying upon its surface. The wrath of God in the seven last plagues had been visited upon the inhabitants of the earth, causing them to gnaw their tongues from pain and to curse God. The false shepherds had been the signal objects of Jehovah's wrath. Their eyes had consumed away in their holes, and their tongues in their mouths, while they stood upon their feet. After the saints had been delivered by the voice of God, the wicked multitude turned their rage upon one another. The earth seemed to be deluged with blood, and dead bodies were from one end of it to the other.

"The earth looked like a desolate wilderness. Cities and

villages, shaken down by the earthquake, lay in heaps. Mountains had been moved out of their places, leaving large caverns. Ragged rocks, thrown out by the sea, or torn out of the earth itself, were scattered all over its surface. Large trees had been uprooted and were strewn over the land. Here is to be the home of Satan with his evil angels for a thousand years. Here he will be confined, to wander up and down over the broken surface of the earth and see the effects of his rebellion against God's law. For a thousand years he can enjoy the fruit of the curse which he has caused. Limited alone to the earth, he will not have the privilege of ranging to other planets, to tempt and annoy those who have not fallen.

"During this time, Satan suffers extremely. Since his fall his evil traits have been in constant exercise. But he is then deprived of his power, and left to reflect upon the part which he has acted since his fall, and to look forward with trembling and terror to the dreadful future, when he must suffer for all the evil that he has done and be punished for all the sins that he has caused to be committed.

"I heard shouts of triumph from the angels and from the redeemed saints, which sounded like ten thousand musical instruments, because they were to be no more annoyed and tempted by Satan and because the inhabitants of other worlds were delivered from his presence and his temptations.

"Then I saw thrones, and Jesus and the redeemed saints sat upon them; and the saints reigned as kings and priests unto God. Christ, in union with His people, judged the wicked dead, comparing their acts with the statute book, the Word of God, and deciding every case according to the deeds done in the body." [13] " 'Behold ye,' said the angel, 'the saints, in unison with Jesus, sit in judgment, and mete out to the wicked according to the deeds done in the body, and that which they must receive at the execution of the judgment is set off against their names.' [14]

"Then they meted out to the wicked the portion which they must suffer, according to their works; and it was written against their names in the book of death. Satan also and his angels were judged by Jesus and the saints. Satan's punishment was to be far greater than that of those whom he had deceived. His suffering would so far exceed theirs as to bear no comparison with it.

"After all those whom he had deceived had perished, Satan was still to live and suffer on much longer.

"After the judgment of the wicked dead had been finished, at the end of one thousand years, Jesus left the city, and the saints and a train of angelic host followed Him. Jesus descended upon a great mountain, which as soon as His feet touched it, parted asunder and became a mighty plain. Then we looked up and saw the great and beautiful city, with twelve foundations, and twelve gates, three on each side, and an angel at each gate. We cried out, 'The city! the great city! it is coming down from God out of heaven!' And it came down in all its splendor and dazzling glory and settled in the mighty plain which Jesus had prepared for it." [15]

Resurrection of the Wicked

Then, in terrible, fearful majesty, Jesus called forth the wicked dead; and they came up with the same feeble, sickly bodies that went into the grave. What a spectacle! What a scene! At the first resurrection all came forth in immortal bloom; but at the second the marks of the curse are visible on all.

"The kings and noblemen of the earth, the mean and low, the learned and unlearned, come forth together. All behold the Son of man; and those very men who despised and mocked Him, who put the crown of thorns upon His sacred brow, and smote Him with the reed, behold Him in all His kingly majesty. Those who spit upon Him in the hour of His trial now turn from His piercing gaze and from the glory of

His countenance. Those who drove the nails through His hands and feet now look upon the marks of His crucifixion. Those who thrust the spear into his side behold the marks of their cruelty on His body. And they know that He is the very one whom they crucified and derided at His expiring agony.

"And then there arises a long protracted wail of agony, as they flee to hide from the presence of the King of kings and Lord of lords.

"All are seeking to hide in the rocks, to shield themselves from the terrible glory of Him whom they once despised. And, overwhelmed and pained with His majesty and exceeding glory, they with one accord raise their voices, and with terrible distinctness exclaim, 'Blessed is He that cometh in the name of the Lord!'

"Then Jesus and the holy angels, accompanied by all the saints, again go to the city, and the bitter lamentations and wailings of the doomed wicked fill the air. Then I saw that Satan again commenced his work. He passed around among his subjects, and made the weak and feeble strong, and told them that he and his angels were powerful. He pointed to the countless millions who had been raised. There were mighty warriors and kings who were well skilled in battle and who had conquered kingdoms. And there were mighty giants and valiant men who had never lost a battle. There was the proud and ambitious Napoleon, whose approach had caused kingdoms to tremble. There stood men of lofty stature and dignified bearing, who had fallen in battle while thirsting to conquer. As they come forth from their graves, they resume the current of their thoughts where it ceased in death. They possess the same desire to conquer which ruled when they fell. Satan consults with his angels, and then with those kings and conquerors and mighty men. Then he looks over the vast army, and tells them that the company in the city is small and feeble, and that they can go up and take it, and cast out its inhabitants, and possess its riches and glory themselves.

Earth's Last War

"Satan succeeds in deceiving them, and all immediately begin to prepare themselves for battle. There are many skillful men in that vast army, and they construct all kinds of implements of war. Then with Satan at their head, the multitude move on. Kings and warriors follow closely after Satan, and the multitude follow after in companies. Each company has its leader, and order is observed as they march over the broken surface of the earth to the Holy City.

"Jesus closes the gates of the city, and this vast army surround it, and place themselves in battle array, expecting a fierce conflict. Jesus and all the angelic host and all the saints, with the glittering crowns on their heads, ascend to the top of the wall of the city. Jesus speaks with majesty, saying, 'Behold, ye sinners, the reward of the just! And behold, My redeemed, the reward of the wicked!'

"The vast multitude behold the glorious company on the walls of the city. And as they witness the splendor of their glittering crowns and see their faces radiant with glory, reflecting the image of Jesus, and then behold the unsurpassed glory and majesty of the King of kings and Lord of lords, their courage fails. A sense of the treasure and glory which they have lost rushes upon them, and they realize that the wages of sin is death. They see the holy, happy company whom they have despised, clothed with glory, honor, immortality, and eternal life, while they are outside the city with every mean and abominable thing." [16]

"Satan seems paralyzed as he beholds the glory and majesty of Christ. He who was once a covering cherub remembers whence he has fallen. A shining seraph, 'son of the morning'; how changed, how degraded! From the council where once he was honored, he is forever excluded. He sees another now standing near to the Father, veiling His glory. He has seen the crown placed upon the head of Christ by an angel of lofty stature and majestic presence, and he knows that the exalted position of this angel might have been his." [17]

"The spirit of rebellion, like a mighty torrent, again bursts forth. Filled with frenzy, he determines not to yield the great controversy. The time has come for a last desperate struggle against the King of heaven. He rushes into the midst of his subjects and endeavors to inspire them with his own fury and arouse them to instant battle. But of all the countless millions whom he has allured into rebellion, there are none now to acknowledge his supremacy. His power is at an end. The wicked are filled with the same hatred of God that inspires Satan; but they see that their case is hopeless, that they cannot prevail against Jehovah. Their rage is kindled against Satan and those who have been his agents in deception, and with the fury of demons they turn upon them." [18] "But fire from God out of heaven is rained upon them, and the great men, and mighty men, the noble, the poor and miserable, are all consumed together. I saw that some were quickly destroyed, while others suffered longer. They were punished according to their deeds done in the body. Some were many days consuming, and just as long as there was a portion of them unconsumed, all the sense of suffering remained. Said the angel, 'The worm of life shall not die; their fire shall not be quenched as long as there is the least particle for it to prey upon.'

"Satan and his angels suffered long. Satan bore not only the weight and punishment of his own sins, but also of the sins of the redeemed host, which had been placed upon him; and he must also suffer for the ruin of souls which he has caused. Then I saw that Satan and all the wicked host were consumed, and the justice of God was satisfied; and all the angelic host, and all the redeemed saints, with a loud voice said, 'Amen!'

"Said the angel, 'Satan is the root, his children are the branches. They are now consumed root and branch. They have died an everlasting death. They are never to have a resurrection, and God will have a clean universe.'

"I then looked and saw the fire which had consumed the wicked, burning up the rubbish and purifying the earth. . . . Again I looked and saw the earth purified. There was not a single sign of the curse. The broken, uneven surface of the earth now looked like a level, extensive plain. God's entire universe was clean, and the great controversy was forever ended. Wherever we looked, everything upon which the eye rested was beautiful and holy. And all the redeemed host, old and young, great and small, cast their glittering crowns at the feet of their Redeemer, and prostrated themselves in adoration before Him, and worshiped Him that liveth forever and ever.

"The beautiful new earth, with all its glory, was the eternal inheritance of the saints. The kingdom and dominion, and the greatness of the kingdom under the whole heaven, was then given to the saints of the Most High, who were to possess it forever, even forever and ever." [19]

"Then we began to look at the glorious things outside of the city. There I saw most glorious houses, that had the appearance of silver, supported by four pillars set with pearls most glorious to behold. These were to be inhabited by the saints. In each was a golden shelf. I saw many of the saints go into the houses, take off their glittering crowns and lay them on the shelf, then go out into the field by the houses to do something with the earth; not as we have to do with the earth here; no, no. A glorious light shone all about their heads, and they were continually shouting and offering praises to God.

"I saw another field full of all kinds of flowers, and as I plucked them, I cried out, 'They will never fade.' Next I saw a field of tall grass, most glorious to behold; it was living green and had a reflection of silver and gold, as it waved proudly to the glory of King Jesus.

"Then we entered a field full of all kinds of beasts—the lion, the lamb, the leopard, and the wolf, all together in perfect union. We passed through the midst of them, and they followed on peaceably after. Then we entered a wood, not like the dark woods we have here; no, no, but light, and all over glorious; the branches of the trees moved to and fro, and we all cried out, 'We will dwell safely in the wilderness and sleep in the woods.' We passed through the woods, for we were on our way to Mount Zion.

"As we were traveling along, we met a company who also were gazing at the glories of the place. I noticed red as a border on their garments; their crowns were brilliant; their robes were pure white. As we greeted them, I asked Jesus who they were. He said they were martyrs that had been slain for Him. With them was an innumerable company of little ones; they also had a hem of red on their garments.

"Mount Zion was just before us, and on the mount was a glorious temple, and about it were seven other mountains, on which grew roses and lilies. And I saw the little ones climb, or, if they chose, use their little wings and fly, to the top of the mountains and pluck the never-fading flowers. There were all kinds of trees around the temple to beautify the place; the box, the pine, the fir, the olive, the myrtle, the pomegranate, and the fig tree bowed down with the weight of its timely figs—these made the place all over glorious. And as we were about to enter the holy temple, Jesus raised His lovely voice and said, 'Only the 144,000 enter this place,' and we shouted 'Alleluia.'"

Describing the temple, she continued, overcome by its beauty:

"The temple was supported by seven pillars, all of transparent gold, set with pearls most glorious. The wonderful things I there saw I cannot describe. Oh, that I could talk the language of Canaan, then could I tell a little of the glory of the better world. I saw there tables of stone in which the names of the 144,000 were engraved in letters of gold.

"After we beheld the glory of the temple, we went out, and Jesus left us and went to the city. Soon we heard His lovely voice again, saying, 'Come, My people, you have come out of great tribulation, and done My will; suffered for Me; come in to supper and I will gird Myself and serve you.' We shouted, 'Alleluia! glory!' and entered into the city. And I saw a table of pure silver; it was many miles in length, yet our eyes could extend over it. I saw the fruit of the tree of life, the manna, almonds, figs, pomegranates, grapes, and many other kinds of fruit. I asked Jesus to let me eat of the fruit. He said, 'Not now. Those who eat of the fruit of this land go back to earth no more. But in a little while, if faithful, you shall both eat of the fruit of the tree of life and drink of the water of the fountain.' And He said, 'You must go back to the earth again and relate to others what I have revealed to you.' " [20]

Epilogue

WHEN THE UNCHECKED wails of the eternally doomed echo sadly through the vastness of limitless space, creating an almost unending tidal wave of agony that will engulf other inhabited worlds, telling them of the end of sin on Planet Earth, the last scene of the cosmic tragedy between good and evil will have been played.

"The field of the controversy between Christ and Satan," Ellen once said sorrowfully, "is the lesson book of the universe." And she submitted her visions and her gift of prophecy to all for an exhaustive examination.

That she was indeed a prophet and not merely a psychic becomes abundantly clear to anyone studying her life and prophecies, especially when the tests of a true prophet are applied. Not only did she *surpass* the psychics in her strict adherence to these inspired criteria, but her supernormal vision went beyond theirs in all dimensions, not just in those limited to time.

225

Within the secret corridors of her mortal mind, she witnessed the dawn of history; she trod the world scene, and ended *not* just with revelations of final destruction and total devastation, but with a divinely inspired view of an earth made new and an award awaiting the just. On many occasions she felt part of the remnant of humanity, fleeing the distressing scenes, traveling mentally to the promised land. And spasms of overwhelming joy and gratitude surged through her being as she walked the streets of gold, far beyond the glittering chasms of Orion.

"Heaven is cheap enough whatever sacrifice we may make to obtain it," she once said gratefully after one of those memorable visits.

That sincerity and understanding caused her to pen these words, no one will ever doubt. To her, the "hereafter" was a reality, just as much as she said it could be for every one of us.

Her principles for extending our meager present-day life span into the aeons of time were simply worded; not beyond human reach, but supported by incentives so overwhelming, pointing toward a reward so limitless, that it seems entirely out of the range of mere human comprehension.

As prerequisites she listed strict adherence to Biblical principles; acceptance of Christ and dependence on His power; active involvement in the cosmic battle of the ages; reliance on the words of the prophets who speak with the authority of God; and a responsible reaction to the warnings relayed through them.

That Ellen White managed to retain her tranquil outlook, her confidence in mankind and unimpaired mental vigor throughout her many years of public involvement is nothing short of a miracle and understood best in the light of the reality of her day-by-day close communion with the Eternal.

As a *channel* for Godly intelligence, she became the relay point through which messages of encouragement, and often warning and rebuke, were transmitted; yet at the same time she served as *target* of her own revelations, as they were directed to humanity *without exception*. At other times she served as unchallenged confidante of God, and as such shared secret knowledge hidden from mankind up to that time.

So awesome and terrifying were some of the scenes that invaded her mind, had it not been for the supernatural strength supplied, her life might have ended in a mental breakdown. But she survived, calm, collected and strengthened in her belief.

Was her total commitment worth it?

It undoubtedly was, and furthermore, the results bear out the correctness of the Source that moved her as she and her husband and their associates pioneered the establishment of what is now a world religious movement with its vast publishing, educational and medical program. Today, 1972, fifty-seven years after her pen was laid down, her "spiritual estate" has grown to a missionary movement that encompasses 193 countries The material printed by the 46 publishing companies that have grown out of the inspired counsel is issued in 266 tongues. In education, too, her guidance has left its mark, for two Seventh-day Adventist universities, and 460 colleges and academies now encircle the globe, and the consistent growth taking place in the enrollment at its more than 4,100 elementary schools promises much for the development of this educational system.

Her health counsel has also been taken seriously, and, as a result, the original Battle Creek Sanitarium became the spark that has ignited a fire, for the Church now operates 138 fully equipped hospitals, 166 clinics, dispensaries and other medical programs, reaching all the way from Loma Linda University in Southern California, with its medical and dental schools, to the Saigon Adventist Hospital in South Vietnam.

And they've all been called into existence for the sake of "Total Involvement."

Was she truly inspired? Was she truly "led"?

When the counsels of her visions were heeded, prosperity marked the work. When neglected, the result has been great loss. The Author of Prophecy, in speaking of his messengers, declared, "By their fruits ye shall know them" (Matt. 7:20). The Scripture declares, "Believe His Prophets, so shall ye prosper" (11 Chr. 20:20).

The record speaks for itself.

Partial Bibliography of Ellen G. White Books

Acts of the Apostles. Mountain View, Calif.: Pacific Press Publishing Association, 633 pp.
> A commentary on the lives, work and writings of the apostles during the first century of the Christian era. Volume four of the "Conflict of the Ages" series.

Christ's Object Lessons. Washington, D. C.: Review and Herald Publishing Association, 436 pp.
> A treatise on the parables.

Counsels on Diet and Foods. Washington, D. C.: Review and Herald Publishing Association, 511 pp.
> A posthumous reference work presenting the Ellen G. White counsels relative to diet and foods in topical order.

The Desire of Ages. Mountain View, Calif.: Pacific Press Publishing Association, 863 pp. New York: Pyramid Publications, paperback.
> Presenting the life, teachings and miracles of Jesus Christ. Volume Three of the "Conflict of the Ages" series.

Early Writings. Washington, D. C.: Review and Herald Publishing Association, 316 pp.

A composite work presenting three early Ellen G. White books: *A Sketch of the Christian Experience and Views of Ellen G. White* (1851); *Supplement* (1854); and *Spiritual Gifts*, Vol. 1, *The Great Controversy*, presenting the 1858 great controversy vision.

Education. Mountain View, Calif.: Pacific Press Publishing Association, 324 pp.

Setting forth a philosophy of education which involves not only mental development, but the spiritual and physical as well.

Fundamentals of Christian Education. Nashville, Tenn.: Southern Publishing Association, 576 pp.

A posthumous work embodying the voluminous Ellen G. White writings on education appearing in Seventh-day Adventist journals.

The Great Controversy. Mountain View, Calif.: Pacific Press Publishing Association, 719 pp. New York: Pyramid Publications, paperback.

The fifth volume of the "Conflict of the Ages" series, tracing the battle between the forces of righteousness and the forces of evil from the destruction of Jerusalem in A. D. 70 to the earth made new. Also available under the title of *The Triumph of God's Love*.

Ministry of Healing. Mountain View, Calif.: Pacific Press Publishing Association, 540 pp.

Mrs. White's major volume dealing with health, stressing nutrition and physiology.

Patriarchs and Prophets. Mountain View, Calif.: Pacific Press Publishing Association, 762 pp. Washington, D. C.: Review and Herald Publishing Association.

Volume One of the "Conflict of the Ages" series portraying

early world history, drawing lessons from the experience of men of old and paralleling Bible history to the time of King David.

Selected Messages. Washington, D. C.: Review and Herald Publishing Association, 2 vols., 762 pp.
Posthumous works comprised of pertinent Ellen G. White materials drawn from periodical articles, out-of-print books and manuscript sources.

Story of Prophets and Kings. Mountain View, Calif.: Pacific Press Publishing Association, 733 pp.
Deals with the experience of Israel from the time of King David to the birth of Jesus Christ, and drawing lessons from lives of the key figures participating in their history. The second volume of the "Conflict of the Ages" series.

Steps to Christ. Mountain View, Calif.: Pacific Press Publishing Association, 128 pp. Washington, D. C.: Review and Herald Publishing Association, Nashville, Tenn.: Southern Publishing Association.
A thirteen-chapter presentation portraying the simple steps to a meaningful Christian life. Published initially by Fleming H. Revell. Now issued in one hundred languages and very widely distributed.

Testimonies for the Church. Mountain View, Calif.: Pacific Press Publishing Association, 9 vols., 5058 pp.
Originally issued as pamphlets and small books published over a span of 55 years. These "testimonies" became the vehicle of communication between Ellen White and the Seventh-day Adventist Church by which she imparted messages of inspiration, directives, counsels and warnings recorded particularly for the church and its members.

Thoughts from the Mount of Blessing. Mountain View, Calif.: Pacific Press Publishing Association, 172 pp.
A commentary of Christ's Sermon on the Mount.

Notes

INTRODUCTION

1. Ellen G. White, *Early Writings*, pp. 39-40.
2. *The Review and Herald*, July 26, 1906.
3. Ellen G. White, *The Great Controversy*, p. 678.

CHAPTER ONE

1. Ellen G. White Manuscript, 1902, p. 114.
2. Ellen G. White, *Evangelism*, p. 27.
3. Ellen G. White, *Testimonies*, Vol. 9, 1909, p. 92.
4. Francis D. Nichol, *The Midnight Cry*, pp. 34, 35.
5. LeRoy Edwin Froom, *The Conditionalist Faith of Our Fathers*, pp. 1053, 1055.
6. *Ibid.*, p. 1057.

CHAPTER TWO

1. Ellen G. White, *Life Sketches*, pp. 34-36.
2. *Ibid.*, p. 36.

3. *Ibid.*, p. 37.
4. Ellen G. White, Letter 33, 1847
5. Ellen G. White, Letter 37, 1890.
6. *Ibid.*
7. *Ibid.*
8. Arthur L. White, *Messenger to the Remnant*, p. 30.
9. Ellen G. White, Letter 2, 1874.
10. Ellen G. White, *Life Sketches*, p. 107.
11. *Ibid.*, p. 109.
12. *Ibid.*
13. *Ibid.*, p. 125.
14. *Ibid.*, p. 142.
15. *Ibid.*, p. 143.
16. *Ibid.*, pp. 165-166.
17. *The Signs of the Times*, September 14, 1876.
18. William C. White, *The Review and Herald*, February 10, 17, 1938; also *The Spirit of Prophecy Treasure Chest*, pp. 33, 34.
19. *Ibid.*
20. *Ibid.*
21. Ellen G. White, *Life Sketches*, pp. 249, 251.
22. *Ibid.*, pp. 256, 257.
23. William C. White, *The Review and Herald*, February 10, 17, 1938; also *The Spirit of Prophecy Treasure Chest*, pp. 36, 37.
24. *Ibid.*
25. *Ibid.*
26. Ellen G. White, *Testimonies*, Vol. 2, pp. 371, 372.
27. *Ibid.*, p. 487.
28. Ellen G. White, Manuscript 82, 1901.
29. Ellen G. White, Letter 89a, 1894.
30. Ellen G. White, Letter 113, 1897.
31. Ellen G. White, Manuscript 4, 1895.
32. *The Review and Herald*, June 14, 1906.
33. *Ibid.*, July 26, 1906
34. *Ibid.*, October 8, 1867.
35. Ellen G. White, Letter 28, 1906.
36. Ellen G. White, Letter 105, 1900.
37. Ellen G. White, Letter 2d, 1892.
38. Ellen G. White, Letter 16c, 1892.
39. Arthur L. White, *Messenger to the Remnant*, p. 111.
40. *Colporteur Evangelist*, p. 36.
41. *The Review and Herald*, July 26, 1906.

42. Ellen G. White, *Testimonies*, Vol. 9, pp. 65, 66.
43. Ellen G. White, *Life Sketches*, pp. 444-445.
44. *Ibid.*, p. 445.

CHAPTER THREE

1. H. M. S. Richards, Jr., *Occult Explosion*, pp. 32, 33.
2. The New English Bible, Isa. 46:9-10.
3. Ellen G. White, *The Great Controversy*, Introduction, p. v.
4. *Ibid.* Introduction, pp. x, xi.
5. D. A. Delafield, *The Spirit of Prophecy Treasure Chest*, p. 31.
6. Francis D. Nichol, *The Midnight Cry*, pp. 263, 264.
7. *Ibid.*, p. 266.
8. Francis D. Nichol, Ellen G. White and Her Critics, pp. 161, 162.
9. J. N. Loughborough, *The Great Second Advent Movement*, p. 203.
10. Ellen G. White, *Early Writings*, pp. 14-20.
11. Ellen G. White, Manuscript 16, 1894. Also, *Messenger to the Remnant*.
12. Martha D. Amadon, "Mrs. E. G. White in Vision," Notebook Leaflets Misc. No. 1.
13. M. G. Kellogg, M.D., *The Spirit of Prophecy Treasure Chest*, p. 24.
14. Ellen G. White, *Testimonies*, Vol. 5, p. 658.
15. *The Review and Herald*, February 28, 1856, p. 171.
16. *The Spirit of Prophecy Treasure Chest*, p. 21.
17. J. N. Loughborough, *The Great Second Advent Movement*, p. 211.
18. *The Review and Herald*, June 9, 1874.

CHAPTER FOUR

1. John Janvier Black, M.D., *Forty Years in the Medical Profession*, 1900, p. 126.
2. J. H. Kellogg, M.D., *The Health Reform*, Battle Creek, January, 1876.

3. Worthington Hooker, M.D., *Rational Therapeutics*, 1857, pp. 13, 14.

4. *The Family Medicine Chest Dispensatory*, 1835.

5. Mrs. E. P. Miller, M.D., "Herald of Health," *The Health Reform*, September, 1866.

6. Ellen G. White, *Counsels on Diet and Foods*, p. 344.

7. Jackson A. Saxon, M.D., *Medical Science and the Spirit of Prophecy*.

8. Dr. Clive McCay, *The Review and Herald*, February 12, 1959.

9. Ellen G. White, *Counsels on Diet and Foods*, p. 267.

10. Ellen G. White, *Ministry of Healing*, p. 313.

11. *The Washington Post*, June 16, 1971.

12. Ludwick Gross, M.D., "Theory of Viral Etiology Gains Momentum," *Journal of the American Medical Association*, December 1, 1956.

13. Robert J. Huebner, "Simply Infectious Diseases," *Newsweek*, March 27, 1961.

14. *Newsweek*, April 6, 1964; also *Time*, April 13, 1964.

15. *The New York Times*, April 23, 1964.

16. Ellen G. White, *An Appeal to Mothers*, p. 27.

17. Ellen G. White, *Selected Messages*, Book 2, pp. 447, 449.

18. Ellen G. White, *Spiritual Gifts*, Vol. 4A, p. 128.

19. Ellen G. White, *Temperance*, p. 64.

20. Alton Ochsner, M.D., *Smoke Signals*, July-August, 1962, p. 1.

21. Ellen G. White, *Child Guidance*, p. 444.

22. *These Times*, December, 1970, pp. 22, 23, 24.

23. Ellen G. White, *Temperance*, p. 59.

24. Ellen G. White, *The Ministry of Healing*, p. 344.

25. Ellen G. White, *Temperance*, pp. 23, 24.

26. Microvascular Research; also *Listen*, December, 1969.

27. *Ibid.*, p. 24.

28. *University Scope* (Loma Linda, Calif.: Loma Linda University), Vol. 4, No. 10, May 10, 1967.

29. Ellen G. White, *Ministry of Healing*, p. 334.

30. Ellen G. White, *Selected Messages*, Bk. 2, p. 431.

31. *Ibid.*, p. 442.

32. Ellen G. White, *The Adventist Home*, p. 257.

33. Ellen G. White, *Patriarchs and Prophets*, p. 561.

34. Leland H. Scott, *Child Development*, 1967, pp. 371, 372.

35. Dr. Jesse D. Rising, "Drugging During Pregnancy," *Time*, October 27, 1958.

36. Thomas M. Rivers, "Radiation, Strong Drugs & Alcohol, *The National Foundation.*

37. *Journal of the American Medical Association,* June 3, 1961, p. 783.

38. Ellen G. White, *Testimonies,* Vol. 2, p. 61.

39. Ellen G. White, *Counsels on Diet and Foods,* pp. 393, 394.

40. *The Review and Herald,* July 13, 1961, p. 3.

41. *Today's Health,* February, 1970, p. 88.

42. *Medical Tribune,* July 10, 1969.

43. Ellen G. White, *Counsels on Diet and Foods,* p. 328.

44. Ellen G. White, *Counsels on Health,* p. 154.

45. Ellen G. White, *Ministry of Healing,* pp. 301, 302.

46. *Signs of the Times,* February, 1970.

47. Ellen G. White, *Testimonies,* Vol. 7, p. 82.

48. Ellen G. White, *Ministry of Healing,* p. 365.

49. Ellen G. White, *Country Living,* p. 29.

50. Ellen G. White, *Selected Messages,* Bk. 2, p. 52.

51. Jack Shepherd, *Look,* April 21, 1970, p. 23.

52. Bryan W. Ball, *These Times,* April, 1971, p. 11.

53. Ellen G. White, *Child Guidance,* p. 447.

54. Ellen G. White, *Testimonies,* Vol. 3, pp. 138, 139.

55. *Ibid.,* p. 157.

56. Ellen G. White, *Education,* p. 209.

57. Ellen G. White, *Testimonies,* Vol. 3, pp. 138, 139.

58. Ellen G. White, *Ministry of Healing,* p. 462.

59. Ellen G. White, *Education,* p. 104.

CHAPTER FIVE

1. Daniel Logan, *The Reluctant Prophet,* p. 127.

2. Rene Noorbergen with Jeane Dixon, *My Life and Prophecies,* pp. 98, 99.

3. *Ibid.,* p. 122.

4. *Ibid.,* p. 154.

5. Ellen G. White, *Life Sketches,* p. 162.

6. Ellen G. White, *Early Writings,* p. 146.

7. Ellen G. White, *The Story of Redemption,* p. 26.

8. *Ibid.,* p. 28.

9. Ellen G. White, *Early Writings,* pp. 146, 147.

10. Ellen G. White, *The Story of Redemption*, pp. 29, 30.
11. Ellen G. White, *Early Writings*, pp. 147, 148.
12. Ellen G. White, *The Story of Redemption*, p. 35.
13. Ellen G. White, *Early Writings*, pp. 148, 149.
14. Ellen G. White, *The Story of Redemption*, p. 42.
15. Ellen G. White, *Early Writings*, pp. 149, 150.
16. *Ibid.*, pp. 150, 151, 152, 153.
17. Ellen G. White, *Life Sketches*, p. 162.
18. *Ibid.*, p. 162.
19. New English Bible, Rev. 16:13-15.
20. Matt. 24:24, 25.
21. Ellen G. White, *The Desire of Ages*, p. 631.
22. Rev. 13:13, 14.
23. Ellen G. White, *Early Writings*, p. 86.
24. Ellen G. White, *Early Writings*, p. 59.
25. *Ibid.*, p. 88.
26. *Ibid.*, pp. 86, 87.
27. Ellen G. White, *The Great Controversy*, p. 588.
28. *Ibid.*
29. Ellen G. White, *The Desire of Ages*, p. 258.
30. Ellen G. White, *The Great Controversy*, pp. 588, 589.
31. *Ibid.*, p. 589.
32. *Ibid.*, pp. 589, 590.
33. *Ibid.*, p. 588.
34. *Ibid.*, p. 604.
35. *Ibid.*, p. 588.
36. Ellen G. White, *Medical Ministry*, pp. 101, 102.
37. Ellen G. White, *The Great Controversy*, p. 561.
38. LeRoy Edwin Froom, *Spiritualism Today*, p. 12.
39. *Ibid.*, p. 7.
40. Russell S. Waldorf, "Spiritual Healing," *Centennial Book of Modern Spiritualism in America*, p. 204.
41. *Spiritualist Manual*, p. 116.
42. Roy Allan Anderson, *Secrets of the Spirit World*, p. 21.
43. Rene Noorbergen with Jeane Dixon, *My Life and Prophecies*, p. 153.
44. Rene Noorbergen, *You Are Psychic*, p. 154.
45. *Ibid.*, p. 156.
46. *Spiritual Frontiers*, Vol. 3, No. 3, May-June, 1958, p. 2.
47. *Ibid.*
48. J. B. Rhine, "Survival—Science Looks At Life After Death,"

The American Weekly, December 8, 1957, p. 9.
    49. Alson J. Smith, *Religion and the New Psychology,* 1951, p. 151.
    50. *Ibid.,* p. 174.
    51. *Psychic Pitfalls,* London, 1954, pp. 269-270.
    52. *Ibid.*
    53. D. Mona Berry, *What Is Spiritualism?* pp. 38, 39.
    54. *Beware Familiar Spirits,* 1938, p. 83.
    55. *The Teachings and Phenomena of Spiritualism,* p. 72.

CHAPTER SIX

    1. Ellen G. White, *Testimonies,* Vol. 5, p. 473.
    2. *Ibid.,* pp. 450, 451.
    3. Ellen G. White, *The Great Controversy,* 1884, Vol. 4, pp. 337-338.
    4. D. B. Ray, *The Papal Controversy,* 1892, p. 179.
    5. *Catholic Virginian,* October 3, 1947.
    6. Dr .Edward T. Hiscox, *The Baptist Manual,* in paper read before a New York Ministers Conference, November 13, 1893.
    7. Schaff Herzog, *Encyclopedia of Religious Knowledge,* 1891 ed., s.v., "Sunday."
    8. T. M. Morer, *Dialogues on the Lord's Day,* 1701.
    9. Martin Luther, *Augsburg Confession of Faith,* Art. 28, par. 9.
    10. Hutton Webster, Ph.D., *Rest Days,* pp. 220, 221.
    11. Ellen G. White, *The Great Controversy,* p. 592.
    12. Fernando Chaij, *Preparation for the Final Crisis,* p. 186.
    13. *The Seventh-day Adventist Bible Commentary,* Vol. 7, p. 977; *The Review and Herald,* December 18, 1888.
    14. Ellen G. White, *Story of Prophets and Kings,* p. 184.
    15. Ellen G. White, *The Great Controversy,* p. 591.
    16. Jeffrey Furst, *Edgar Cayce, the Story of Jesus,* p. 42.
    17. Ellen G. White, *Testimonies,* Vol. 5, p. 451.
    18. *Ibid.,* Vol. 1, pp. 353, 354.
    19. Ellen G. White, *The Great Controversy,* p. 635.
    20. *Liberty,* May-June, 1963, p. 22.
    21. Editorial in *Christian Heritage,* June, 1964, p. 5.
    22. Ellen G. White, *The Great Controversy,* p. 571.
    23. *Our Sunday Visitor,* A Catholic Magazine, July 31, 1960.
    24. Father Gustave Weigel, S.J., *An American Dialogue,* pp. 218, 220.

25. Father Bernard Leeming, S.J., *The Catholic News*, Thursday, July 25, 1963.

26. Ellen G. White, *The Great Controversy*, p. 592.

27. Richard Cardinal Cushing, *Sign*, a Catholic magazine, October, 1961.

28. Rev. 12:7-9.

29. Mark 13:21-27. New English Bible.

30. Rev. 6: 12, 13.

31. Robert Sears, *Wonders of the World*, p. 50.

32. *Ibid.*, p. 58.

33. *Ibid.*, p. 381.

34. *Encyclopedia Americana*, 1831 ed., s.v. "Lisbon," note.

35. A. R. Spofford and Charles Gibbon, *The Library of Choice Literature*, Vol. VII, p. 162.

36. Noah Webster, "Vocabulary of the Names of Noted Persons and Places," *An American Dictionary of the English Language*, 1882.

37. *The Essex Antiquarian*, Vol. 3, No. 4, April, 1899, pp. 53, 54.

38. Samuel Williams, *Memoirs of the American Academy of Arts and Sciences*, Vol. 1, pp. 234, 235.

39. Ellen G. White, *The Great Controversy*, p. 307.

40. Isaiah Thomas, *Massachusetts Spy; or American Oracle of Liberty*, Vol. 10, No. 472, (May 25, 1780).

41. Samuel Tenny, *Collections of Massachusetts Historical Society for the Year 1792*, Vol. 1, pp. 97, 98.

42. *New York Journal of Commerce*, Vol. 8, No. 534 (November 14, 1883), p. 2.

43. F. Reed, *Christian Advocate and Journal*, December 13, 1833.

44. R. M. Devens, *American Progress, or The Great Events of the Greatest Century*, Chap. 28, par. 1-5.

45. Elijah H. Burritt, *The Geography of the Heavens*, p. 163.

46. Denison Olmsted, *The Mechanism of the Heavens*, p. 328.

47. Ruth Montgomery, *A Gift of Prophecy*, pp. 179, 180.

48. *Ibid.*, pp. 180, 181.

49. *Ibid.*, p. 181.

50. Rene Noorbergen with Jeane Dixon, *My Life and Prophecies*, p. 187.

51. Rene Noorbergen, *You Are Psychic*, p. 168.

52. Ellen G. White, *The Great Controversy*, p. 624.

53. *Ibid.*

54. *Ibid.*, pp. 553, 554.

55. *Ibid.*, p. 624.

56. *Ibid.*, p. 593.

CHAPTER SEVEN

1. Ellen G. White Estate, *Notes & Papers*, p. 300.
2. Ellen G. White, *Early Writings*, pp. 45, 55.
3. *Ibid.*, pp. 251, 252.
4. *Ibid.*, pp. 254-256.
5. *Ibid.*, pp. 277-287.
6. Ellen G. White, *The Great Controversy*, p. 644.
7. Ellen G. White, *Early Writings*, pp. 287, 288.
8. Ellen G. White, *My Life Today*, p. 352.
9. Ellen G. White, *Early Writings*, pp. 16, 17.
10. Ellen G. White, *The Great Controversy*, p. 647.
11. Ellen G. White, *Patriarchs and Prophets*, p. 62.
12. Ellen G. White, *The Great Controversy*, pp. 647, 648.
13. Ellen G. White, *Early Writings*, pp. 288-291.
14. *Ibid.*, pp. 52, 53.
15. *Ibid.*, p. 291.
16. *Ibid.*, pp. 19-20, 31.
17. *Ibid.*, pp. 292-294.
18. Ellen G. White, *The Great Controversy*, p. 669.
19. *Ibid.*, pp. 671, 672.
20. Ellen G. White, *Early Writings*, pp. 18-19.

We'd love to send you a free catalog of titles we publish
or even hear your thoughts, reactions, criticism,
about things you did or didn't like about this
or any other book we publish.

Just write or call us at:

TEACH Services, Inc.
254 Donovan Road
Brushton, New York 12916-9738
1-800/367-1998

http://www.TEACHServicesInc.com